INSIGHTS ON JOURNALISM AND HUMAN RIGHTS

Bringing together 17 authors from diverse perspectives, *Insights on Journalism and Human Rights* offers an accessible introduction to the characteristics and complexities of reporting human rights issues in a changing media environment.

Organised into three sections, this book begins by mapping the field of human rights and journalism, outlining the evolving interaction between journalists and the human rights movement, and summarising the main theories and debates surrounding this relationship. Chapters then focus on journalists who find themselves at the centre of human rights violations and explore the challenges they face when covering human rights abuses, including their own safety and responsibilities. The final section of the book scrutinises the media's treatment of various human rights-related issues such as terrorism, missing people, climate change, and migration, and identifies weaknesses and gaps in their coverage.

Featuring case studies, points for discussion, and further reading suggestions throughout, *Insights on Journalism and Human Rights* is recommended reading for advanced students, educators, and researchers in this field.

Sanem Şahin is Senior Lecturer and Researcher in the School of English and Journalism at the University of Lincoln, UK.

Journalism Insights

The Journalism Insights series provides edited collections of theoretically grounded case study analyses on an eclectic range of journalistic areas, from peace and conflict reporting to fashion and sports reporting.

The series has a bias towards the contemporary, but each volume includes an important historical, contextualising section. Volumes offer international coverage and focus on both mainstream and 'alternative' media, always considering the impact of social media in the various fields.

The volumes are aimed at both undergraduate and postgraduate students on journalism as well as media and communication programmes who will find the texts original, interesting and inspirational.

For information on submitting a proposal for the series, please contact the Series Editor Richard Lance Keeble, of the University of Lincoln and Liverpool Hope University, at RKeeble@lincoln.ac.uk

Insights on Science Journalism
Edited by Felicity Mellor

Insights on Literary Journalism
Edited by Kevin M. Lerner

Insights on Journalism and Human Rights
Edited by Sanem Şahin

For more information visit: https://www.routledge.com/Journalism-Insights/book-series/JI

INSIGHTS ON JOURNALISM AND HUMAN RIGHTS

Edited by Sanem Şahin

LONDON AND NEW YORK

Designed cover image: natasaadzic/Getty Images
First published 2025
by Routledge
4 Park Square, Milton Park, Abingdon, Oxon OX14 4RN

and by Routledge
605 Third Avenue, New York, NY 10158

Routledge is an imprint of the Taylor & Francis Group, an informa business

© 2025 selection and editorial matter, Sanem Şahin; individual chapters, the contributors

The right of Sanem Şahin to be identified as the author of the editorial material, and of the authors for their individual chapters, has been asserted in accordance with sections 77 and 78 of the Copyright, Designs and Patents Act 1988.

All rights reserved. No part of this book may be reprinted or reproduced or utilised in any form or by any electronic, mechanical, or other means, now known or hereafter invented, including photocopying and recording, or in any information storage or retrieval system, without permission in writing from the publishers.

Trademark notice: Product or corporate names may be trademarks or registered trademarks, and are used only for identification and explanation without intent to infringe.

British Library Cataloguing-in-Publication Data
A catalogue record for this book is available from the British Library

ISBN: 9781032662572 (hbk)
ISBN: 9781032662541 (pbk)
ISBN: 9781032662589 (ebk)

DOI: 10.4324/9781032662589

Typeset in Galliard
by Apex CoVantage, LLC

In memory of Brian Winston (1941–2022)

A leading scholar, mentor, colleague, and friend.

Your wisdom, guidance, and support have been invaluable.

CONTENTS

List of figures ix
List of tables x
List of contributors xi

1 Introduction 1
  Sanem Şahin

PART I

2 Key debates on the relationship between media and
  human rights 13
  Ekaterina Balabanova

3 A rights-based approach to the safety of journalists 27
  Sara Torsner

4 Human rights and journalism: under pressure when
  national interests are at stake 42
  Aidan White

5 The double-edged sword of human rights news 58
  Matthew Powers

PART II

6 Women journalists and online harassment: a human rights approach 75
Susana Sampaio-Dias, Maria João Silveirinha and João Miranda

7 Forced displacement of journalists and human rights 91
Sanem Şahin

8 Media's responsibility to report (R2R): the case for an international legal obligation 106
Lorenzo Fiorito and Senthan Selvarajah

9 The challenges of reporting human rights in conflicts: towards a human rights journalism approach 120
Ibrahim Seaga Shaw

PART III

10 Reporting asymmetrical conflict in the media: how poorly written stories impact the right to know 139
Barry Turner

11 Journalism and disappearances in México 151
Siria Gastelum and Darwin Franco

12 Reporting on climate change through the lens of human rights 167
Jhesset Thrina Enano

13 Migration and forced displacement: transnational phenomena challenging journalism research and education 183
Susanne Fengler and Monika Lengauer

14 Conclusion 198
Sanem Şahin

Index *202*

FIGURES

9.1 Human Wrongs Journalism frames   127
9.2 Human Rights Journalism frames   128
11.1a and b   Mural for missing people in Culiacán, Sinaloa   160

TABLES

9.1 Human Wrongs Journalism (HWJ) vs Human Rights
     Journalism (HRJ)   124
12.1 Journalists interviewed for the chapter   171

CONTRIBUTORS

Ekaterina Balabanova is Professor of Politics and Media at the University of Liverpool. Her research interests include public and policy debates on migration and refugees, human rights campaigning and communication of human rights issues by business, government and non-government organisations. Her work explores how rights-based arguments and international norms feature and are strengthened or weakened in media coverage. She is the author of The Media and Human Rights: The Cosmopolitan Promise (Routledge, 2014).

Jhesset Thrina Enano is an independent multimedia journalist and educator from Manila, Philippines. Her current reporting work examines the intersections of climate change and environmental issues with human rights, policy, gender, culture, and science. Her writing and visual work have been published in The Washington Post, National Geographic, Mongabay, Rest of World, Philippine Daily Inquirer, and Rappler. In 2022, she was a finalist in the Emerging Journalist category of the Covering Climate Now Journalism Awards. Jhesset is also a journalism lecturer at the University of the Philippines' College of Mass Communication, where she teaches courses on environmental journalism and news reporting and research.

Susanne Fengler is the academic director of the Erich Brost Institute for International Journalism (www.brost.org) at TU Dortmund University and is a full professor for international journalism at the Institute of Journalism, TU Dortmund University, Germany. She has directed numerous comparative research projects in the field of media and migration, media accountability, and foreign coverage. Among her recent key publications are the *Global Handbook of Media Accountability* and the UNESCO Handbook *Reporting on Migrants* *and Refugees* She has directed two graduate schools and established with EU funds an E-Learning Portal for journalism students in all 27 EU states on EU coverage. She edits two book series at VS Springer on journalism and international communication.

Lorenzo Fiorito (LL.M) is a legal editor in London and a researcher at the Centre for Media, Human Rights, and Peacebuilding, UK. He has served as an NGO representative at the UN Human Rights Council and the World Trade Organization. Since 2005, Lorenzo has contributed to small press and community media on issues of human rights, writing from Canada, Switzerland, and the UK. His most recent publications include Dynamics of the Changing Global Order (Lexington, 2023), as a chapter contributor and co-editor.

Darwin Franco is a professor and researcher at the University of Guadalajara (Mexico). He is a member of the National System of Researchers, Level II. In addition to this, he is a journalist specialising in human rights and coverage of forced disappearances. He is also the founder of the independent digital media ZonaDocs (www.zonadocs.mx).

Siria Gastelum is the Director of Resilience at the Global Initiative. Siria started documenting community responses to organised crime in her own native state of Sinaloa, Mexico, where she launched the #GIResilience Project in 2017. The #GIResilience Project was selected to be presented during the 2018 UN General Assembly in New York at the UN Solutions Summit and, in 2019, the #GIResilience Project became the Resilience Fund.

Monika Lengauer is affiliated with the Erich Brost Institute for International Journalism at the Institute of Journalism, TU Dortmund University, Dortmund, Germany. She contributes as a senior research fellow to research on international journalism with a focus on migration and forced displacement as well as media accountability, and with geographical emphases on the Arab World, Africa and Southeast Asia. Her contribution as a lecturer was acknowledged by a Teaching Award in 2020.

João Miranda is a professor on the faculty of arts and humanities of the University of Coimbra and a researcher at the Centre for Interdisciplinary Studies – CEIS20 (Portugal). His research interests include the socio-professional dimension of journalistic activity, media accountability and regulation, practices and cultures of journalism, and critical issues concerning algorithmic automation of media processes. He is also involved in research projects focused on media literacy and trust, as well as online violence against journalists.

Matthew Powers is a professor in the Department of Communication at the University of Washington in Seattle, where he also co-directs the Center for Journalism, Media and Democracy. He is author of NGOs as Newsmakers: The Changing Landscape of International News (2018, Columbia), co-editor with Adrienne Russell of Rethinking Media Research for Changing Societies (2020, Cambridge) and co-author with Sandra-Vera Zambrano of The Journalist's Predicament: Difficult Choices in a Declining Profession (2023, Columbia). His current research examines the feminisation of political journalism in the United States.

Sanem Şahin is a senior lecturer in the School of Education and Communication at the University of Lincoln. Her research focuses on peace and conflict reporting, journalistic roles, marginalised communities, and exiled journalists. Her first monograph, *Journalism Matters: Peace and Conflict Reporting in Cyprus*, was published by Palgrave MacMillan in 2022.

Susana Sampaio-Dias is a senior lecturer in journalism at the School of Film, Media, and Communication at the University of Portsmouth, United Kingdom. Her areas of research and teaching specialisation include journalism and human rights, press freedom, safety of journalists, and gender equality in journalism. Her first monograph, *Reporting Human Rights*, was published by Peter Lang in 2016. She earned her PhD from Cardiff University, School of Journalism, Media, and Culture. Prior to her academic career, she worked as a journalist and news producer for RTP (Rádio e Televisão de Portugal), the Portuguese public service broadcaster.

Senthan Selvarajah is a co-director at the Centre for Media, Human Rights and Peacebuilding, UK; CEO at the Gate Foundation, UK; and PhD supervisor for Unicaf University. Senthan's experience spans over 20 years as a journalist, researcher, consultant, and academic. He has published several books, numerous book chapters, and journal articles.

Ibrahim Seaga Shaw is Chairman and Information Commissioner of the Right to Access Information Commission in Sierra Leone and Chair, Graduate Programme, Faculty of Communications, Media, and Information Studies, Fourah Bay College, University of Sierra Leone. He was Senior Lecturer in media and politics at Northumbria University, UK, and served as the Secretary General of the International Peace Research Association (IPRA) between 2012 and 2016. He is the author of five books, including *Business Journalism: A Critical Political Economy Approach* (2016) published by Routledge and *Human Rights Journalism* (2012) published by Palgrave, and over 45 academic articles and book chapters. He holds a PhD from the Sorbonne in Paris. He is also a journalist of over 20 years in Sierra Leone, France and the UK, and publisher/CEO of the Expo Media Limited, which publishes Expo Magazine (monthly) and the Expo Times newspaper in Sierra Leone.

Maria João Silveirinha is a retired associate professor from the University of Coimbra and is currently a researcher at ICNova, working in the field of Communication and Media Studies. She holds a PhD in Communication Sciences from the Universidade Nova de Lisboa in Lisbon. She is also the current vice-president of the Portuguese Association of Studies on Women (APEM), as well as chief editor of ex aequo journal. Her research areas focus on feminist media studies, news practices and culture, and political communication. Among her published work are her books Media, Identities and Politics, Women and the Media. She was PI on financed projects on Media and Gender, European Identity and Media, and gender hate against journalists.

Sara Torsner is a postdoctoral research fellow with the Centre for Freedom of the Media (CFOM), School of Journalism, Media and Communication, University of Sheffield, UK. Sara is the co-founder of the Journalism Safety Research Network, which is hosted by CFOM. Her research focuses on understanding: the communicative conditions under which the news media operates; risk to journalistic practice via restrictions and attacks on its communicative capacity; alongside the consequences of such constraints for the quality of collective associative life.

Barry Turner is a former senior lecturer in media law and human rights law at the University of Lincoln. He is also a member of the Royal Institute of International Affairs and of the Royal United Services Institute.

Aidan White is President of the Ethical Journalism Network, which he founded in 2012, and is an advisor to the Fetisov Journalism Awards. He is a former UK journalist who worked with The Guardian and the Financial Times from 1979–1987. He was the General Secretary of the International Federation of Journalists from 1987 to 2012. He is a joint founder of the International Freedom of Expression Exchange (1993) and the International News Safety Institute (2003) and has written extensively on ethics, human rights and accountable journalism.

1
INTRODUCTION

Sanem Şahin

This book is put together to explore, discuss and evidence the close relationship between journalism and human rights. At the time of writing, the communication of global human rights concerns demonstrates the importance of paying attention to this relationship. Ongoing armed conflicts and atrocities, climate-related disasters, increasing economic inequalities, attacks on women and LGBTQ+ rights and efforts to limit freedom of expression through surveillance and censorship are some of the main human rights issues that journalists bring to our attention. It is through journalism that we learn about local, national and global events, connect with other people's stories and engage in discussions and campaigns for change. However, it is because of its role in creating awareness and power in safeguarding human rights that journalism is often attacked and controlled by those who want to hide their abuse of power. Consider wars, for example: How can we get an accurate and comprehensive picture of what's happening in wars without independent journalism? How do we learn the actions, including human rights violations, of the parties involved in conflicts? An example is Israel's restrictions on foreign journalists entering Gaza during its military campaign during the 2023/24 conflict. After the Hamas attack on Israel on 7 October 2023 which killed about 1,200 people and took more than 250 others as hostages to Gaza, Israel denied foreign journalists access to Gaza without the Israeli army escorting them, citing security concerns. Meanwhile, it committed war crimes and crimes against humanity during its military operations in Gaza (OHCHR 2024). Yet, at the time of writing, foreign media are not allowed in Gaza to report them. Those who are in Gaza do their job in challenging conditions, and by July 2024, more than 116 journalists and media workers were killed (Committee to Protect Journalists 2024).

Journalism's role in human rights is not limited to wars and conflicts. We often associate human rights violations with authoritarian and undemocratic countries, but even in peaceful and democratic ones, journalism faces challenges in performing its role properly. Media freedom is increasingly under attack even in these countries (UNESCO 2022; Reporters Without Borders 2024; Day, Otto and Simon 2024). A report on media freedom in the European Union (Liberties Media Freedom Report 2024) showed that media pluralism, freedom of expression and journalists' safety as major concerns in Europe. It highlighted the need for urgent action to protect media freedom to effectively safeguard human rights and democratic values.

Journalism and human rights support and reinforce each other. As rights and freedoms benefit from journalism's scrutiny, journalism relies on human rights to function and fulfil its responsibilities. For example, freedom of expression is crucial for journalists to perform their professional roles. They can question, investigate and communicate information that is in the public interest without fear of reprisal or punishment. That is why the abuse of human rights by states starts with restrictions on media freedom. Those in power control the media by curtailing media freedom through various means, such as censorship, regulation, economic and legal pressure and violence, to reduce the risk of being challenged by critical reporting. The aim is to create a chilling effect to hinder the media from criticising and investigating human rights abuses.

Human rights refer to the rights and freedoms of individuals and communities, including specific groups such as women, children, people with disabilities, etc. Enshrined in the Universal Declaration of Human Rights (UDHR), they are protected and defined by many conventions, charters, treaties, laws and institutions of monitoring and policymaking. They set a framework for the fundamental rights and freedoms of individuals and communities to protect them from unfair treatment and act as universal legal guarantees of their freedoms and dignity. However, despite these intentions and ideas, there are challenges and concerns about their implementation, enforcement and effective progression (De Frouville 2019). Consistent human rights abuses, states' refusal to enforce or comply with the agreements they signed and continuing inequalities around the world undermine the trust in the ability of human rights to encourage a social transformation (Langford 2018). The concept of universality is also questioned as the human rights framework is seen as a Western project, imposing its values on other cultures (Langford 2018; Mende 2021).

Today, human rights are facing new challenges. Sabatini (2023, 3) lists these risks as 'increased geopolitical competition with new powers whose views of state sovereignty are at odds with human rights obligations, the rise of xenophobic and populist domestic movements, and the spread of surveillance technologies' that affect people's freedom and dignity. Other issues, such as climate change and increased migration, are linked to these threats and raise questions about the effectiveness, purpose and functionality of human rights in tackling them. There are continuing debates about whether and how human rights should be reformed (Sabatini 2023).

The media and journalism's relationship to human rights is not just limited to being able to report their abuses. Through their story selection, framing and treatment, they play a part in the communication processes that influence the public's understanding of the concepts and practices of human rights. Journalism, media and human rights scholars (see Balabanova 2015; Sampaio-Dias 2016; Tumber and Waisbord 2017) have studied the media's role and power in protecting rights and freedoms and influencing the public's understanding of human rights. They question journalists and the media's responsibilities in protecting human rights and democratic values, study the media's rights and freedoms, examine how issues like ownership, privacy and technology affect their performance and explore the effects of media coverage on public and human rights.

The risks and dangers journalism faces are a growing concern among professionals and scholars. Declining media freedom, violence against journalists, worsening working conditions and erosion of public trust are some of the threats journalists experience. Reports (UNESCO 2022; Reporters Without Borders 2024) show that press freedom is threatened by governments and political authorities' hostile actions and increased control of media. Restriction of media freedoms using legal actions, such as defamation laws or Strategic Lawsuits Against Public Participation (SLAPP), criticising and discrediting journalists, increased surveillance and censorship and supporting pro-government media and ownership are some of the ways employed to control media criticism and to limit journalists' ability to scrutinise power (Freedom House 2019; OHCHR 2022).

It is not just state or political authorities that intimidate journalists. Militias and political and organised crime groups also pose threats to journalists by using violence and other harassment tactics to endanger them. In today's digital media environment, with their increased visibility, journalists are also victims of online hostility by individuals (Hiltunen 2019; Nilsson and Örnebring 2016; Waisbord 2020). Violence against journalists has become a big problem. Journalists are attacked physically (e.g. killing, beating, or other bodily harm), psychologically (e.g. attacks to impact journalists' mental and emotional well-being), digitally (e.g. online harassment, surveillance), financially (e.g. threats to their employment, precarious work conditions) and by using legal means SLAPP: (e.g. legal efforts to silence journalists such as SLAPP) (Harrison and Torsner 2022; Slavtcheva-Petkova et al. 2023; Media4Democracy 2020). They are also targeted because of their gender, race, religion, ethnicity and sexuality (Waisbord 2022; Posetti et al. 2021). Journalists' safety is an important element of media freedom, and without free media, there can be no pluralism, independence or democracy. Therefore, when they are attacked, it should be seen not just as violence against individual journalists but also against media freedom and communities' right to information as they hinder them from keeping the public informed (Harrison and Torsner 2022).

Attacks, intimidation and threats can create a culture of fear among journalists, undermining their performance of democratic functions. Impunity or exemption from punishment encourages and permits violence against journalists (Relly and González de Bustamante 2017). When perpetrators go unpunished, it creates a chilling effect among journalists. Seeing victims without justice can have longer-term effects on them with personal and professional consequences. They reconsider their roles when selecting which stories to report and change their practices, self-censor, reduce their interaction with the audience or exit the profession. When they can no longer work independently and safely, journalists are forced to be displaced (Schönert 2022; Yeğinsu 2020). As a result, important stories are not investigated, the truth is not told, and the public's right to information is prevented, creating an undemocratic environment open to abuse of power.

Digital developments and new media have presented both opportunities and challenges to human rights. People can access, produce and disseminate information, interact with others and share their opinions. However, these technologies are also used to violate and restrict rights. Data and privacy protection, surveillance, censorship and online violence are some of the main concerns. Digital media have also transformed human rights reporting, creating new opportunities and challenges. Journalists are no longer the only gatekeepers, content producers or disseminators of news on human rights. Other actors, such as nongovernmental organisations (NGOs) and local activists or individuals, also produce and disseminate information on human rights issues using various tools, channels and platforms. They can record and report human rights violations, which amplifies and diversifies the voices, perspectives and ways of storytelling on human rights. For example, videos recorded by citizens can provide first-hand evidence of human rights abuses, pushing them into public attention and prompting action (Ristovska 2018; Allan 2017). Journalists collaborate with citizens and NGOs to tell these stories, which enhances their access to information and victims. However, these technologies also present risks and threats to journalists, such as increased surveillance and campaigns of misinformation and disinformation aiming to silence and discredit them. Online gendered violence targeting women journalists not only creates a chilling effect among them but also undermines democratic rights such as media freedom and the public's right to access information (Posetti et al. 2021).

The transformations in global political, cultural and technological environments encourage us to rethink the meaning and scope of human rights. There is more awareness that human rights are not just issues concerning distant undemocratic countries but are problems also affecting democratic ones.

Topics like environment, health, migration and poverty are increasingly discussed within the human rights framework. For example, media coverage of climate change as a human rights issue has increased. Reports on how climate change is threatening communities' access to food, water and housing and forcing them to migrate have become more visible. Similarly, the impact of the COVID-19 pandemic on individuals and communities and states' responsibilities to protect them are discussed from the human rights perspective. The absence of support for vulnerable people, domestic violence during lockdowns and lack of access to healthcare for certain communities were some of the issues raised by monitoring institutions and reported by the media.

Journalists' role in reporting human rights is clear: they investigate and document human rights violations and bring them to the public's attention to create awareness and hold those who abuse their power accountable. When journalists decide which stories to cover, they also determine how to define and disseminate the problem to the public. It is the awareness of their and the media's influence on public opinion and knowledge that raises the question of journalists' roles and responsibilities concerning human rights issues. Is it their job to promote human rights by seeking stories about this issue? Should they treat them the same way as they do other stories or approach them differently? These are personal and professional decisions journalists should make individually, depending on their perception of their responsibilities, ethical standards and the journalism culture in which they work. Regardless, truth is the basis of journalists' duty. For example, the International Federation of Journalists (IFJ) lists 'respect for the facts and for the right of the public to truth is the first duty of the journalist' as the first item in their Global Charter of Ethics for Journalists (International Federation of Journalists 2019) to demonstrate the importance of reporting facts accurately. Journalists have an interest in the public knowing the truth and defending human rights because when the rights and freedoms of journalists and communities are restricted, the public's right to know also suffers.

This book

In this book, journalists and scholars specialising in media and human rights issues provide their critical observations and assessments. The result is an edited collection of diverse perspectives broadening our understanding of the complex relationship between human rights and journalism. It offers theoretical debates on the changing interaction between journalism and the human rights movement and identifies the problems and criticisms related to human rights coverage in the news, including the quantity and quality of it. The chapters discuss how journalists see and perform their role concerning human rights, underline their safety concerns and investigate the reflection of various human rights in the news media. They present a collection of current debates and developments on journalism and human rights.

The book is organised into three sections to discuss the main theories and debates on human rights and journalism, journalists' role perceptions and practices and the representation of various human rights in the news media. The first section presents the main ideas and arguments on human rights and journalism and identifies the main problems and criticisms. It starts with Ekaterina Balabanova's chapter outlining the key issues concerning the relationship between human rights and the media. It examines the development of media coverage as a research field and discusses the impact of global issues like inequality, populism, authoritarianism, social media, big tech and climate change on the international human rights system. Stressing the role the media play in the protection of the integrity of the human rights system, Balabanova provides examples of media's influence in either undermining or supporting human rights.

The safety of journalists is a continuous concern, despite various attempts and debates about how to tackle this problem. Sara Torsner adopts a rights-based approach, which considers the attacks on journalists not just violations of individual journalists' human rights but also the public's right to information. Using two case studies, the UN's Sustainable Development Goal (SDG) Indicator 16.10.1 and the Committee to Protect Journalists' (CPJ) 'Journalists Killed' dataset, she highlights the gaps in data collection efforts and argues for a more holistic documentation of the societal implications of human rights violations against journalists.

In the third chapter, Aidan White points out the connection between ethical journalism and human rights and stresses journalists' role as independent providers of ethical and reliable information. This role becomes crucial, especially during wars which present many risks and dangers to journalists. However, journalists are also victims of human rights abuses, and impunity for crimes against journalists is an increasing concern among journalists and human rights organisations. White argues that despite many initiatives to protect journalists, national strategic, political and commercial interests take precedence over the defence of the rights of journalists and therefore, there is a need for stronger international legal instruments to protect journalists.

Matthew Powers discusses the positive and negative effects of the changes in media, advocacy, politics and digital technology on human rights coverage. He examines how the shifts in the transformations in both journalism and non-governmental organisations (NGOs) impact human rights news, which he describes as a double-edged sword for human rights reporting. Digital technologies offer NGOs the opportunity to produce and disseminate their media materials, as well as the chance to bypass traditional media. They also help to diversify human rights coverage by exposing audiences to a wider range of institutional voices. However, it is still journalists who decide the agenda and definition of human rights news, and their reliance on official sources can result in the coverage being biased and the scope of topics being limited.

The second section puts journalists at the centre of human rights violations. The chapters in this part focus on journalists when their rights are violated, exploring the challenges and dilemmas they experience when covering human rights abuses. Susana Sampaio-Dias, Maria João Silveirinha and João Miranda investigate discrimination and misogynistic abuse women journalists experience. They examine online violence against women journalists as a violation of human rights and discuss its emotional and psychological toll. Normalisation of such violence results in desensitisation and underreporting. They argue for the adoption of a gender-sensitive and intersectional approach to tackle the violence women journalists face in their private and public spheres.

Sanem Şahin's chapter is on the forced displacement of journalists. Journalists flee their home countries for various reasons such as conflict, violence, persecution, human rights violations or disasters caused by humans or nature. Focusing on exiled journalists in the UK, the chapter discusses how forced displacement affects journalists as displaced people, professionals and individuals and its impact on their human rights.

Lorenzo Fiorito and Senthan Selvarajah examine journalists' responsibility to report (R2R) human rights violations. They state that R2R is not only a moral duty but also a legal obligation for journalists. Journalists have a legal responsibility to report on atrocities and human rights violations; otherwise, they can be complicit in these crimes. Fiorito and Selvarajah argue that the idea of R2R is grounded in the concept of the Responsibility to Protect (R2P), and together with Human Rights Journalism (HRJ), it can promote awareness and accountability for human rights violations.

Ibrahim Seaga Shaw criticises traditional conflict reporting for focusing on visible violence while ignoring the structural and cultural problems that lead to the conflict. Describing such journalism as Human Wrongs Journalism (HWJ), he proposes Human Rights Journalism (HRJ) as a model to address the problems and shortcomings of mainstream media's reporting of human rights. He studies the local media coverage of the violent protests in Sierra Leone in 2022 to see which model of journalism applies to the reporting of human rights violations.

The fourth section explores the media coverage of various human rights-related issues and identifies its weaknesses, gaps and problems. Barry Turner focuses on terrorism and examines how media coverage can impact people's right to know. He remarks that defining terrorism can be a complex process, as what counts as terrorism can shift. That is why accurate and informative reporting is essential in helping the public understand terrorism. When the news media exaggerates threats or uses tropes and cliches, they not only disseminate misinformation but also glorify terrorism. As Turner remarks, 'it is the role of serious journalists to report the news, not dramatize it'.

Siria Gastelum and Darwin Franco's chapter examines the role of journalists in the disappearance crisis in Mexico, largely due to the 'war on drugs'.

Journalists play a crucial part in highlighting these human rights violations, but at the same time face significant risks and violence themselves from both state and non-state actors. Despite this, they collaborate with families who are searching for their loved ones to report their stories. Gastelum and Franco share examples of initiatives, such as *Hasta Encontrarles*, in which journalists not only cover the news of disappearances but also provide families with tools and resources to advocate for their cause for justice.

In recent years, the impact of climate change on human rights has been one of the widely discussed topics. Jhesset Thrina Enano's chapter presents the experiences of journalists from various countries who cover the link between environmental problems and human rights. These journalists document how climate change affects fundamental human rights, including the rights to life, health, shelter, food and water. Enano outlines the challenges they face personally and professionally as they witness the exacerbation of violations of human rights by climate crisis.

In the final chapter, Susanne Fengler and Monika Lengauer explain the importance of responsible and human rights-based journalism especially when covering migration and forced displacement. They underline the need for journalism training for responsible and human rights-based storytelling and argue that journalism education supported by mass communication research can help produce such stories. They present the UNESCO Handbook for Journalism Educators "Reporting on Migrants and Refugees" (Fengler, Lengauer and Zappe 2021) and CoMMPASS (Communicating Migration and Mobility: E-Learning Programs and Newsroom Applications for Sub-Saharan Africa- https://commpass.org/) projects as examples of resources supporting journalism educators globally.

References

Allan, Stuart. 2017. "Citizen Witnessing of Human Rights Abuses." In *The Routledge Companion to Media and Human Rights*, edited by Howard Tumber and Silvio Waisbord, 1st ed., 347–56. London: Routledge.

Balabanova, Ekaterina. 2015. *The Media and Human Rights: The Cosmopolitan Promise*. London: Routledge.

Committee to Protect Journalists (CPJ). 2024. "Journalist Casualties in the Israel-Gaza War." *CPJ*, August 23, 2024. https://www.cpj.org/journalist-casualties-israel-gaza-war.

Day, Jonathan, Franziska Otto, and Eva Simon. 2024. *Liberties Media Freedom Report 2024*. Civil Liberties Union for Europe (Liberties). https://dq4n3btxmr8c9.cloudfront.net/files/flccsm/Media_freedom_Report2024.pdf.

De Frouville, Olivier. 2019. "The Universal Declaration of Human Rights at 70: The Challenges That Await the UN." *The Conversation*, April 15. https://theconversation.com/the-universal-declaration-of-human-rights-at-70-the-challenges-that-await-the-un-115032

Fengler, Susanne, Monika Lengauer, and Anna-Carina Zappe, eds. 2021. Reporting on Migrants and Refugees: Handbook for Journalism Educators. Paris: UNESCO. https://unesdoc.unesco.org/ark:/48223/pf0000377890.

Freedom House. 2019. "Freedom and the Media 2019: A Downward Spiral." *Freedom House*. https://freedomhouse.org/sites/default/files/2020-02/FINAL07162019_Freedom_And_The_Media_2019_Report.pdf.
Harrison, Jackie, and Sara Torsner. 2022. *Safety of Journalists and Media Freedom: Trends in Non-EU Countries From a Human Rights Perspective*. Brussels: European Union.
Hiltunen, Ilmari. 2019. "Experiences of External Interference Among Finnish Journalists: Prevalence, Methods and Implications." *Nordicom Review* 40 (1): 3–21. https://doi.org/10.2478/nor-2018-0016.
International Federation of Journalists (IFJ). 2019. "The IFJ Global Charter of Ethics for Journalists." *Adopted at the 30th IFJ World Congress in Tunis*, June 12. https://www.ifj.org/who/rules-and-policy/global-charter-of-ethics-for-journalists.
Langford, Malcolm. 2018. "Critiques of Human Rights." *Annual Review of Law and Social Science* 14: 69–89. http://dx.doi.org/10.1146/annurev-lawsocsci-110316-113807.
Löfgren Nilsson, M., and H. Örnebring. 2016. "Journalism Under Threat: Intimidation and Harassment of Swedish Journalists." *Journalism Practice* 10 (7): 880–90. https://doi.org/10.1080/17512786.2016.1164614.
Media4Democracy. 2020. *Protecting the Safety of Journalists, Protecting Freedom of Expression: A Handbook for EU Delegations*. Brussels: European Union. https://doi.org/10.2841/580755.
Mende, Janne. 2021. "Are Human Rights Western: And Why Does It Matter? A Perspective From International Political Theory." *Journal of International Political Theory* 17 (1): 38–57. https://doi.org/10.1177/1755088219832992.
OHCHR. 2022. "Ensuring Media Freedom and Safety of Journalists Requires Urgent Concrete Action Backed by Political Will: UN Expert." *UN Human Rights Council*, June 14. https://www.ohchr.org/en/press-releases/2022/06/ensuring-media-freedom-and-safety-journalists-requires-urgent-concrete.
OHCHR. 2024. "Israeli Authorities, Palestinian Armed Groups Are Responsible for War Crimes, Other Grave Violations of International Law, UN Inquiry Finds." *UN Human Rights Council*, June 12. https://www.ohchr.org/en/press-releases/2024/06/israeli-authorities-palestinian-armed-groups-are-responsible-war-crimes#:~:text=In%20relation%20to%20Israeli%20military,%2C%20forcible%20transfer%2C%20sexual%20violence%2C.
Posetti, Julie, Nabeelah Shabbir, Diana Maynard, Kalina Bontcheva, and Nermine Aboulez. 2021. *The Chilling: Global Trends in Online Violence Against Women Journalists*. Paris: UNESCO.
Relly, J. E., and C. González de Bustamante. 2017. "Global and Domestic Networks Advancing Prospects for Institutional and Social Change: The Collective Action Response to Violence Against Journalists." *Journalism and Communication Monographs* 19 (2): 84–152. https://doi.org/10.1177/1522637917702618.
Reporters Without Borders (RSF). 2024. "2024 World Press Freedom Index: Journalism Under Political Pressure." *RSF*. https://rsf.org/en/2024-world-press-freedom-index-journalism-under-political-pressure?year=2024&data_type=general.
Ristovska, Sandra. 2018. "The Rise of Eyewitness Video and Its Implications for Human Rights: Conceptual and Methodological Approaches." In *Making Human Rights News: Balancing Participation and Professionalism*, edited by John Crothers Pollock and Morton E. Winston, 41–54. London: Routledge.
Sabatini, Christopher. 2023. "Introduction." In *Reclaiming Human Rights in a Changing World Order*, edited by Christopher Sabatini, 1–11. London: Chatham House.
Sampaio-Dias, Susana. 2016. *Reporting Human Rights*. New York: Peter Lang.
Schönert, U. 2022. *Exile Journalism in Europe: Current Challenges and Support Programmes*. Hamburg: Körber-Stiftung.

Slavtcheva-Petkova, Vera, Jyotika Ramaprasad, Nina Springer, Sallie Hughes, Thomas Hanitzsch, Basyouni Hamada, Abit Hoxha, and Nina Steindl. 2023. "Conceptualizing Journalists' Safety Around the Globe." *Digital Journalism* 11 (7): 1211–29. https://doi.org/10.1080/21670811.2022.2162429.

Tumber, Howard, and Silvio Waisbord. 2017. *The Routledge Companion to Media and Human Rights*. London, New York: Routledge.

UNESCO. 2022. *Journalism Is a Public Good: World Trends in Freedom of Expression and Media Development, Global Report 2021/2022.* Paris: UNESCO.

Waisbord, Silvio. 2020. "Mob Censorship: Online Harassment of US Journalists in Times of Digital Hate and Populism." *Digital Journalism* 8 (8): 1030–46. https://doi.org/10.1080/21670811.2020.1818111.

Waisbord, Silvio. 2022. "Can Journalists Be Safe in a Violent World?" *Journalism Practice* 16 (9): 1948–55. https://doi.org/10.1080/17512786.2022.2098524.

Yeğinsu, Can. 2020. *Report on Providing Safe Refuge to Journalists at Risk*. International Bar Association Human Rights Institute. Accessed July 12, 2024. https://www.ibanet.org/Safe-Refuge-report-launch-2020.

PART I

2
KEY DEBATES ON THE RELATIONSHIP BETWEEN MEDIA AND HUMAN RIGHTS

Ekaterina Balabanova

Introduction

On 10 December 2023, the world marked the 75th anniversary of the Universal Declaration of Human Rights (UDHR). While the system, created after the end of World War II, has developed significantly over time since then, the idea of human rights remains politically charged. In what ways does the media sustain or erode the international system of human rights, and how are these dynamics changing in the 21st century? This chapter will answer that question by focusing on recent developments in scholarship, exploring how contemporary challenges and political trends impact upon our understanding of the relationship between human rights and the media.

This is important because we are told that the international human rights system is in jeopardy. Many argue we are facing unprecedented political threats to some of the key human rights structures that protect people (Jones and Malcorra 2020; Sabatini 2022). The role of the media is central to this because of the importance of public confidence in human rights when political actors may seek to avoid or undermine them to satisfy their own ends. Adopting a human rights lens or perspective can challenge entrenched and powerful interests. The need for a free and independent media to protect human rights has long been recognised (and is enshrined in Article 19 of the UDHR), but the media also provides fertile ground for alternative ideas and narratives about human rights to propagate and spread.

For most of those alive in the world today, human rights have been ever-present, but history shows how controversial and precarious the very idea of human rights can be. In 1795, the British philosopher Jeremy Bentham described the famous forerunner of the UDHR – the French Revolution's

DOI: 10.4324/9781032662589-3

'Declaration of the Rights of Man and Citizen' – as 'nonsense upon stilts'! He railed against what he saw as a very dangerous idea: that humans have innate, natural rights. A British critique of the notion of human rights has arguably continued ever since, given oxygen by tabloid articles about the 'madness' of human rights and 'lefty lawyers' who bring forward cases based on them. For some politicians, the problem with human rights is the principle that they apply to everyone, and that means they can stop them from doing what they want. But it seems that where you fall on the political spectrum will not only affect the way you think about human rights (Braun and Arves 2017), but it is likely that it is entrenched and reinforced by the kinds of partisan media being consumed, particularly when they are driven by aggressive social media algorithms (Wilson et al. 2020).

The rest of the chapter explores media and human rights as a field of research (Section 1), before examining the role of the media in the current challenges facing the international human rights system (Section 2), and then providing some examples of the ways in which the media can undermine and erode support for, or provide the space to resist and defend the integrity of, human rights (Section 3).

'Media and human rights' as a field of research

While there has been an undeniable interest in the topic of human rights across the media and an increase in human rights coverage from the 1990s (Barnhurst 2016; Riffe et al. 2018; Ramos et al. 2007), this has not correlated with accurate and informed coverage. Despite the attention given, research has argued that media fail to report much that ought to be known (Brandle 2018; Maier 2021), the coverage is full of misunderstandings, myths and misconceptions (Cole 2010; Internews 2012), and this is further exacerbated by engrained media considerations (Galtung and Ruge 1965) alongside the role states play as information gatekeepers (Bennett et al. 2008). Rather alarmingly, recent research also suggests that the media coverage of human rights issues is declining both in amount and depth in British and American news outlets, and whatever limited coverage there is does not use the actual frame of human rights (Brandle 2018).

As Tumber and Waisbord (2017, 3) point out, '[t]he media magnify the presence of certain human rights problems whilst minimizing the relevance of others'. Western media coverage tends to be dominated by civil and political concerns, whereas social, economic and cultural abuses are absent or largely ignored (Ovsiovitch 1993; Ramos et al. 2007). But even within these parameters studies have consistently found a weak correlation between the severity of physical violence and media attention (Caliendo et al. 1999; Cole 2010; Ramos et al. 2007), leading Maier (2021, 1625) to conclude that 'violations of human rights are a weak predictor of news coverage'. Media attention usually remains focused on a few nations that are already in the Western media spotlight (Thrall et al. 2014; Wu 2000), such as Syria and Libya, whereas human rights violations are overlooked in other countries like Myanmar, Sudan, Congo or Yemen (Maier 2021). Brandle (2018) proposes that it is the relative socio-economic privilege of those involved that matters the most when human rights violations are covered – in the words of Dowler (2004, 94), 'the motto "it bleeds it leads" . . . is not entirely accurate. It really depends on who is bleeding'.

It is certainly the case that not all human rights issues satisfy media criteria for newsworthiness. News values (Galtung and Ruge 1965; Harcup and O'Neil 2001; O'Neill and Harcup 2009), working as 'a system of criteria which are used to make decisions about the inclusion and exclusion of material' that 'transcend individual judgments, although of course they are to be found embodied in every news judgment made by particular journalists' (Palmer 2000, 45), ensure that issues that are less visible or processes that are slow are rarely covered. Human rights coverage has to fight for space with other news and the pressure to deliver dramatic images and sensational coverage in a highly competitive news environment militates against deeper and more explanatory coverage. Ultimately, news values serve as a tool to 'translate untidy reality into neat stories with beginnings, middles and denouements' and by doing this they tend to 'reinforce conventional opinions and established authority' (Curran and Seaton 2003, 336). This lends support to those who argue that official government priorities are significant determinants of media coverage. Herman and Chomsky in their manufacturing consent/propaganda model are very clear that through the 'selection of topics' (as one of a number of ways) media act to 'inculcate and defend the economic, social, and political agenda of privileged groups that dominate the domestic society and the state' (1988, 298). In a similar vein, Bennett et al. (2008, 189), point out that 'instead of careful and continuous scrutiny, the press shows moments of critical independence within an overall pattern of dependence on government for the raw materials of news and the legitimization of "acceptable" viewpoints'.

This would spell bad news for the understanding of human rights and the overall international human rights agenda as the examples of the US and UK demonstrate how human rights are focused on when discussing issues in foreign countries, but switch to civil and political rights lens when responding to domestic concerns (Brandle 2015, 2018). Underlying this is the assumption that violations of human rights occur abroad, that the international regime of human rights standards does not trigger national responsibilities. It is tempting to attribute this to a confusion of what and where human rights are, with many journalists, politicans and civil society actors having only a 'superficial grasp of the institutional apparatus of human rights' (ICHRP 2002, 19) and not being familiar with the 1948 UDHR and other international human rights treaties and mechanisms (Internews 2012). It is also possible, however, to see this as a way of avoiding implementing meaningful protections for human rights in domestic politics (Brandle 2018).

Media do not seem to challenge this narrative often and effectively. If, as Sampaio-Dias (2016, 190) found, '"human rights" is not a topic in itself, but something undeniably present when addressing certain issues', then the perception of which issues are to be seen within or outside this framework matters. Brandle's (2018, 171) study on the coverage of human rights in the USA and UK based on data from 1990–2009 and then 2010–2016 concludes that 'not only do news outlets generally still not cover human rights, even when they do, it is almost exclusively as foreign news. Human rights is overall not a frame that journalists reach for, especially for domestic issues'.

The media and the 'turning tide' on human rights

The 75th anniversary of the UDHR was a moment for many to reflect on the state of the international system of human rights. It was not meant to be seen as a 'celebration' (Farge 2023), mainly due to the fact that it was overshadowed by a long list of troubling issues. These included the still-fresh trauma of the global COVID-19 pandemic that had exacerbated structural inequalities, putting human rights 'to the test' (Spadaro 2020), the growing urgency of the human rights and social justice impacts of climate change (Levy and Patz 2015) and the rise of populist political forces who adopt an increasingly selective, instrumental or downright antagonistic approach to human rights (Alston 2017).

Perhaps most troubling, however, was the extraordinarily high number of violent conflicts and wars taking place when the date of the anniversary fell. According to the Uppsala Conflict Data Program, in 2022–2023 these were at their highest level since the end of the Cold War. Many of these conflicts – notably those in Ethiopia, Sudan, Myanmar and Syria, the ongoing invasion of Ukraine by Russia (which began in 2022) and the ground offensive being conducted by Israel in Gaza – were marked by serious and ongoing violations of human rights.

It is hardly surprising, then, that a recent international initiative led by Chatham House and the Brookings Institute to explore the state of the international human rights system began with the depressing observation that 'the tide has turned' (Sabatini 2022, xiii) against human rights. This was attributed to three longer-term trends: the rise of China (which prioritises economic, but denies political and civil rights), the ability of anti-democratic forces to take advantage of new technologies, and an increasing ambivalence in the 21st century towards human rights from those traditionally seen as 'upholders of the UN declaration', i.e. 'The West'. Others have called this a 'crisis of multilateralism' (Jones and Malcorra 2020).

The role of the media is generally held to be central to the first two of these trends. The ability of authoritarian and anti-democratic regimes to ignore or reject human rights is regularly traced to suppression of a free and independent media (Repucci 2019). In her 2022 report on the promotion and protection of the right to freedom of opinion and expression, Irene Khan, the UN's Special Rapporteur, pointed to a long list of factors behind the claim that 'media freedom and the safety of journalists are in dangerous decline in almost every region of the world' (Khan 2022, 3). These include increasing control of public media by state authorities (e.g. in Central and Eastern Europe), persecution and attacks (often misogynistic) aided and abetted by new laws criminalising and harassing journalists, restrictions on media freedom, targeted surveillance and censorship. In addition to these, a key theme in the report was that every one of these problems has been accelerated and exacerbated by the rise of new technologies and digital media (Khan 2022).

Perhaps more insidious but equally threatening are the ways in which the media is heavily implicated in the third trend Sabatini (2022) identified: a loss of interest in international human rights. His point was specifically in relation to the powerful states in the international community who are traditionally seen as supporters of the system, but there is evidence that this is more widespread. Public opinion and public support for human rights are closely linked to the way issues are presented and discussed in different forms of media, and this has implications for the full range of democratic and non-democratic societies. In the former, there is evidence in the US, for example, of continued support for human rights assessments and conditionality to be part of foreign policy (Allendoerfer 2017). But within the human rights community there is growing recognition that work is needed to maintain and build public support for human rights, to develop strong narratives addressing local needs, spoken by people other than the usual suspects from the global north NGOs (Logan 2019). Trust and confidence in the United Nations (UN), as with domestic institutions, is fairly low, but this is a long-standing pattern and there is not much evidence that this has changed dramatically (Trithart and Case 2023).

The problem of a lack of public support also presents challenges in more authoritarian states or in the Global South where the human rights of marginalised communities are at stake. Take, for example, the controversial Anti-Homosexuality Bill (AHB) in Uganda which introduced the death penalty for 'repeat offenders'. The international response, which was to cut foreign aid, fuelled a national tabloid campaign in the country and arguably led to it being passed in 2013 (although it was subsequently repealed) (Dasandi and Erez 2023).

Central to maintaining public support is public faith and trust in the legitimacy of human rights structures at national and international levels. Here, the implications and impacts of wars and conflicts and how these are dealt with by the international community become an important area for discussions about the international human rights system. The full-scale military invasion of Ukraine by Russia in February 2022 violated many principles of international law and was roundly condemned at the UN General Assembly.[1] Yet it divided the international community into at least three groups: those who support Ukraine, those who defend Russia's right to invade and others who prefer to stay non-aligned (Haddad 2023). Those who line up behind Russia are not necessarily opposing the existence of international human rights 'but rather raise objections to their arbitrary application' (Suami 2023). The military response by Israel in Gaza to terrorist attacks committed by Hamas on 7 October 2023 also led to an urgent response from the international community, but here there was even greater division: 44 states chose to abstain (including the UK) and 14 voted against (including the US) a UN General Assembly resolution on 27 October 2023 demanding that 'all parties immediately and fully comply with their obligations under international law'.[2] The two conflicts, and the reaction by the international community, are important for understanding the way human rights form part of the international system.

Commentators have argued that responses to these two conflicts by Western governments illustrate double standards on human rights (O'Callaghan et al. 2023), particularly on the part of the US (Noor 2024) and UK. The manner in which these conflicts are discussed by mainstream media in liberal democracies is central to such accusations. Research comparing US media coverage of the Russia-Ukraine conflict and Saudi-led intervention in Yemen found extensive bias in terms of volume of coverage and greater emphasis on human rights in the former, whereas the latter was described in more neutral terms, with harms suffered by civilians described as 'largely incidental' (Bachman and Brito Ruiz 2024).

According to the Centre for Media Monitoring (CfMM),[3] UK media coverage of the Gaza conflict had an anti-Palestinian bias characterised by selective usage of emotive language and with poor practice in use of sources and fact-checking (Hanif 2024). These findings are echoed in a larger study in the US that used natural language processing to analyse a large historical data-set of coverage in the *New York Times* (Jackson 2024), finding 'disproportionate use of the passive voice to refer to negative or violent action perpetrated towards Palestinians' alongside 'more negative and violent rhetoric in reference to Palestinians compared to Israelis' (Jackson 2024, 130).

Understanding media's role in the erosion and resistance around human rights

In 2015, the United Nations Sustainable Development Goals (SDGs) were launched with the aim of meeting a range of targets by 2030 (the Agenda for Sustainable Development).[4] Progress has been slow: in an event on the SDGs held in 2023 (at the halfway point to Agenda 2030), UN Secretary-General

António Guterres lamented that only 12% of the targets were on track.[5] The SDG Media Compact initiative was then launched in 2018 by the UN in recognition of the central role that media could play in supporting and furthering progress on the SDGs, and by 2023 this was hailed as a success, growing to nearly 400 members from the media and entertainment sectors.[6] Yet it is often claimed that media coverage of certain issues erodes or undermines basic human rights.

Take, for example, migration – identified as a key (and cross-cutting) issue in the SDGs.[7] The SDG declaration recognised refugees, internally displaced persons and migrants as vulnerable groups, but there is evidence from around the world that media coverage is problematic. Research from Chile found that media coverage of migration increased negative perceptions of the topic (Scherman et al. 2022), and evidence from Norway and the UK suggest it propagates racism (Ranji and Archetti 2024; Połońska-Kimunguyi 2022). Comparative analysis looking at 11 European and African countries shows different preoccupations in media coverage between 'sending' and 'receiving' countries, but found that none meaningfully addressed root causes (Fengler et al. 2022).

Why does media coverage generally eschew a human rights 'lens' for migration and refugee issues? One main reason is simply the nature of the political debate. Politicians avoid justifications for their policies and programmes in this area based on human rights: they prefer to either securitise the issue or resort to economic arguments, and this is echoed and amplified in media coverage of both left- and right-leaning publications (Balch and Balabanova 2016). There are also less visible ways in which a human rights approach is eroded or undermined in the media. Research on the UK and Hungary (Balabanova and Balch 2020) identified a number of ways in which foundational ideas underpinning the international refugee regime were being attacked during Europe's so-called 2015–2016 'migrant crisis'. Commitments around the norm of asylum (obligations of states towards refugees that reach their territories) and burden-sharing (between states), were implicitly rejected across the two countries by reframing refugees as 'illegal migrants' engaging in criminality, or connecting the issue with human trafficking and smuggling and metaphors of war.

The result is that the media act as convenient cover for political 'solutions' which actively and deliberately reduce or avoid human rights commitments. The EU-Turkey readmission deal, reached in 2016 in response to the large increase in refugees arriving in Europe from Syria, was described by Eve Geddie, Director of Amnesty International, EU, as an 'abject failure' which 'failed to respect the rights of refugees and migrants and failed to provide alternative safe passage to Europe for people seeking protection'.[8] In 2024, the UK's 'Rwanda Plan', which aimed to deport asylum-seekers to Rwanda without processing their claims, was described by Michael O'Flaherty, Council of Europe Commissioner for Human Rights, as raising 'major issues about the human rights of asylum seekers and the rule of law more generally' (CoE 2024).

New vs 'legacy' media?

How does the rise of new forms of digital media affect the media-human rights nexus? This is perhaps the area where gaps in our knowledge and understanding are most obvious. In the age of social media, big data and artificial intelligence (AI), there appear to be multiple possibilities but also new, unprecedented challenges. The evidence is fairly clear in terms of impact on news comsumption: the advent of digital media is linked to the long-term decline of the news industry and what are now described as 'legacy' media. In parallel, while sales of newspapers, numbers of journalists and audiences for mainstream broadcast and press reduce, numbers using social media increase, but people are not consuming news at these sites (Kuper 2024). Nevertheless, research continues to point to the importance of legacy media in political agenda-setting (Langer et al. 2021).

Aside from how media is consumed, the way content is created has also been permanently altered by the development of new technologies. The power of AI to create, moderate, censor and surveil news content has led to fears about increasing levels of 'automated journalism', and the ability of authoritarians to use these tools for repression and denial of free expression (Haas 2020). Studies suggest audiences find it quite difficult to distinguish computer from human-generated content (Wölker and Powell 2021), and this has led to calls for regulators to find new safeguards to protect freedom of expression (Llansó et al. 2020; Minow 2021). Debates are ongoing about the role of platforms in spreading mis-/disinformation, interfering in elections, promoting and inciting violence against marginalised groups while in the process collecting huge quantities of personal information about their users with no transparency over how this data is subsequently stored or shared (Galvin 2019).

Another important aspect of digital media is the role of user-generated content, the speed with which stories and comments can go 'viral' and the consequences of this for how we understand freedom of expression and what 'media' is. This has fuelled new challenges such as the so-called 'free speech crisis' in the UK and US, which has drawn academics very much into the complex debate about what is now dubbed 'cancel culture' as part of the wider debate on free speech and academic freedom (Bacevic 2024). A more positive feature of citizen engagement via digital media is the potential to operate as a sort of 'early warning system'. Evidence suggests analysis of social media and big data can play a vital role in anticipating, analysing and responding to human rights issues in different parts of the world. This can include faster mobilisation following humanitarian crises (Prøitz 2018), better documentation of human rights abuses during wars and conflicts (Cottle 2011), providing accessible space for political expression and organisation of protests and demonstrations (Lee 2018; Valenzuela 2013) and acting as a tool for grassroots activists for human rights campaigning (Briones et al. 2013; Hall 2019).

The example of refugees and human rights provides some useful insights into some of these issues and shows how new and legacy media interconnect.

In the context of very negative reactions to a large number of refugees arriving in Europe in 2015–2016, the hashtag #refugeeswelcome emerged as an important signal of resistance: synonymous with digital activism and the power of social media. It has been described as an example where the general public express their reaction to 'a highly mediatized and emotionally charged event in a manner that creates the impression of a monolithic voice arising from social media' (Barisione et al. 2019).

The #refugeeswelcome 'moment' in September 2015 has been the subject of a number of studies to show how social media and user-generated content can create 'an alternative narrative of the refugee crisis through solicitations of sympathy and prominent calls-to-action' (Nerghes and Lee 2019). This is often compared favourably to so-called 'mainstream media', where there is a bank of research showing coverage is divisive, racist and how it politicises and securitises the issue (Georgiou and Zaborowski 2017; Balabanova and Balch 2020; Berry et al. 2015).

More than an alternative narrative, the hashtag campaign is associated with digital activism leading to actual political change – where, according to some, its power in 'raising awareness and in placing such issues on political agendas . . . cannot be contested' (Nerghes and Lee 2019, 284). Indeed, it is claimed that the hashtag #refugeeswelcome spread to other social media platforms (Facebook, YouTube, Instagram, etc.) and then into the 'offline public sphere', becoming a 'politically relevant slogan'. From these readings, the social media environment becomes a veritably cosmopolitan space where the 'moral shock' of different communities can be transformed, enabling 'solidarity and collective action frames' to be constructed across differences (Bakardjieva 2020).

In relation to the media-human rights nexus, the success of campaigns such as #refugeeswelcome then symbolise a partial reconfiguration of power, where digital activism can help overturn established policy responses. But there remain questions about how meaningful this impact really is. While there was a definite #refugeeswelcome moment in 2015, in the decade since then, the steady hardening of borders (in the UK, Germany and across Europe and North America) suggests that while digital media undoubtedly provide human rights advocates with new weapons and some new victories, there remains an underlying pattern of 'cosmopolitan promise' unfulfilled (Balabanova 2014). As with television and the internet in the 20th century, new forms of media and technology in the 21st century may be raising hopes and expectations of global citizenship and solidarity that then seem to fail to fully materialise.

Conclusions

The breadth and complexity of this field make it impossible to cover all the different issues and implications that arise from the relationship between media and human rights in a single chapter. The focus here has been on summarising some of the key debates and highlighting a growing body of scholarship that points to a vibrant and dynamic research area. Many of the findings from these studies indicate we are in a uniquely interesting moment for both the human rights and media systems. The former is under extraordinary and increasing pressure, while developments in the latter add, but also complicate, this situation.

The chapter covered multiple different areas of interest in relation to the media and human rights field. Different types of human rights (economic, social, political, civic, cultural), governments (from democratic to non-democratic) and political challenges (from climate change to refugees, from global health to conflict) naturally lead to different issues and research questions in relation to the media and human rights. This is beyond the possible for a chapter-length piece such as this, but the key debates and issues selected for discussion here try to highlight and illuminate a range of pathways of interest that reflect the most pressing concerns, challenges and debates.

Discussion points

1. Can we predict what types of roles media will play in relation to upholding or eroding human rights if we know enough about any given country's political and geographical context?
2. How convincing are causal arguments linking the co-emergence of new/social/digital media with what some have described as a 'turning tide' against international human rights?
3. Why is it so hard to maintain a human rights frame in the public debate when it comes to policies on migration and refugees?

Further reading

Balabanova, E., and A. Balch. 2020. "Norm Destruction, Norm Resilience: The Media and Refugee Protection in the UK and Hungary During Europe's 'Migrant Crisis'." *Journal of Language and Politics* 19 (3): 413–35.

Dasandi, N., and L. Erez. 2023. "The Flag and the Stick: Aid Suspensions, Human Rights, and the Problem of the Complicit Public." *World Development* 168.

Haas, J. 2020. *Freedom of the Media and Artificial Intelligence*. Office of the OSCE Representative on Freedom of the Media, Organisation for Security and Cooperation in Europe. https://www.osce.org/files/f/documents/4/5/472488.pdf.

Notes

1 See resolution adopted by the General Assembly on March 2, 2022, Aggression Against Ukraine, A/RES/ES-11/1.

2 Resolution ES-10/21, 10th emergency special session of the United Nations General Assembly relating to the Israel–Hamas war, October 27, 2023.
3 Centre for Media Monitoring (CfMM) was created by the Muslim Council of Britain in 2018 to monitor British media coverage of Muslims and Islam.
4 Adopted at the United Nations Sustainable Development Summit on September 25, 2015.
5 https://press.un.org/en/2023/sgsm21776.doc.htm.
6 https://www.un.org/sustainabledevelopment/sdg-media-compact-about/.
7 SDG 10 ('to reduce inequality within and among countries'), Target 10.7 ('facilitate orderly, safe, regular and responsible migration and mobility of people, including through the implementation of planned and well-managed migration policies').
8 https://www.amnesty.org/en/latest/press-release/2021/03/eu-anniversary-of-turkey-deal-offers-warning-against-further-dangerous-migration-deals/.

References

Allendoerfer, M. G. 2017. "Who Cares About Human Rights? Public Opinion About Human Rights Foreign Policy." *Journal of Human Rights* 16 (4): 428–51.
Alston, P. 2017. "Dialogue on Human Rights in the Populist Era (Lecture, Given at the London School of Economics on 1 December 2016)." *Journal of Human Rights Practice* 9: 1–15.
Bacevic, J. 2024. "No Such Thing as Free Speech? Performativity, Free Speech, and Academic Freedom in the UK." *Law and Critique*. Early Access.
Bachman, J. S., and E. Brito Ruiz. 2024. "The Geopolitics of Human Suffering: A Comparative Study of Media Coverage of the Conflicts in Yemen and Ukraine." *Third World Quarterly* 45 (1): 24–42.
Bakardjieva, M. 2020. "'Say It Loud, Say It Clear . . .': Concerting Solidarity in the Canadian Refugees Welcome Movement (2015–2016)." *Canadian Review of Sociology/Revue canadienne de sociologie* 57: 632–55.
Balabanova, E. 2014. *The Media and Human Rights: The Cosmopolitan Promise*. Routledge.
Balabanova, E., and A. Balch. 2020. "Norm Destruction, Norm Resilience: The Media and Refugee Protection in the UK and Hungary During Europe's 'Migrant Crisis'." *Journal of Language and Politics* 19 (3): 413–35.
Balch, A., and E. Balabanova. 2016. "Ethics, Politics and Migration: Public Debates on the Free Movement of Romanians and Bulgarians in the UK, 2006–2013." *Politics* 36 (1): 19–35.
Barisione, M., A. Michailidou, and M. Airoldi. 2019. "Understanding a Digital Movement of Opinion: The Case of #RefugeesWelcome." *Information, Communication & Society* 22 (8): 1145–64.
Barnhurst, K. G. 2016. "The Problem of Modern Locations in US News." *International Journal of Media & Cultural Politics* 12 (2): 151–69.
Bennett, W. L., R. G. Lawrence, and S. Livingston. 2008. *When the Press Fails: Political Power and the News Media From Iraq to Katrina*. University of Chicago Press.
Berry, M., I. Garcia-Blanco, and K. Moore. 2015. *Press Coverage of the Refugee and Migrant Crisis in the EU: A Content Analysis of Five European Countries*. Report Prepared for the United Nations High Commission for Refugees. https://www.unhcr.org/media/press-coverage-refugee-and-migrant-crisis-eu-content-analysis-five-european-countries.
Brandle, S. 2015. *Television News and Human Rights in the US & UK: The Violations Will Not Be Televised*. Routledge.
Brandle, S. 2018. "Media Coverage of Human Rights in the US and UK: The Violations Still Won't Be Televised (Or Published)." *Human Rights Review* 19 (2): 167–91.

Braun, J., and S. Arves. 2017. "Tailoring the Message: How the Political Left and Right Think Differently About Human Rights." *Open Global Initiative*. https://www.openglobalrights.org/Tailorin-%20the-message-How-the-political-left-and-right-think-differently-about-human-rights/.

Briones, R., S. Madden, and M. Janoske. 2013. "Kony 2012: Invisible Children and the Challenges of Social Media Campaigning and Digital Activism." *Journal of Current Issues in Media & Telecommunications* 5 (3).

Caliendo, S. M., M. P. Gibney, and A. Payne. 1999. "'All the News That's Fit to Print?' New York Times Coverage of Human Rights Violations." *Harvard International Journal of Press/Politics* 4: 48–69.

CoE. 2024. *Serious Human Rights Concerns About United Kingdom's Rwanda Bill*. Statement, Commissioner for Human Rights (Michael O'Flaherty), Council of Europe. https://www.coe.int/en/web/commissioner/-/serious-human-rights-concerns-about-united-kingdom-s-rwanda-bill.

Cole, W. M. 2010. "No News is Good News: Human Rights Coverage in the American Print Media, 1980–2000." *Journal of Human Rights* 9 (3): 303–25.

Cottle, S. 2011. "Media and the Arab Uprisings of 2011: Research Notes." *Journalism* 12 (5): 647–59.

Curran, J., and J. Seaton. 2003. *Power Without Responsibility: The Press, Broadcasting and New Media in Britain*. Routledge.

Dasandi, N., and L. Erez. 2023. "The Flag and the Stick: Aid Suspensions, Human Rights, and the Problem of the Complicit Public." *World Development* 168.

Dowler, K. 2004. "Dual Realities? Criminality, Victimization, and the Presentation of Race on Local Television News." *Journal of Crime and Justice* 27 (2): 79–99.

Farge, E. 2023. "UN Marks 75 Years of Human Rights Declaration in Shadow of Gaza." *Reuters*, December 11. https://www.reuters.com/world/un-marks-75-years-human-rights-declaration-shadow-gaza-2023-12-11/.

Fengler, S., M. Bastian, J. Brinkmann, A. C. Zappe, V. Tatah, M. Andindilile, E. Assefa, M. Chibita, A. Mbaine, L. Obonyo, and M. Lengauer. 2022. "Covering Migration – In Africa and Europe: Results From a Comparative Analysis of 11 Countries." *Journalism Practice* 16 (1): 140–60.

Galtung, J., and M. H. Ruge. 1965. "The Structure of Foreign News: The Presentation of the Congo, Cuba and Cyprus Crises in Four Norwegian Newspapers." *Journal of Peace Research* 2: 64–91.

Galvin, M. 2019. "Human Rights in Age of Social Media, Big Data, and AI." *The National Academies of Sciences, Engineering, and Medicine*, September 23. https://www.nationalacademies.org/news/2019/09/human-rights-in-age-of-social-media-big-data-and-ai.

Georgiou, M., and R. Zaborowski. 2017. *Media Coverage of the "Refugee Crisis": A Cross-European Perspective*. Council of Europe Report (DG1(2017)03). Council of Europe.

Haas, J. 2020. "Freedom of the Media and Artificial Intelligence." Report by Julia Haas, Office of the OSCE Representative on Freedom of the Media, Organisation for Security and Cooperation in Europe. https://www.osce.org/files/f/documents/4/5/472488.pdf.

Haddad, M. 2023. "Where Does Your Country Stand on the Russia-Ukraine War?" *Al-Jazeera News*, February 16. https://www.aljazeera.com/news/2023/2/16/mapping-where-every-country-stands-on-the-russia-ukraine-war.

Hall, N. 2019. "Norm Contestation in the Digital Era: Campaigning for Refugee Rights." *International Affairs* 95 (3): 575–95.

Hanif, F. 2024. *Media Bias Gaza 2023–24*. Centre for Media Monitoring (CfMM). https://cfmm.org.uk/resources/publication/cfmm-report-media-bias-gaza-2023-24/.

Harcup, T., and D. O'Neil. 2001. "What is News? Galtung and Ruge Revisited." *Journalism Studies* 2 (2): 261–80.

International Council on Human Rights Policy (ICHRP). 2002. *Journalism, Media and the Challenge of Human Rights Reporting*. ICHRP.

Internews. 2012. *Speak Up, Speak Out: A Toolkit for Reporting on Human Rights Issues*. Washington: Internews.

Jackson, H. M. 2024. "*The New York Times* Distorts the Palestinian Struggle: A Case Study of Anti-Palestinian Bias in US News Coverage of the First and Second Palestinian Intifadas." *Media, War & Conflict* 17 (1): 116–35.

Jones, B., and S. Malcorra. 2020. "Competing for Order: Confronting the Long Crisis of Multilateralism." Brookings and IE University School of Global and Public Affairs, Part of the Series: 'Competitive Multilateralism: Revitalization and Realism in an Era of Global Tension'.

Khan, I. 2022. "Reinforcing Media Freedom and the Safety of Journalists in the Digital Age." Report of the Special Rapporteur on the Promotion and Protection of the Right to Freedom of Opinion and Expression, United Nations Human Rights Council, Fiftieth Session, June 13– July 8, 2022 Agenda Item 3.

Kuper, S. 2024. "No News is Bad News." *Financial Times Magazine*, March 21. https://www.ft.com/content/451e7466-7a91-4784-aa37-02993ff0fc9e.

Langer, A. I., and J. B. Gruber. 2021. "Political Agenda Setting in the Hybrid Media System: Why Legacy Media Still Matter a Great Deal." *The International Journal of Press/Politics* 26 (2): 313–40.

Lee, S. 2018. "The Role of Social Media in Protest Participation: The Case of Candlelight Vigils in South Korea." *International Journal of Communication* 12: 1523–40.

Levy, B., and J. Patz. 2015. "Climate Change, Human Rights, and Social Justice." *Annals of Global Health* 81 (3): 310–22.

Llansó, E., J. van Hoboken, P. Leerssen, and J. Harambam. 2020. "Artificial Intelligence, Content Moderation, and Freedom of Expression." Transatlantic Working Group (TWG) on Content Moderation Online and Freedom of Expression. https://www.ivir.nl/publicaties/download/AI-Llanso-Van-Hoboken-Feb-2020.pdf.

Logan, J. 2019. "New Year, New Human Rights Narratives?" *Open Global Rights*. https://www.openglobalrights.org/new-year-new-human-rights-narratives/.

Maier, S. R. 2021. "News Coverage of Human Rights: Investigating Determinants of Media Attention." *Journalism* 22 (7): 1612–28.

Minow, M. 2021. *Saving the News: Why the Constitution Calls for Government Action to Preserve Freedom of Speech*. Oxford University Press.

Nerghes, A., and J. S. Lee. 2019. "Narratives of the Refugee Crisis: A Comparative Study of Mainstream Media and Twitter." *Media and Communication* 7 (2): 275–88.

Noor, I. J. 2024. "Challenging the American Empire: A History of Hypocrisy and Double Standards in Human Rights." *Tapestries: Interwoven Voices of Local and Global Identities* 13 (1): Article 3.

O'Callaghan, S., A. Khan, K. Nwajiaku-Dahou, T. Tindall, L. Fouad, and C. Milesi. 2023. "Humanitarian Hypocrisy, Double Standards and the Law in Gaza." Expert Comment, ODI Website (Formerly the Overseas Development Institute). https://odi.org/en/insights/humanitarian-hypocrisy-double-standards-and-the-law-in-gaza/.

O'Neill, D., and T. Harcup. 2009. "News Values and Selectivity." In *The Handbook of Journalism Studies*, edited by K. Wahl-Jorgensen and T. Hanitzsch, 161–74. Routledge.

Ovsiovitch, J. S. 1993. "News Coverage of Human Rights." *Political Research Quarterly* 46: 671–89.

Palmer, J. 2000. *Spinning into Control: News Values and Source Strategies*. Leicester University Press.

Połońska-Kimunguyi, E. 2022. "Echoes of Empire: Racism and Historical Amnesia in the British Media Coverage of Migration." *Humanities and Social Sciences Communications* 9 (3).

Prøitz, L. 2018. "Visual Social Media and Affectivity: The Impact of the Image of Alan Kurdi and Young People's Response to the Refugee Crisis in Oslo and Sheffield." *Information, Communication & Society* 21 (4): 548–63.

Ramos, H., J. Ron, and O. N. T. Thoms. 2007. "Shaping the Northern Media's Human Rights Coverage, 1986–2000." *Journal of Peace Research* 44 (4): 385–406.

Ranji, B., and C. Archetti. 2024. "The Details That Matter: Racism in Norwegian Media During the Covid-19 Pandemic." *Media, Culture & Society* 46 (7): 1397–413. https://doi.org/10.1177/01634437241241482.

Repucci, S. 2019. "Freedom and the Media 2019: A Downward Spiral." Report Essay Published in the 'Freedom and the Media 2019' Report, Freedom House, June. https://freedomhouse.org/sites/default/files/2020-02/FINAL07162019_Freedom_And_The_Media_2019_Report.pdf.

Riffe, D., S. Kim, and M. R. Sobel. 2018. "News Borrowing Revisited: A 50-Year Perspective." *Journalism and Mass Communication Quarterly* 95 (4): 909–29.

Sabatini, C., ed. 2022. *Reclaiming Human Rights in a Changing World Order*. London: Chatham House; Washington: Brookings Institution Press. https://www.chathamhouse.org/2022/10/reclaiming-human-rights-changing-world-order.

Sampaio-Dias, S. 2016. *Reporting Human Rights*. Peter Lang.

Scherman, A., N. Etchegaray, I. Pavez, and D. Grassau. 2022. "The Influence of Media Coverage on the Negative Perception of Migrants in Chile." *International Journal of Environmental Research and Public Health* 19 (13): 8219.

Spadaro, A. 2020. "COVID-19: Testing the Limits of Human Rights." *European Journal of Risk Regulation* 11 (2): 317–25.

Suami T. 2023. "Dead or Alive? Global Constitutionalism and International Law After the Start of the War in Ukraine." *Global Constitutionalism* 1–30.

Trithart, A., and O. Case. 2023. "Do People Trust the UN? A Look at the Data." *IPI Global Observatory*, February 22. https://theglobalobservatory.org/2023/02/do-people-trust-the-un-a-look-at-the-data/.

Tumber, H., and S. Waisbord, eds. 2017. *The Routledge Companion to Media and Human Rights*. Routledge.

Valenzuela, S. 2013. "Unpacking the Use of Social Media for Protest Behavior: The Roles of Information, Opinion Expression, and Activism." *American Behavioral Scientist* 57 (7): 920–42.

Wilson, A., V. Parker, and M. Feinberg. 2020. "Polarization in the Contemporary Political and Media Landscape." *Current Opinion in Behavioral Sciences* 34: 223–28.

Wölker, A., and T. E. Powell. 2021. "Algorithms in the Newsroom? News Readers' Perceived Credibility and Selection of Automated Journalism." *Journalism* 22 (1): 86–103.

Wu, H. 2000. "Systemic Determinants of International News Coverage: A Comparison of 38 Countries." *Journal of Communication* 50 (2): 110–30.

3
A RIGHTS-BASED APPROACH TO THE SAFETY OF JOURNALISTS

Sara Torsner

Introduction

This chapter unpacks the meaning of a rights-based approach to the safety of journalists and demonstrates its value in understanding key considerations relating to the manifestations and consequences of human rights violations targeting journalists. In doing so, it proposes that a rights-based perspective, grounded in international human rights standards, can inform the development of an evaluative framework to support a better empirical understanding of journalism safety problems and ultimately facilitate their more effective redress. A rights-based approach combines two central issues which together form the justificatory rationale for the protection of journalists under international human rights law. The first is recognition of the individual journalist as a holder of human rights, such as rights to expression and publication, and acknowledgement that journalists should be able to exercise their individual rights and journalistic practice without undue interference. The second is understanding that infringements of the rights of journalists impede the capacity of the public to receive and exchange information and ideas. In this way, international human rights law recognises that breaches of the rights of journalists not only represent an attack on the rights of individual journalists but also on the instrumental role that journalism plays in upholding the collective right of all members of society to stay informed. Differently expressed, safeguarding journalists can be understood to span two interrelated dimensions of significance – the standing of the individual journalist as a *rights-holder* and the role the journalist plays as a *rights-protector* on behalf of the public. The former refers to the rights held by journalists by virtue of being a human being. The latter to the specific role journalists play in realizing the collective dimensions of rights to freedom of expression and to information, as a means to keep society well-informed.

Accordingly, any comprehensive empirical account of threats to the safety of journalists needs to capture both how violations of the rights-holding status of journalists are manifest and how the wider societal consequences of such violations impact the rights-protecting role of journalists. However, current data gathering initiatives documenting safety violations against journalists do not systematically and explicitly focus on the role journalists play as rights-protectors. The argument put forward here is that by adopting a rights-based outlook – combining the dimensions of the *journalist as rights-holder* and the *journalist as rights-protector* – we can build an evaluative framework which can function as a future-facing path for a more holistic assessment and empirical documentation of threats to the safety of journalists. Ultimately, then, the value of the rights-based approach and its wider consideration of societies to engage in meaningful communication and exchange of ideas is its ability to support the development of a more comprehensive empirical evidence base. Such empirical evidence can in turn inform advocacy and policy efforts to push for stronger accountability mechanisms to ensure that duty-bearing states live up to their obligations to protect journalists under international law.

To this end, the following steps will be undertaken in this chapter: First, providing an understanding of the meaning of a rights-based approach alongside its application to issues related to the safety of journalists as established in international human rights law. Second, two case studies will be discussed as a means to understand the value and limitations of current efforts to monitor threats to the safety of journalists in supporting a holistic empirical understanding of safety threats to journalists from a rights-based perspective. The first of these case studies is the Sustainable Development Goal (SDG) Indicator 16.10.1, a UN-led rights-based agenda to achieve global systematic monitoring of occurrences of human rights violations against journalists. The second case study is the "Journalists Killed" data set compiled by press freedom watchdog the Committee to Protect Journalists (CPJ, https://cpj.org/).

Finally, a case will be made for an expanded monitoring agenda by demonstrating how a rights-based perspective can open up possibilities and pave the way for strengthened and broadened documentation of rights violations against journalists. In doing so, the chapter discusses the work of Forbidden Stories (https://forbiddenstories.org/), a network of investigative journalists aiming to protect, pursue and publish the work of journalists facing threats, prison or murder.

By taking these steps we can better comprehend the insidious nature of human rights violations against journalists, and more specifically deepen our understanding of the chilling – or deterring – effect these have on journalistic expression and by extension the harm it causes the public's capacity to stay informed.

The meaning of a rights-based approach and its application to matters of journalism safety

Whilst no single definition of a rights-based approach exists, the UN identifies a set of applicable key characteristics (UN 2003). Accordingly, the UN's Human Rights-Based Approach (HRBA) can be summarised as a 'framework for the process of human development that is normatively based on international human rights standards and operationally directed to promoting and protecting human rights' (UN n.d.a). Correspondingly, a rights-based approach can be understood as placing international human rights – such as the right to life and liberty, freedom from slavery and torture, as well as the freedom to opinion and expression[1] – centre stage in relation to any given situation or issue. As such it can be applied to various fields, decision-making processes and policies to ensure the protection and realisation of fundamental human rights (see e.g., Landman 2006, 136).

A rights-based approach on the one hand seeks to protect the fundamental rights of individuals and groups – the claims of rights-holders – as enshrined in the Universal Declaration of Human Rights (UDHR), human rights treaties and other international human rights instruments. On the other hand, it aims to ensure that states and non-state actors – as duty-bearers – meet their obligations to respect, protect and fulfil these rights (UN n.d.a). In this light, a rights-based approach to the safety of journalists needs to begin with a consideration of the standing of journalists as rights-holders. Human rights bodies have adopted a broad and functional definition of journalists as

> individuals who observe and describe events, document and analyse events, statements, policies, and any propositions that can affect society, with the purpose of systematising such information and gathering of facts and analyses to inform sectors of society or society as a whole.
>
> *(UNHRC 2012, 3)*

Accordingly, journalism is understood as 'a function shared by a wide range of actors, including professional full-time reporters and analysts, as well as bloggers and others who engage in forms of self-publication' (HRC 2011, 11).

While journalists have rights (as noted earlier) simply by virtue of being human, infringements of the rights of a journalist also prevent journalists from performing their professional role of publicising and disseminating information in the public interest. By extension, then, curtailment of journalistic expression is therefore understood to have an added dimension of significance as 'attacks on the function of journalism itself in a democracy' (Parmar 2014, 20), ultimately jeopardizing the capacity of society at large to be kept informed. Put another way, journalists are in fact facilitating a form of rights-protection on behalf of members of society when it comes to protecting the public's right to exchange and receive information and ideas. That is, they both rely on and at the same time promote and protect freedom of expression. Article 19 (2) of the International Covenant on Civil and Political Rights (ICCPR) codifies the right to freedom of expression:

> Everyone shall have the right to freedom of expression; this right shall include freedom to seek, receive and impart information and ideas of all kinds, regardless of frontiers, either orally, in writing or in print, in the form of art, or through any other media of his choice.
>
> *(UNGA 1976)*

Importantly, the right has been interpreted to apply not only to '"information" or "ideas" that are favourably received or regarded as inoffensive or as a matter of indifference, but also to those that offend, shock or disturb the State or any sector of the population' (ECtHR 1976, para. 49). In essence, freedom of expression is widely understood as 'a foundational human right of the greatest importance' (Mendel 2010, 1) and as integral to the realisation of all human rights (UNGA 1946, para. 1), including rights to freedom of assembly and association (HRC 2011, para. 4).

Central to the understanding of the societal importance of freedom of expression is that the right does not only apply to the person expressing or disseminating information and ideas, but it extends to the collective capacity of a public 'to seek and receive information and ideas' (Mendel 2010, 4). This is sometimes referred to as the principle of 'the right to know' (Stiglitz 1999), which recognises that '[i]mplicit in freedom of expression is the public's right to open access to information and to know what Governments are doing on their behalf' (ECOSOC 2000, 54), as well as 'to participate in decision-making processes' (ECOSOC 2000, 62). This then underpins the understanding that restrictions of an individual's right to freedom of expression 'not only [violate] the right of that individual . . ., but also the right of all others to "receive" information and ideas' (IACtHR 1985, 8–9). The particular importance of journalism for effective freedom of expression as expressed in international human rights law can be understood through the notions of press freedom and the accompanying right to information. UNESCO (2015, 19) refers to press freedom and the right to information as corollaries of the general right to freedom of expression with press freedom being understood here as 'the freedom to publish to a wider audience' or 'the right to impart information on a mass scale'. Therefore,

> [t]he status of press freedom designates the particular use of this right of expression on public media platforms, where its social visibility and significance means that press freedom serves as a barometer of the wider right to freedom of expression.
>
> *(UNESCO 2018, 20)*

Journalists then can be described as performing a key role as agents of free expression on behalf of others and as potential mediators of public interchange. Accordingly, an environment where journalists are safe to report is recognised as an important underlying component for ensuring actual press freedom and the wider right to freedom of expression (UNESCO 2014). Thus, in the same way as the right to freedom of expression has both an individual and collective dimension, attacks against journalists violate the journalists' individual rights on the one hand, but they also jeopardize the right of society at large to be kept informed. Importantly the curtailing of journalistic expression is also likely to cause journalists to self-censor out of fear of reprisals and such developments may 'compromise editorial independence and remove ethical choice, as well as limiting the extent of pluralism possible within the media choices available to a society' (UNESCO 2014, 19). This disturbing effect 'is all the more piercing when the prevalence of attacks and intimidation is compounded by a culture of legal impunity for their perpetrators' (McGonagle 2013, 4). As noted earlier, another way to put this is to see the individual journalist practitioner as a holder of fundamental rights, and as facilitating a form of rights protection on behalf of members of society when it comes to protecting the public's right to receive information and ideas.

Drawing on this understanding, then, it is possible to establish a basic evaluative framework that recognises what can be described as a 'special status' of journalists. Hence any evaluation of threats to journalists and the practice of free and independent journalism has to recognise the safe practice of journalism as a form of 'rights protection' with regard to freedom of expression and the public's right to receive information and ideas.

The argument put forward here therefore is that because of the instrumental role and societal value of journalism in realizing effective freedom of expression and access to information in societies, journalism, as an everyday practice, should be understood as always serving a rights-protecting role on behalf of all members of society.[2] To consider the degree to which current empirical evidence accounts for this rights-protecting quality of journalism, the chapter will now examine SDG Indicator 16.10.1, which establishes a monitoring framework of global scope to document threats to the safety of journalists as part of the UN 2030 development agenda. The question then becomes whether the framework can support a comprehensive understanding of the significance of human rights violations against journalists as representing infringements of the *journalist as rights-holder* and the *journalist as rights-protector*.

Case study 1: the SDG 16.10.1 framework to monitor human rights violations against journalists

Monitoring the compliance of duty-bearers with human rights standards by establishing a reliable empirical record of instances of human rights violations is an important tool to strengthen the protection of human rights and realising a human rights-based agenda. Effective human rights documentation can serve as an accountability measure reminding states and other actors of their obligations to uphold human rights. By supporting identification of patterns and trends, monitoring can also inform laws, policies and practices to more effectively protect human rights (OHCHR 2011; Landman and Carvalho 2010).

Previous research has highlighted that current empirical understandings of problems related to the safety of journalists are 'fragmentary', highlighting a

> need [for] comprehensive information that covers the breadth of the issue, and which also allows for the in-depth analysis of causes, consequences, and correctives over time. Such information is indispensable for awareness-raising and capacity-building, as well as for devising and operating mechanisms to ensure the effective protection of journalists and prosecution of their attackers.
> *(Berger 2022, 78; see also: Harrison, Maynard and Torsner 2022; Torsner 2017)*

In this context, the UN 2030 Sustainable Development Goals (SDG) Agenda, Indicator 16.10.1 proposes an important rights-based agenda for the global systematic monitoring of human rights violations against journalists covering the: 'Number of verified cases of killing, kidnapping, enforced disappearance, arbitrary detention and torture of journalists, associated media personnel, trade unionists and human rights defenders in the previous 12 months' (UNDESA n.d.a). As expressed by Berger, this monitoring agenda represents crucial recognition of the fact that safety for journalists constitutes a necessary condition for sustainable and human rights-centred development. It is also significant because it articulates a commitment by duty-bearing states to safeguard journalists as part of their work to actualize the SDG Agenda:

> it is a 'big deal' to have the safety of journalists, and the monitoring thereof, recognised within the UN's current development agenda. . . . This gives journalists' safety a particular framing that is both significant conceptually and politically, thereby enabling new opportunities to cast light on its relevance as an issue to society.
> *(2022, 79)*

Adopted by all UN member states in 2015, the UN SDG Agenda is a comprehensive plan of action to respond to urgent global challenges such as improving health and education, reducing inequality, fostering economic growth, as well as addressing environmental degradation and climate change. Progress (and setbacks) are assessed across 17 interconnected SDGs[3] with specified formulated targets (UNDESA n.d.b). As part of this framework of indicators, threats to the safety of journalists have been included under SDG 16, which seeks to promote 'peace, justice and strong institutions', and Target 16.10, which specifies 'public access to information and fundamental freedoms' as a prerequisite to achieve the goal's overarching objectives (UNDESA n.d.a).

Combined, indicator 16.10.1, which tracks occurrences of human rights violations against journalists as outlined earlier, and indicator 16.10.2,[4] which catalogues changes regarding the status of the legal protection of access to information, signal how well societies 'respect and uphold individual rights, as well as the right to privacy, freedom of expression, and access to information' (UN n.d.b) (as captured by Target 16.10).

SDG 16.10.1 specifically measures the enjoyment of fundamental rights by actors, including journalists, 'who actively defend human rights' (OHCHR 2023). As such, the indicator covers violations of rights such as freedom of opinion and expression and access to information. While the indicator assesses the degree to which the rights-holding status of the individual journalists is upheld in this way, the framework also recognizes that these violations 'not only have a direct impact on victims' enjoyment of rights but have a massive inhibiting effect on the general population (OHCHR n.d.b). Subsequently, it is the significance of these violations of the rights of journalists in terms of how these impede the capacity of the public to effectively enjoy rights to freedom of expression and to receive and exchange information and ideas which makes them particularly important to document. The framework thus recognises the two dimensions of significance mentioned previously in this chapter. However, while violations against journalists as holders of rights are assessed, the rights-protecting role of journalists is only implicitly embedded into the framework, and not expressly measured.

The UN's systematically collected data on SDG 16.10.1 is currently only available on one type of violation targeting journalists, namely instances of killings (Berger 2022). This data is compiled by UNESCO which keeps a record of journalists killed since 1993 in the organisation's 'Observatory of Killed Journalists' (UNESCO n.d.). As discussed elsewhere (Harrison, Maynard and Torsner 2022; see also, Berger 2022), lack of data availability across the full range of categories of human rights violations covered in SDG 16.10.1, remains a challenge to achieving comprehensive and standardised globalised monitoring of the safety of journalists in line with the indicator.

The current data on killings collected by UNESCO represent high-level statistical counts. This means that what is accounted for is the number of instances of killings occurring in countries and globally. In addition to this statistical count of the number of killings, the UNESCO Observatory also provides some additional data disaggregation such as information regarding the gender of the journalist, whether the journalist killed was staff or freelance, what type of media they worked for and whether the killing took place in a conflict zone or not.[5] However, while UNESCO only records cases where a journalist has been confirmed as having been killed as a result of their work, no information is provided on the underlying motives of perpetrators.

Furthermore, no details are provided on what type of journalistic activities the killed journalist was undertaking, including what kind of journalistic beats or stories they were working on. This is information that could arguably support a better understanding of the rights-protecting role of journalists, and what kind of information society is at risk of losing out on.

While this means that the rights-protector role is not expressly documented in the UNESCO data, the Methodological Guidance Note on SDG Indicator 16.10.1 (OHCHR n.d.b) provides insights into how data collection for the indicator can be further developed to that end. The guidance uses the 'Who did What to whom, Where and Why?'[6] framework as a starting point for classifying a human rights violation as a statistical event. Accordingly, this analytical construct can be summarized to cover information on the perpetrator (Who did), the violation type (What), information about the victim (To whom), the incident date (When), and finally the context of the incident (Why), including information on the motive (link to journalistic activities and violation of fundamental right) as well as the thematic area of engagement of the victim.

This guidance is clearly focused on facilitating effective monitoring of human rights violations as per the definition and scope of SDG 16.10.1. Interestingly however, the 'Why-dimension' opens up possibilities to consider how human rights documentation on violations against journalists could be expanded to not only record the nature of the human rights abuse itself but to take into account what kind of journalistic information is censored when journalists are targets of human rights violations. Systematically documenting what kind of journalistic information is suppressed can arguably support a better understanding of how such abuse impacts the capacity of the public to stay well-informed. While this why-dimension currently is not covered in UNESCO's data, the monitoring work of press freedom watchdog CPJ provides an opportunity to explore possibilities to more effectively document the chilling effect of human rights violations against journalists on the public's ability to stay informed, and ultimately the rights-protecting role of journalists.

Case study 2: the CPJ data set on journalist killings

A number of civil society organisations around the world carry out crucial work to document threats to the safety of journalists. While these organisations employ diverse methodological approaches to undertake such monitoring,[7] the shared rationale for this collective documentation effort is commonly grounded in the rights-based arguments for safeguarding journalistic practice as articulated in international human rights law.[8] Statistical tallies covering the type and incidence of targeted attacks on journalists compiled by these organisations represent one of the primary sources of empirical evidence through which we can understand whether safety for journalists is improving or deteriorating (Torsner 2017).

Out of the wealth of statistical accounts collated by press freedom organisations internationally and nationally, the CPJ dataset on "Journalists Killed" (CPJ n.d.a) is one of the most comprehensive global datasets; it provides a systematic open access record (starting in 1992) of journalist killings, the most serious type of human rights violation. The CPJ's data collection methodology is also a commonly adopted approach amongst other civil society data collectors. As such, it has broader relevance and application when it comes to illustrating the value and limitations of human rights documentation practices.

The CPJ methodology is designed to record statistical count data of the number of killings on country-level, as well as additional categories of information in a similar way as the UNESCO-provided data previously discussed. The CPJ investigates and verifies the circumstances behind each case of a journalist fatality before it is recorded. The organisation considers a case 'confirmed' if it can be ascertained that the journalist in question 'was murdered in direct reprisal for his or her work; in combat or crossfire; or while carrying out a dangerous assignment' (CPJ).[9] Whereas the UNESCO data set – as previously noted – does not record information on the perpetrator likely responsible for the killing, the CPJ provides such information through the category 'suspected source of fire in killings of journalists'. This category covers political groups, government officials, military officials, paramilitary groups, criminal groups, mob violence and local residents engaged in violence triggered by news coverage. CPJ also documents the judicial process for each confirmed murder case to track the status of judicial resolution.[10] What makes the CPJ data set an interesting case is thus the fact that the recorded instances of killings are disaggregated to provide additional information on the previously discussed dimension of 'Why' journalists are attacked, as well as what type of journalistic work the targeted journalist was undertaking.

The obvious value of the CPJ tally as outlined thus far is reflected in its ability to systematize key information related to the circumstances of a deadly attack on a journalist through numeric representations and in doing so it generates comparative understanding showing which countries are the most dangerous ones for journalists, who the perpetrators are, what kind of job roles place journalists most at risk, and, how impunity rates for journalist killings fluctuate over time and across country contexts. In doing so, the emphasis of the tally is on detailed information on lethal human rights violations on the rights-bearing journalist.

Interestingly, an additional category of information included in the CPJ dataset can be understood to document attacks on journalists as rights-protectors on behalf of the public's right to know. This category of information records the journalistic beat the killed journalist was reporting on and covers issues related to business, corruption, crime, culture, human rights, politics or sports. The CPJ data shows that out of 1551 cases of journalist killings between 1992–2023, journalists involved in political journalism were most at risk of being targeted with lethal violence. 45% of journalists killed reported on stories connected to politics. The second most dangerous beat was war reporting (41%) followed by covering human rights issues (22%), corruption (21%), crime (19%), culture (12%), business (6%) and sports (3%).

In providing some basic information regarding what topic the killed journalist was covering, the dataset can in fact be used to establish an understanding not only of which journalistic beats are particularly risky but also to begin uncovering what kind of information the public loses out on when a journalist is killed. However, while the systematic inclusion of information on the journalistic beat in this way has the potential to support wider comprehension of the problem, the fact that only rudimentary information is currently made available by the organisation prevents any in-depth understanding of the work the journalist was pursuing, and which resulted in them being attacked.

This is a limitation with monitoring practices: While in-depth qualitative reports and specific data sets currently provide insights into the ways reporting on various topics, such as environmental issues (RSF 2020, 2021; Schwartzstein 2020), crime and corruption (Article 19, 2022; CPJ 2023; RSF 2018a; Transparency International 2020) as well as gender-related beats (RSF 2018b; Posetti et al. 2021), expose journalists to a range of human rights violations, a comprehensive account of how such violations effectively deny members of society access to public interest information is currently missing. In short, the consequences of these assaults remain unexamined in any systematic manner.

Towards an expanded rights-based empirical agenda for the more holistic documentation of threats to the safety of journalists

By combining categories of information that can facilitate a better understanding of how rights violations against journalists compromise both the status of the journalist as a rights-bearer and their role as rights-protectors, the CPJ data set provides an important step towards a comprehensive rights-based approach to monitor violations against journalists. In practical terms, however, the question becomes how the current evidence base can be strengthened and further expanded to capture in more detail not only the nature of human rights violations against journalists but the negative consequences of these on the public's capacity to stay informed.

To further illustrate the value of such an expanded rights-based empirical agenda for documenting human rights violations against journalists, the work of Forbidden Stories can be used to start building a picture of how attacks on journalists are in essence nothing other than an attempt to silence a news story and relatedly demonstrate the value of broadening the empirical documentation of threats to the safety of journalists to cover the rights-protecting role of journalism.

Founded in 2015, Forbidden Stories is a non-profit global network of journalists that utilize collaborative investigative journalism to pursue investigations of reporters who have been murdered, jailed or threatened and by doing so 'mak[ing] visible and impactful the work of reporters who can no longer investigate' (Forbidden Stories n.d.a). The goal of Forbidden Stories is ultimately 'to keep stories alive and to make sure that a maximum number of people have access to independent information on crucial topics, including the environment, health, human rights, and corruption' (Forbidden Stories n.d.a). By pursuing the stories of journalists who have been prevented from reporting, Forbidden Stories 'sends a powerful message to the enemies of press freedom that killing the journalist won't kill the story' while working both to 'deter . . . violence against journalists and ensur[ing] access to crucial information for millions of citizens around the world' (Forbidden Stories, n.d.a). In this way, the objectives of Forbidden Stories switch attention to the rights protecting properties of journalism. The story survives and rights abusers are further exposed.

For example, it is through the vehicle of investigative journalism that exposes rights abusers and their threats to the public that Forbidden Stories have pursued projects like 'The Raphael Project' (Forbidden Stories n.d.b.). 'The Raphael Project' is the continuation of the work of murdered Colombian journalist Rafael Moreno to shine a light on the detrimental health and environmental consequences of mining activities in northern Colombia. 'The Cartel Project' (Forbidden Stories n.d.c) is another example where Forbidden Stories took up the work of murdered journalist Regina Martínez on Mexican drug cartels and their political connections around the world. In essence, the rights protecting aspects of the stories 'survive beyond borders, beyond governments, beyond censorship' (Forbidden Stories n.d.a).

Whereas Forbidden Stories pursues an admirable journalistic mission to continue the stories of silenced journalists, the aim of the organisation is clearly not focused on building a systematic record of the ways in which the rights-protecting role of journalists is compromised. While moving towards such monitoring is currently purely a theoretical proposition, the work of Forbidden Stories helps us understand the value of a broadened rights-based approach to documenting threats to the safety of journalists.

Conclusion

As demonstrated in this chapter, an expanded rights-based empirical agenda needs to combine two interrelated issues: Recognition of the standing of the journalist practitioner as a holder of fundamental rights and recognition of the societal value of journalistic practice, as translated into the role of journalists as rights-protectors. The former is a matter of rights derived from the status of the journalist as a human being, while the latter is derived from the right of the public to be 'well informed citizens'. Obviously, these dimensions overlap and combine and yet current methodological approaches to empirical data gathering tend to favour a more one-dimensional approach – emphasising breaches of human rights of individual journalists. Interestingly, the documentation efforts of CPJ and the journalistic work of Forbidden Stories point to the value of a more multidimensional approach that enables us to also systematically document how the right to receive information is restricted via violations of the rights of journalists. This basic fact is often overlooked in empirical evaluations of threats to journalists and journalism. And yet by taking both the status of the journalist as a rights-holder and rights-protector into consideration, we can begin to understand and measure the nature and extent of the wider significance, including intangible phenomena like 'the chilling effect' of rights violations against journalism on the quality of communicative life.

Discussion questions

1. Why is it important to view the safety of journalists as a human rights issue? What fundamental human rights are particularly relevant to journalists?
2. What are the primary threats to journalist safety worldwide? Are there certain regions of the world where journalists face greater risks? Why?
3. What role do governments play in protecting or endangering journalists?
4. How can we measure the effectiveness of efforts to protect journalists?

Further reading

McGoldrick, Dominic. 2022. "Thought, Expression, Association, and Assembly." In *International Human Rights Law*, edited by Daniel Moeckli, Sangeeta Shah, Sandesh Sivakumaran, and David Harris, 4th ed. Oxford: Oxford University Press.

Harrison, Jackie, and Sara Torsner. 2022. "Safety of Journalists and Media Freedom: Trends in Non-EU Countries From a Human Rights Perspective." https://www.europarl.europa.eu/thinktank/en/document/EXPO_BRI(2022)702562.

UNESCO. "UN Plan of Action on the Safety of Journalists and the Issue of Impunity." CI-12/CONF.202/6. https://unesdoc.unesco.org/ark:/48223/pf0000384476.

United Nations High Commissioner for Human Rights. n.d. "How International Human Rights Standards and Mechanisms Help Protect Journalists." https://www.ohchr.org/sites/default/files/documents/issues/ruleoflaw/How-HR-standards-mechanisms-protect-journalists.pdf.

Notes

1 See the ICCPR (UNGA 1976) for the full list.
2 This can be contrasted with OHCHR's (n.d.a) seemingly more narrow interpretation of who is a 'human rights defender' which states that journalists 'In their

general role, ... are not human rights defenders. However, many journalists do act as defenders, for example when they report on human rights abuses and bear witness to acts that they have seen'.
3 For a full list of the 17 SDGs see UNDESA (n.d.b).
4 The second indicator, SDG 16.10.2, assesses the 'Number of countries that adopt and implement constitutional, statutory and/or policy guarantees for public access to information' (OHCHR 2021).
5 In addition to the statistical records of killings UNESCO also provides a digital library of responses from states on the judicial status of cases of killings which has been condemned by UNESCO.
6 For more information on this monitoring framework see Landman and Carvalho (2010).
7 For an overview of the range of actors and diversity in methodological approaches used see Torsner (2017).
8 See for example the mission statements by press freedom organisations CPJ (https://cpj.org/about/video/#values) and Reporters Without Borders (RSF) (https://rsf.org/en/who-are-we).
9 To take these categories in turn "murder" is understood to capture the targeted killing of a journalist as a result of their journalistic work. Both intentional and non-intentional killings are included. The category "crossfire/combat" covers killings occurring on a battlefield or in a military context whereas "dangerous assignment" includes deaths occurring in connection to covering a demonstration, riot, clashes between rival groups and mob situations. The category includes 'assignments which are not expected to entail physical risk but turn violent unexpectedly'.
10 Categories of information recorded are: complete impunity (no convictions have been obtained); partial justice (some but not all of those responsible have been convicted; typically, assassins are convicted but not those who ordered the killing); and full justice (everyone responsible is convicted, including perpetrators and those who commissioned them).

References

Article 19. 2022. "Italy: Lawsuits, Threats of Violence and Organised Crime Hinder Journalists." https://www.article19.org/resources/italy-lawsuits-threats-of-violence-and-organised-crime-hinder-journalists/.
Berger, Guy. 2022. "New Opportunities in Monitoring Safety of Journalists Through the UN's 2030 Sustainable Development Agenda." *Media and Communication* 8 (1): 78–88.
CPJ. n.d.a. "Journalists Killed Since 1992." https://cpj.org/data/killed/all/?status=Killed&motiveConfirmed%5B%5D=Confirmed&type%5B%5D=Journalist&start_year=1992&end_year=2024&group_by=year.
CPJ. n.d.b. "Our Mission." https://cpj.org/about/video/#values.
CPJ. 2023. "Violence Against Netherlands' Journalists Dims a Beacon of Press Freedom." https://cpj.org/2023/08/violence-against-netherlands-journalists-dims-a-beacon-of-press-freedom/.
ECOSOC. 2000. "Civil and Political Rights Including the Question of: Freedom of Expression." *Commission on Human Rights.* https://undocs.org/en/E/CN.4/2000/63.
ECtHR. 1976. "Case of Handyside v. United Kingdom. Application No. 5493/72." https://hudoc.echr.coe.int/eng#{%22itemid%22:[%22001-57499%22]}.
Forbidden Stories. n.d.a. "About Us." https://forbiddenstories.org/about-us/.
Forbidden Stories. n.d.b. "The Rafael Project." https://forbiddenstories.org/case/the-rafael-project/.
Forbidden Stories. n.d.c. "The Cartel Project." https://forbiddenstories.org/case/the-cartel-project/.

Harrison, Jackie, Diana Maynard, and Sara Torsner. 2022. "Strengthening the Monitoring of Violations Against Journalists Through an Events-Based Methodology." *Media and Communication* 8 (1): 89–100.
HRC. 2011. "General Comment No. 34: Article 19, Freedoms of Opinion and Expression." https://www.undocs.org/CCPR/C/GC/34.
IACtHR. 1985. "Advisory Opinion OC-5/85. Compulsory Membership in an Association Prescribed by Law for the Practice of Journalism (Arts. 13 and 29 American Convention on Human Rights)." http://www.corteidh.or.cr/docs/opiniones/seriea_05_ing.pdf.
Landman, Todd. 2006. *Studying Human Rights.* Oxford: Routledge.
Landman, Todd, and Edzia Carvalho. 2010. *Measuring Human Rights.* New York: Routledge.
McGonagle, Tarlach. 2013. "How to Address Current Threats to Journalism?: The Role of the Council of Europe in Protecting Journalists and Other Media Actors." Expert Paper Presented at the Council of Europe Conference of Ministers Responsible for Media and Information Society – Freedom of Expression and Democracy in the Digital Age: Opportunities, Rights, Responsibilities, Belgrade, Serbia, November 2013. https://rm.coe.int/1680484c67.
Mendel, Toby. 2010. "Restricting Freedom of Expression: Standards and Principles. Background Paper for Meetings Hosted by the UN Special Rapporteur on Freedom of Opinion and Expression." http://www.law-democracy.org/live/wp-content/uploads/2012/08/Paper-on-Restrictions.10.03.22.rev_.pdf.
OHCHR. n.d.a. "About Human Rights Defenders Special Rapporteur on Human Rights Defenders." https://www.ohchr.org/en/special-procedures/sr-human-rights-defenders/about-human-rights-defenders.
OHCHR. n.d.b. "Statistical Classification Framework and Methodological Guidance Note on SDG Indicator 16.10.1 Number of Verified Cases of Killing, Kidnapping, Enforced Disappearance, Arbitrary Detention and Torture of Journalists, Associated Media Personnel, Trade Unionists and Human Rights Advocates in the Previous 12 Months." https://www.ohchr.org/sites/default/files/Documents/Issues/HRIndicators/SDG_Indicator_16_10_1_Guidance_Note.pdf.
OHCHR. 2011. "Basic Principles of Human Rights Monitoring." https://www.ohchr.org/sites/default/files/Documents/Publications/Chapter02-MHRM.pdf.
OHCHR. 2021. "SDG Indicator Metadata." https://unstats.un.org/sdgs/metadata/files/Metadata-16-10-02.pdf.
OHCHR. 2023. "Conflict-Related Deaths of Civilians." https://www.ohchr.org/sites/default/files/documents/issues/hrindicators/2023_Infographics_OHCHR%20Indicators.pdf.
Parmar, Sejal. 2014. "The Protection and Safety of Journalists: A Review of International and Regional Human Rights Law." Background Paper Presented at the Seminar and Inter-regional Dialogue on the Protection of Journalists: Towards an Effective Framework of Protection for the Work of Journalists and an End to Impunity, Strasbourg, Germany, November 2014. https://www.inter-justice.org/pdf/Sejal_Parmar_Protection_and_Safety_of_Journalists.pdf.
Posetti, Julie, Nabeehla Shabbir, Diana Maynard, Kalina Bontcheva, and Nermine Aboulez. 2021. "The Chilling: Global Trends on Online Violence Against Women Journalists; Research Discussion Paper." https://unesdoc.unesco.org/ark:/48223/pf0000377223.
RSF. n.d. "Who Are We?" https://rsf.org/en/who-are-we.
RSF. 2018a. "Journalists: The Bête Noire of Organised Crime." https://rsf.org/sites/default/files/en_rapport_mafia_web_0.pdf.
RSF. 2018b. "Women's Rights: Forbidden Subject." https://rsf.org/sites/default/files/womens_rights-forbidden_subject.pdf.

RSF. 2020. "Red Alert for Green Journalism: 10 Environmental Reporters Killed in Five Years." https://rsf.org/en/red-alert-green-journalism-10-environmental-reporters-killed-five-years.
RSF. 2021. "Respect the Right to Cover the Environment, RSF and Journalists Tell COP26." https://rsf.org/en/respect-right-cover-environment-rsf-and-journalists-tell-cop26.
Schwartzstein, Peter. 2020. *The Authoritarian War on Environmental Journalism*. The Century Foundation. https://tcf.org/content/report/authoritarian-war-environmental-journalism/#easy-footnote-bottom-25.
Stiglitz, Joseph. 1999. "On Liberty, the Right to Know, and Public Discourse: The Role of Transparency in Public Life." http://www.internationalbudget.org/wp-content/uploads/On-Liberty-the-Right-to-Know-and-Public-Discourse-The-Role-of-Transparency-in-Public-Life.pdf.
Torsner, Sara. 2017. "Measuring Journalism Safety: Methodological Challenges." In *The Assault on Journalism: Building Knowledge to Protect Freedom of Expression*, edited by Ulla Carlsson and Reeta Pöyhtäri, 129–38. Gothenburg: Nordicom. http://www.unesco.se/wp-content/uploads/2017/04/The-Assault-on-Journalism.pdf.
Transparency International. 2020. "The High Cost Journalists Pay for Reporting on Corruption." https://www.transparency.org/en/news/the-high-costs-journalists-pay-when-reporting-on-corruption.
UN. n.d.a. "Human Rights-Based Approach." https://unsdg.un.org/2030-agenda/universal-values/human-rights-based-approach.
UN. n.d.b. "Sustainable Development Goals. Goal 16: Promote Just, Peaceful and Inclusive Societies." https://www.un.org/sustainabledevelopment/peace-justice/.
UN. 2003. "The Human Rights Based Approach to Development Cooperation Towards a Common Understanding Among UN Agencies." https://unsdg.un.org/resources/human-rights-based-approach-development-cooperation-towards-common-understanding-among-un.
UNDESA. n.d.a. "Sustainable Development Goal 16." https://sdgs.un.org/goals/goal16.
UNDESA. n.d.b. "The 17 Goals." https://sdgs.un.org/goals.
UNESCO. 2014. "World Trends in Freedom of Expression and Media Development." https://unesdoc.unesco.org/ark:/48223/pf0000227025.
UNESCO. 2015. "World Trends in Freedom of Expression and Media Development: Special Digital Focus 2015." http://www.unesco.se/wp-content/uploads/2016/01/World-Trends-in-Freedom-of-Expression-and-Media-Development-2015.pdf.
UNESCO. 2018. "World Trends in Freedom of Expression and Media Development: Global Report 2017/2018." https://unesdoc.unesco.org/ark:/48223/pf0000261065.
UNESCO. n.d. "Observatory of Killed Journalists. Monitoring the Killing of Journalists and Media Workers Across the Globe." https://www.unesco.org/en/safety-journalists/observatory.
UNGA. 1946. "Calling of an International Conference on Freedom of Information." https://www.undocs.org/A/RES/59(I).
UNGA. 1948. *The Universal Declaration of Human Rights (UDHR)*. New York: United Nations General Assembly. https://www.ohchr.org/en/human-rights/universal-declaration/translations/english.
UNGA. 1976. "International Covenant on Civil and Political Rights." https://treaties.un.org/doc/Publication/UNTS/Volume 999/volume-999-I-14668-English.pdf.
UNHRC. 2012. "Report of the Special Rapporteur on Extrajudicial, Summary or Arbitrary Executions, Christof Heyns." https://undocs.org/A/HRC/20/22.

4
HUMAN RIGHTS AND JOURNALISM

Under pressure when national interests are at stake

Aidan White

Introduction

To some people, human rights are the bedrock of civilisation. To others, including some governments, they have well-meaning aspirations, are hopelessly idealistic and get in the way of practical politics. For journalists and news media, they are a protective cloak. They ensure the right to free speech, public access to reliable, fact-based information and above all, they reinforce the social role that journalism plays in society. This chapter looks at how journalism and human rights intersect at a moment of remarkable and historical change in the first decades of the 21st Century. The information and political landscape is being redrawn, posing new questions about journalism, human rights and information policy.

In many parts of the world, there is slippage in attachment to universal values as populism and political attachment to national interests increasingly trump global visions, even on critical concerns for humanity such as climate change, the rights of minorities and the conduct of war. This political shift threatens to destabilise commitments to rights protection. It is also leading to growing collisions at the national level between the law and the work of journalists.

Journalists and human rights defenders understand well the troubling context in which these difficulties arise: a profound internal crisis for news media that threatens the sustainability of independent journalism; rising populism in national politics that is shaking belief in liberal democracy; and increasing public uncertainty in a fragmented and polarised public information space in the wake of the communications revolution of the past 30 years. The global media crisis, which has badly damaged the fabric of independent journalism

DOI: 10.4324/9781032662589-5

and is exacerbated by the actions of ruthless technological media giants, is also important. It means that the question is not just whether human rights law can keep journalists safe, but also whether the social role of media as guardian and watchdog of the rights of others is sustainable.

In this chapter, we explore the linkage and occasional tensions between ethical journalism and human rights and consider whether existing levels of human rights protection are sufficient to protect public information rights and ease the pressure on journalists and news media. In particular, using case studies to illustrate the challenges media face, the questions of the physical safety of journalists and impunity in attacks on media are addressed.

The historical development of ethical journalism, free speech and a rules-based order for human society have gone hand in hand for more than 150 years. Ethical journalism has its roots in notions of universality, both in recognition of fundamental rights and the core values of good journalism – truth-telling, independence, fairness and responsibility. Incremental reforms to strengthen human rights protections have emerged from the horrors of war and historic shifts in economic and political power – from colonialism to globalisation, for example – leading to the rights-based democratic consensus following the Second World War.

Human rights are enshrined in the treaties between states, particularly the Universal Declaration of Human Rights (UDHR in 1948), the International Covenant on Civil and Political Rights (ICCPR in 1966), the European Convention on Human Rights (ECHR in 1954), the African Charter on Human and Peoples' Rights (1981) and the American Convention on Human Rights (1969), all of which guarantee the rights of all people living in the signatory countries. Journalists have a vested interest in the promotion of human rights, particularly the right to free expression under Article 19 of the UDHR and the ICCPR.

These rights, and the linked body of International Humanitarian Law which we shall return to later, are enshrined in national laws but, as with the exercise of journalism, they are influenced by the moral and political realities of modern life. So, within the refreshingly clear commitments to free speech, are let-out clauses that give governments the right to make exceptions and to limit free expression. Article 10 of the ECHR, for example, states that everyone has the right to free expression, but this right may be constrained by overriding national concerns over national security, prevention of disorder or crime and protection of an individual's reputation. These potential limitations on free speech worry journalists, who fear they may rein in legitimate scrutiny of public affairs.

For journalists to make judgments that are morally and legally defensible, they need to be able to work freely. They must be competent, well-trained, informed and, above all, work in conditions which encourage them to act ethically. Too often journalists are constrained by undue political or corporate influence or they come up against the law. This not only leads to self-censorship; it may intimidate and silence the sources upon which journalism depends. Even worse, journalists are victims of violence. Over the past 33 years, almost 3,000 have been targeted and murdered. Many of these deaths have not been properly investigated or explained because of widespread impunity (International Federation of Journalists 2021).

In many countries, populist political movements make the situation worse by fomenting public hostility to critical journalism by targeting independent media. Taking their cue from the great media disrupter Donald Trump in America and the draconian administration of Vladimir Putin, which has put legal chains on media freedom in Russia, the new wave of populist political leaders exploit an emerging 'post-truth' culture and promote their own propaganda, often through state-controlled media or the voluntary compliance of politically-compromised systems of media ownership.

Everywhere, disinformation, fake news, 'alternative facts' and conspiracy theories circulate through online platforms. This creates an unreliable information landscape and weakens confidence in public information, including journalism. Depressingly, multiple surveys and media research indicate that people are mistrustful of media and are turning away from the news (Newman et al. 2022).

At the same time, the work of media and journalists is constrained by poor access to public sources of information; improper use of laws of privacy, defamation and blasphemy; limited protection of journalists' sources; and restrictive laws covering security, terrorism and hate speech. Creating conditions where journalists can work freely, in relative safety and without official and legal obstruction, has become challenging as governments assert that their perceptions of national interests, whether political, economic or strategic, take precedence over the rights of journalists.

Testing relations: ethical journalism and human rights

News media and civil liberties are both rooted in defending the public interest, but there are a number of key areas where ethical and independent reporting comes up against the law, and when that happens it can expose tensions between political interests, human rights and journalism.

News media argue that journalism is a public good, it is not the mouthpiece of government or of corporate power and is an ally of those striving for democracy and human rights protection. But these are meaningless words unless journalists can get hold of facts to tell their stories. The problem is that much of the information journalists need to get their hands on is held by others, particularly the state and public authorities. That is why, for decades, journalists and others have been campaigning for access to public information.

There has been some success. By 2022, according to the free expression group Article 19, some 126 countries, covering most of the world's population, now have freedom of information laws (Article 19 2022). These laws are essential to combat official secrecy. They underpin the peoples' right to know and help journalists to better scrutinise governments and to root out corruption. But prising the fingers of state bureaucrats and secretive government officials off the controls of access to official information remains tricky, even when the law has half-opened the door. Often political and official institutions construct exceptions to the rule of openness. They may restrict access to information related to security and terrorism, for example, or they may establish bureaucratic obstacles to transparency, introducing charges or setting no time limits and making it impossible for reporters working to a deadline. This means that journalists often turn to whistleblowers, people working inside the machinery of government and the state who, very often at risk to themselves and certainly their employment, will break secrecy rules and leak official information. With this in mind, there is a heavy obligation on news media to protect their sources.

Sometimes media fall short. In 1983, for example, to the embarrassment of *The Guardian*, a young woman working as a government clerk was sent to jail after she leaked an internal government document planning a cover-up over the deployment of nuclear missiles. The woman, Sarah Tisdall, was only exposed because *The Guardian* gave in to a court order demanding they hand over the photocopy she had sent. This failure of principle outraged many journalists, but it highlights how media are often caught between sticking by their ethical principles and submitting to draconian secrecy laws (Guardian Research Department 2011). Fast forward 30 years, and the threats posed to whistleblowers remain worryingly in the headlines. American whistleblower Edward Snowden, who in 2010 leaked information about the extensive illegal surveillance by the US National Security Agency on governments, institutions and individuals, is on the run and in permanent exile in Moscow and never expects to see his homeland again (Greenwald et al. 2013).

Another high-profile leaker, Julian Assange, the Australian co-founder of WikiLeaks has, since 2010, been trying to avoid criminal charges in the United States for supplying media with caches of documents exposing serious violations of human rights. He was detained in Britain in 2019 and commenced a five-year battle fighting deportation to the US despite pleas from the UN Special Rapporteur on Torture that the UK Government should halt his extradition because of risks of treatment amounting to torture if he was sent to the US. Finally, after 14 years of legal dispute, his case was resolved when he pleaded guilty to a single charge at a US Court in the Northern Mariana Islands, an American territory in the Pacific, two days after leaving a British prison in June 2024. He was sentenced to time already served and released to fly to his native Australia and reunited with his family. These cases underscore why for decades journalists have been campaigning for the legal right to protect the confidentiality of sources.

Nevertheless, some journalists voluntarily accept, in certain circumstances, exceptions to the principle of source protection (those like Jeremy Bowen and Jackie Rowlands of the *BBC* and Ed Vulliamy of *The Observer* who gave evidence, for example, at the UN War Crimes Tribunal in the Hague in 2002 over atrocities committed in the conflict in former Yugoslavia) or they acknowledge that if a source is to be revealed it must be in strictly controlled circumstances. In Belgium, for instance, the law provides that only a judge can decide to ask a journalist to disclose a source and then only when it is clear that there is a serious physical threat to the public.

Journalists have to be wary of how they use the information they get. Legal pitfalls await at every turn. In particular, there are threats posed by laws of defamation which can be used as blunt weapons by governments and powerful people to hide their mistakes, protect their image and, if they can get away with it, punish intrusive reporters. Around 80 percent of countries still operate laws that criminalise defamation and there is growing evidence of how governments and powerful people exploit the judicial system to restrict the rights of journalists, particularly through the use of so-called SLAPPS – Strategic Lawsuits Against Public Participation (UNESCO 2022).

These laws provide legal loopholes that protect public figures from media scrutiny, even though the application of defamation laws should recognise that people in the public eye, particularly elected officials, must expect more media attention than ordinary people. The threat of mischievous prosecution, which can encourage self-censorship and have a deterrent effect on watchdog journalism, led the European Union in April 2024 to adopt new rules banning abusive use of law to gag journalists (Council of the European Union, European Parliament 2024).

Related to defamation is the problem of insult laws that apply to religion. News media find blasphemy laws particularly difficult to navigate, especially when they provide special protection for the core beliefs of a particular religion, but do not extend the same immunity to other beliefs, including ideas based upon a secular view of the world.

Another area where journalists regularly come up against the law concerns the question of privacy. While most journalists see no contradiction between honest and ethical reporting and legitimate privacy protection, they don't accept that the right to privacy should obstruct the people's right to know, particularly when matters of public interest are at stake. This is one area where human rights are sometimes conflicting and media need to balance competing rights. In practice, when press freedom comes into conflict with the right of individuals to a private life, there is no simple way of making judgments, either in the courtroom or the newsroom, without giving one priority over the other.

The ethical task for journalists is to tell the story that the public needs to know without doing undue damage to the privacy rights of others.

The challenge of mediating conflicting rights is also found in how media deal with hate speech laws. These rules may be useful to tackle racism and are often necessary to cool down passions when there is a risk of community violence, but sometimes hate speech laws go beyond protection from objective harm. They can also constrain the media's responsibility to report freely on speech that tests the boundaries of public tolerance. In dealing with one such example, the European Court of Human Rights ruled that free speech extends also to statements which 'shock, offend or disturb' (European Court of Human Rights 1976). Some countries have vague and loosely defined definitions of hate speech that prohibit any statements which are perceived as offensive. Such rules invite a collision between judges and journalists over where to draw the line. In France, for example, the *Loi sur la liberté de la presse* (*Law on freedom of the press*) prohibits 'attacks against honour' by reason of ethnicity, nationality, race or religion. In other countries, the legacy of history has shaped the legal framework. In countries devastated by the politics of fascism and war, there are laws that prohibit denial of the Holocaust. In Germany, for example, the wearing of Nazi symbols is forbidden. Some people might say that Holocaust deniers should be exposed to public ridicule rather than being prosecuted, but in a time when anti-Semitism and anti-Muslim bias are on the rise, particularly because of conflict in the Middle East, the threats posed generations ago still resonate (Sherwood 2024).

Justice and journalism in times of war

The first decades of the 21st century have seen an increasing focus on the importance of human rights protection, not just in the application of International Human Rights Law but also in International Humanitarian Law, the related body of legal protections for people in times of war and conflict.

Over the years, rigorous enforcement methods have already seen war crime perpetrators jailed and have restrained the freedom of others who are alleged to have committed such crimes. For this reason, the relationship between human rights and journalism in the context of war provides an important context for raising awareness within the public at large about international justice, the need to defend humanitarian law and the pursuit of those who commit crimes of war. But that is not easy, not least because often journalists themselves and the work they do are among the victims of human rights abuse. To do their work, journalists need to be ethically aware, competent in their skills and, above all, able to work in relative safety – even in conflict zones. That has become a major challenge over the past 40 years, during which almost 3,000 journalists and media workers have been recorded by free expression and media support organisations as killed at work, many of them murdered while on assignments or targeted on the battlefield (International Freedom of Expression Exchange n.d.). This is despite legal protections under international law going beyond Article 79 of Additional Protocol I of the Geneva Conventions (1977), which says that journalists in war zones must be treated as civilians and protected as such provided they play no part in the hostilities.

The United Nations has a number of initiatives around the rights and safety of journalists, including World Press Freedom Day (May 3), the International Day to Combat Impunity and Violence Against Journalists (November 2) and, in 2012, the launch of the UN Plan of Action on Safety of Journalists, the first concerted governmental effort to address attacks and impunity of crimes against journalists. In addition, United Nations resolutions, adopted in 2006, 2013 and 2015 have strengthened a growing international consensus that the protection and security of journalists and media staff must be taken seriously. In practical terms, the UN says its plan to keep journalists safe has led to the creation of national safety mechanisms in at least 50 countries, within ten years had reduced the rate of impunity attacks on media staff (UNESCO 2024) and raised awareness about threats to journalists. The issue is also part of the UN Secretary General's call for action on human rights and is part of the 2030 Agenda for Sustainable Development (United Nations 2024).

The reduction in the number of cases of impunity is an important indicator of progress in campaigns to deliver justice to media and journalists subject to violent intimidation, but as recent high-profile killings illustrate, much more needs to be done. It requires political solidarity and depends crucially upon the commitment of individual governments to keep their word and to set aside national strategic and political interests in defence of international law and, in particular, the rights of journalists and freedom of expression. Guy Berger, one of the pioneers of the UN Plan of Action and a former UNESCO Director for Policies and Strategies regarding Information and Communications, said the UN has a viable set of guidelines for safety in reporting and UN resolutions on the issue remain the baseline for governmental policy in two key areas. He explained, 'First, and very important, that journalists are civilians who deserve civilian protection', he said, 'and, secondly, that any killings of journalists in a war situation should not be done with impunity' (Berger, Personal Interview, 2024). The Security Council agreed on this. Other states signed up voluntarily to support this resolution, including Israel (Berger 2024). However, governments can't always be relied upon to keep their word, and Berger cited as an example the actions of Israel during the Gaza conflict (Berger, Personal Interview, 2024).

Israel was one of the states that voluntarily signed up to UN Security Council resolution 2222 (2015), which had been hailed as a milestone in the campaign to protect journalists. It condemned all violations and abuses committed against journalists and affirmed that states must respect and protect journalists as civilians. In the Gaza conflict, however, Israeli armed forces have been accused of killing Palestinian journalists and their families and of targeting media premises, leading to a series of complaints to the International Criminal Court. Allegations of deliberate targeting of journalists and media staff in Gaza have undermined confidence among journalists that Israel is honouring its international commitments. Many hoped that by sharing with Israeli forces information on the location of media offices and where people were working, as well as the wearing of highly visible 'PRESS' markings on the ground, they would be relatively safe. This was not the case.

The priority concern for the Israeli government during the Gaza conflict of 2023/24 has been the management of media activity. It has isolated journalists and media organisations operating inside Gaza and prohibited entry to the conflict zone by foreign correspondents and even Israeli reporters. The only exceptions have been journalists and media who agreed to be strictly controlled. This has meant so-called 'embedding', a process developed during the Iraq war of 2003 which saw journalists travelling with and under the protection of military personnel. In the Israeli case, it also meant allowing official access to editorial material prior to publication. While foreign reporters and media have been kept safely away from the action, the reporters inside Gaza, almost all of them Palestinian and working for local media or freelance for external media, have faced unprecedented attacks.

According to the Committee to Protect Journalists and the International Federation of Journalists, the number of Palestinian journalists and media workers killed, injured or missing in the war is at record levels, higher than at any time since these organisations started gathering and publishing data in 1991 (Committee to Protect Journalists 2024). Journalism has never previously experienced such slaughter in any war zone. By the end of February 2024, more than 100 journalists have been killed, dozens of their family members have died with them and hundreds more have been injured. Many of these victims died working out in the open, with microphones or cameras in hand, and while wearing media insignia as well as body armour.

Each death tells a story, but few match the shocking experience of Weal Dahdouh, the Gaza Bureau chief for Aljazeera, who lost several members of his close family in a series of attacks by the Israeli Defence Force, which Aljazeera alleged was 'systematic targeting' (Al Jazeera 2024). On 25 October, he was on air when he was told by a colleague that his wife, two young children and grandson, had been killed in an Israeli air strike. He paused briefly before returning to the camera to be interviewed. Weeks later he was injured when he and a colleague were hit by an Israeli airstrike while reporting on the bombing of a local school. His colleague was killed. Shortly afterwards, on 7 January, his eldest son and another journalist were killed in a missile strike on their car. They were targeted and killed, said Israeli sources, because they were 'terrorists', something Dahdouh and Aljazeera strongly refute (Al Jazeera 2024).

A number of formal complaints over the targeting of journalists and media from Aljazeera, Reporters Without Borders and the International Federation of Journalists have been submitted to the International Criminal Court alleging war crimes by Israel and Hamas, in the targeting and killing of journalists. Israel has strenuously denied all of these charges.

Justice denied: the impunity challenge for media

Reporting from war zones is a notoriously dangerous assignment for journalists, but even in peace-time, journalists come under fire when they make powerful enemies. Each year scores are killed, often with impunity.

In many cases, such as that of Irish journalist Veronica Guerin, gunned down on the streets of Dublin in 1996 by gangsters she was investigating; or the assassination in 2017 of Maltese journalist Daphne Caruana Galizia by businessmen whose murky dealings she exposed; or the brutal killing of reporter Dominic Phillips and environmentalist Bruno Pereira in 2022 while on the trail of illegal fishing in the Amazon, the killings have reverberated around the world and the killers brought to justice.

But in the vast majority of cases impunity reigns, justice is denied and the killers of journalists go untried and unpunished. The killing of investigative Russian journalist Anna Politkovskya in 2006, for example, led to years of investigation and, finally, the trial and jailing of her assailants. One of them, jailed for 20 years, was pardoned and freed in 2023 by the Russian authorities after serving a tour of duty in Ukraine (Plummer 2023). Not surprisingly, calls from within journalism for an international legal process to eliminate impunity have grown louder. Two cases in recent years have particularly reverberated in both media and human rights circles, underscoring demands to counter the threat that impunity poses to justice, democracy and independent journalism.

The first concerns the distinguished Palestinian-American journalist Shireen Abu Akleh, who on 11 May 2022 joined colleagues on what appeared to be a routine assignment covering a raid by Israeli soldiers inside Jenin, a Palestinian refugee camp, on the West Bank in the Occupied Palestinian territories. By any standards, Abu Akleh, a correspondent for the Aljazeera network, was fully prepared. She had years of experience and was a well-known and respected reporter across the region. She was acutely aware of the risks that Palestinian journalists faced in reporting from the West Bank and Gaza. What she may not have known is that just a month earlier the International Federation of Journalists, the Palestinian Journalists' Syndicate and the International Centre of Justice for Palestinians had submitted a formal complaint to the International Criminal Court alleging war crimes against journalists and a pattern of targeting by Israel's security forces over a number of years (International Federation of Journalists 2022). She was walking alongside her colleague Shatha Hanaysha, a Palestinian journalist, with other correspondents nearby when she was shot and killed. Hanaysha and other colleagues are convinced she was killed by Israeli fire. There was no crossfire, they said. This was no incident of a journalist caught in the middle of a firefight.

The incident triggered a wave of protest from fellow correspondents and international news media. The killing outraged human rights groups and politicians in the United States and led to a number of local and international investigations. Israeli officials, looking for damage limitation, initially said she was killed by Palestinian gunmen. They dismissed claims she was deliberately targeted. However, after carrying out an extensive investigation, the UN Independent International Commission of Inquiry on the Occupied Palestinian Territory, including East Jerusalem and Israel, concluded 'on reasonable grounds that Israeli forces used lethal force without justification under international human rights law, violating her right to life' (United Nations Human Rights Council 2023).

The Israeli government had refused to co-operate with this investigation and even stopped American investigators from the FBI from holding an inquiry into the killing, accusing the US of 'interference in Israel's internal affairs'. This response, putting national sovereignty above the pursuit of justice internationally, highlights for many journalists and human rights defenders how combating impunity becomes impossible when a government declines to co-operate with external law enforcement and the monitoring agencies of the international community. Nevertheless, Israel did admit that it was most likely an Israeli soldier who accidentally fired the fatal shot that killed Akleh. However, no one in the Israeli army has been prosecuted, and there was no announcement of any disciplinary action (Sanchez and Jabari 2023). Despite this, Aljazeera has submitted the case for investigation by the International Criminal Court.

The second case concerns the veteran Saudi journalist, political dissident and author Jamal Khashoggi. When he stepped into the Consulate of Saudi Arabia in Istanbul in Turkey on 2 October 2018, Khashoggi knew he was taking a risk. For years he had been an outspoken opponent of the Saudi regime. He fled the country a year earlier to work freely abroad. But he couldn't have imagined the horror that was waiting for him when he visited the consulate in Turkey to pick up documents related to his planned marriage. Within minutes of his arrival, he was brutally murdered, provoking a global wave of protests and reverberations that may yet lead to changes in international law to tackle impunity in the killing of journalists. Turkish President Recep Tayyip Erdogan, not known for his support for critical journalism, himself condemned the barbarity in the killing of Khashoggi (McKernan 2018).

The assassination led to a painstaking investigation by the UN Special Rapporteur on Extrajudicial, Summary or Arbitrary Killings, who concluded emphatically that Khashoggi's death was purely and simply an act of state murder by Saudi Arabia (United Nations Office of the High Commissioner 2019). Following her six-month investigation, Rapporteur Agnes Callamard reported:

'The circumstances of Mr Khashoggi's death have led to numerous theories and allegations, but none alters the responsibility of the Saudi Arabia State'.

> Saudi state agents, 15 of them, acted under cover of their official status and used state means to execute Mr. Khashoggi. His killing was the result of elaborate planning involving extensive coordination and significant human and financial resources. It was overseen, planned and endorsed by high-level officials. It was premeditated.
>
> *(United Nations Office of the High Commissioner 2019)*

Initially, the Saudi government denied the death, but following a series of shifting explanations, the country's Attorney General admitted that the murder had been premeditated. Later, on 16 November 2018, the Central Intelligence Agency (CIA) reported that Saudi leader Mohammed bin Salman had ordered the assassination (Harris et al. 2018). But this has never been followed up. Instead, on 23 December 2019, a Saudi Arabian court sentenced five officials to death and three others to 24 years in prison. Human rights group Amnesty International described the verdicts as 'a whitewash', stating, 'The trial has been closed to the public and to independent monitors . . . the verdict fails to address the Saudi authorities' involvement' (Amnesty International 2019). On 7 September 2020, a further eight people tied to the murder were sentenced from seven to 20 years, although Saudi Arabia did not name them (Gubash et al. 2020).

In her report, Callamard cited six violations of international law, including the killing of a journalist, by which, she said, the State of Saudi Arabia committed an act inconsistent with a core tenet of the United Nations, the protection of freedom of expression. She concluded: 'The killing of Mr Khashoggi constitutes an international crime over which other States should claim universal jurisdiction.' She called on the major bodies of the UN system – the Human Rights Council, the Security Council or the UN Secretary-General – to conduct an international follow-up criminal investigation, but this was never forthcoming. Callamard noted that apart from statements of concern there were few effective international responses. Nevertheless, she called for the establishment of new mechanisms at the UN level to strengthen the prevention and criminal investigation of targeted killings, and it may be here that a further, more positive chapter in this sorry tale will be written (United Nations Office of the High Commissioner 2019).

Conclusions: improving law and strengthening media voice

The right to report, independently and safely, is paramount for information democracy. It is a right that underpins the social role of news media in defending the rights of others but, as this chapter illustrates, this role is under threat if the legal environment in which media work does not deliver sufficient protection for journalists.

Additionally, the future sustainability of independent news media is also in question in the midst of a communications revolution, driven by the internet and its exploitation by powerful technology companies and their social media platforms. As a result of a transformation of business models, news media have been stripped of vital resources needed to keep public interest journalism alive.

At the same time, with the rise of abusive communications, disinformation and the creation of an information landscape polluted by bias, propaganda and polarised opinion, there is widespread public concern about the quality and integrity of public information. Debates about artificial intelligence, information ethics and regulation of online communications proliferate. The political challenge this poses is how to create a new information environment that will promote and encourage the social role of free and independent journalism and that will reduce the undue pressure on media from narrow political and national interests. With this in mind, the recommendation for new international instruments to counter impunity in the killing of journalists, such as the Khashoggi case, provides an opportunity for concerted international action and recognition that the work of journalists must be protected. This recommendation has been submitted to the Media Freedom Coalition (https://mediafreedomcoalition.org/), a group of around 50 democratic states set up in 2019 which is working in partnership with media and human rights groups to strengthen international protections for free speech and journalism. This coalition has been invited to support the establishment of a rapid response mechanism, underpinned by international law, to tackle impunity.

Although now out of the frontline of international diplomacy in the service of safer journalism, Guy Berger is hopeful.

> There's certainly much going on under the UN plan at the sort of normative level training, capacity building, even some investigations into impunity and so on, but it's time to start asking, will this Media Freedom Coalition lead to a legal mechanism that will be adopted by the United Nations, with an effective mandate that will deliver justice?
>
> *(Berger, Personal Interview, 2024)*

There are many hurdles to overcome – finding a route through the UN system to agree on a new law, and deciding how the mandate for enforcement will be applied – but there is hope that deaths such as those of Khashoggi and Abu Akleh will lead to change that will help to take journalism out of the firing line. While international action can be effective in some areas – peacekeeping, for example – a lack of political will and the overriding importance of protecting national interests leads to inconsistency and hypocrisy among governments in their approach to human rights abuse.

For example, compare the outrage expressed by Western governments to the warmongering and targeted assassination of political opponents by the government of Vladimir Putin, including international sanctions and arms supplies to Ukraine, with the hand-wringing, silence and collective looking the other way which has followed the killing of Jamal Khashoggi by Saudi Arabia, or the muted response to the excesses of Israel in the cases of Shireen Abu Akleh and other journalists targeted in Gaza.

The feeble enforcement of international humanitarian law through the courts means that good journalism and credible news reporting remain the essential guarantors of justice in cases of human rights abuse.

Berger, himself a former journalist exiled during the Apartheid years, knows that public opinion mobilised through the truth-telling of news media remains of paramount importance. He cites as an example the complaint tabled in early 2024 by the South African government to the International Court of Justice (ICJ) in The Hague, accusing Israel of breaching the International Genocide Convention over its actions in Gaza. The court will take years to come to a conclusion, but in an interim statement the ICJ ordered Israel to 'take all measures within its power' to prevent the commission of acts prohibited in the Convention, in particular killings, causing serious physical or mental harm, the deliberate infliction of conditions of life calculated to bring about the physical destruction of the population in whole or in part (Sagoo and Bar-Yaacov 2024).

> This is purely a public opinion victory. It's not a legal victory because there's no compulsion that goes with it, but as I know from my own experience in dealing with Apartheid, this kind of coverage of human rights abuses has impact.
>
> *(Berger, Personal Interview, 2024)*

Journalism used alongside a robust mechanism for applying and enforcing international law can ensure that governments become more willing to hold themselves to account. As Berger explains:

When I was in exile in the United Kingdom, I was receiving smuggled footage of atrocities and this was used for news broadcasts on the BBC and Channel 4. This journalism helped create better public understanding of the nature of Apartheid. It wasn't the use of law that ended Apartheid, but it was the creation of an international climate that basically led President Reagan in the US to tell the South Africans 'I can't bankroll you anymore'. They panicked and settled.

(Berger, Personal Interview, 2024)

But it is a distant dream. With populism on the march and both human rights and free journalism under pressure, few governments, even those at the top of the pyramid of democracy, are ready to sacrifice their national and strategic interests in the cause of press freedom or the meaningful enforcement of international humanitarian law. As a result, public opinion, mobilised through the truth-telling of news media, remains the frontline defender of human rights.

Discussion questions

- How does the issue of impunity in crimes against journalists impact the field of journalism? What measures can be taken to address this problem?
- In what ways has the rise of populism and national interests over global visions affected the protection of human rights and the work of journalists?
- How can governments better uphold their commitments to international law and the rights of journalists? What challenges might they face in doing so?

Further reading

Barry, James. 2007. "States Turn a Blind Eye to Attacks on Journalist Press Freedom." In *UNESCO Conference Report: Safety of Journalists and Impunity*, edited by Barry James. UNESCO. https://unesdoc.unesco.org/ark:/48223/pf0000156773.

International Media Support (IMS), Defending Journalism. 2020. *Shared Responsibility: Safeguarding Press Freedom in Perilous Times*. IMS, May 2020. https://www.mediasupport.org/publication/shared-responsibility-safeguarding-press-freedom-in-perilous-times/.

Office of the UN High Commissioner for Human Rights (OHCHR). n.d. *Human Rights, Impunity and Safety of Journalists*. OHCHR. https://www.ohchr.org/en/safety-of-journalists.

White, Aidan. 2011. *Ethical Journalism and Human Rights: Issue Discussion Paper (CommDH/IssuePaper (2011))*. Commissioner for Human Rights, Council of Europe. https://rm.coe.int/16806da54a.

References

Al Jazeera. 2024. "Al Jazeera Firmly Rejects Israeli Occupation Forces' Attempt to Justify Its Crimes." *Al Jazeera*, February 15. https://network.aljazeera.net/en/press-releases/al-jazeera-firmly-rejects-israeli-occupation-forces%E2%80%99-attempt-justify-its-crimes.

Amnesty International. 2019. "Saudi Arabia: Khashoggi Verdict a Whitewash." *Amnesty International*, December 23. https://www.amnesty.org/en/latest/press-release/2019/12/khashoggi-verdict/.

Article 19. 2022. "Right to Information Around the World." https://www.article19.org/right-to-information-around-the-world/.

Berger, Guy. Personal Interview With the Author, February 15, 2024.

Committee to Protect Journalists (CPJ). 2024. "Full Coverage: Israel-Gaza War." *CPJ*. https://cpj.org/full-coverage-israel-gaza-war/.

Council of the European Union, European Parliament. 2024. "Directive (EU) 2024/1069 on Protecting Persons Who Engage in Public Participation From Manifestly Unfounded Claims or Abusive Court Proceedings ('Strategic Lawsuits Against Public Participation')." *Official Journal of the European Union*, April 16. https://www.europeansources.info/record/directive-eu-2024-1069-on-protecting-persons-who-engage-in-public-participation-from-manifestly-unfounded-claims-or-abusive-court-proceedings-strategic-lawsuits-against-public-participatio/#:~:text=Summary%3A,against%20public%20participation%20%2D%20SLAPPs.

European Court of Human Rights. 1976. "Handyside v. United Kingdom. Judgment." December 7. https://hudoc.echr.coe.int/eng#{%22itemid%22:[%22001-57499%22]}.

Greenwald, Glenn, Ewen MacAskill, and Laura Poitras. 2013. "Edward Snowden: The Whistleblower Behind the NSA Surveillance Revelations." *The Guardian*, June 11. https://www.theguardian.com/world/2013/jun/09/edward-snowden-nsa-whistleblower-surveillance.

Guardian Research Department. 2011. "22 October 1983: Sarah Tisdall." *The Guardian*, June 3. https://www.theguardian.com/theguardian/from-the-archive-blog/2011/jun/03/guardian190-sarah-tisdall-1983.

Gubash, Charlene, Doha Madani, and Saphora Smith. 2020. "Saudi Court Issues Final Verdicts for 8 People in Death of Journalist Jamal Khashoggi." *NBC News*, September 8. https://www.nbcnews.com/news/world/final-verdicts-issued-jamal-khashoggi-murder-case-n1234567.

Harris, Shane, Greg Miller, and Josh Dawsey. 2018. "CIA Concludes Saudi Crown Prince Ordered Jamal Khashoggi's Assassination." *The Washington Post*, November 16. https://www.washingtonpost.com/national-security/2018/11/16/cia-concludes-saudi-crown-prince-ordered-jamal-khashoggis-assassination/.

International Federation of Journalists (IFJ). 2021. *White Paper on Global Journalism*. Brussels: International Federation of Journalists, IFJ, March 31. https://www.ifj.org/media-centre/reports/detail/ifj-white-paper-on-global-journalism/category/publications.

International Federation of Journalists (IFJ). 2022. "Palestine: ICC Case Filed Over Systematic Targeting of Palestinian Journalists." *IFJ*, April 26. https://www.ifj.org/media-centre/news/detail/category/press-releases/article/palestine-icc-case-filed-over-systematic-targeting-of-palestinian-journalists.

International Freedom of Expression Exchange. n.d. "No Impunity." Accessed August 22, 2024. https://ifex.org/campaigns/no-impunity/.

McKernan, Bethan. 2018. "Jamal Khashoggi: Erdoğan Rejects Saudi Account of Killing." *The Guardian*, October 23. https://www.theguardian.com/world/2018/oct/23/jamal-khashoggi-erdogan-rejects-saudi-account-of-killing.

Media Freedom Coalition. Accessed August 22, 2024. https://mediafreedomcoalition.org/.

Newman, Nic, Richard Fletcher, Craig T. Robertson, Kirsten Eddy, and Rasmus Kleis Nielsen. 2022. *Digital News Report 2022*. Oxford: Reuters Institute for the Study of Journalism. https://doi.org/10.60625/risj-x1gn-m549.

Plummer, Robert. 2023. "Anna Politkovskaya: Russian Convicted of Journalist Murder Gets Pardon." *BBC News*, November 14. https://www.bbc.co.uk/news/world-europe-67414517.

Sagoo, Rashmin, and Nomi Bar-Yaacov. 2024. "South Africa's Genocide Case Against Israel: The International Court of Justice Explained." *The Chatham House*, February 21. https://www.chathamhouse.org/2024/01/south-africas-genocide-case-against-israel-international-court-justice-explained.

Sanchez, Raf, and Lawahez Jabari. 2023. "A Year After Shireen Abu Akleh's Killing, Her Family Pushes for Justice." *NBC News*, May 11. https://www.nbcnews.com/news/world/shireen-abu-akleh-killing-fbi-justice-israel-military-palestinians-rcna83089.

Sherwood, Harriet. 2024. "Huge Rise in Antisemitic Abuse in UK Since Hamas Attack, Says Charity." *The Guardian*, February 15. https://www.theguardian.com/news/2024/feb/15/huge-rise-in-antisemitic-abuse-in-uk-since-hamas-attack-says-charity.

UNESCO. 2022. "Defamation Laws and SLAPPs Increasingly Misused to Curtail Freedom of Expression." December 8. https://www.unesco.org/en/articles/defamation-laws-and-slapps-increasingly-misused-curtail-freedom-expression.

UNESCO. 2024. "Basic Texts Related to the Safety of Journalists." May 17, 2024. https://www.unesco.org/en/safety-journalists/basic-texts.

United Nations. 2024. *Secretary-General's Call to Action for Human Rights*. United Nations. https://www.un.org/en/content/action-for-human-rights/index.shtml.

United Nations Human Rights Council. 2023. "Report of the Independent International Commission of Inquiry on the Occupied Palestinian Territory, Including East Jerusalem, and Israel." September 5. https://documents.un.org/doc/undoc/gen/n23/260/71/pdf/n2326071.pdf.

United Nations Office of the High Commissioner (OHCHR). 2019. *Khashoggi Killing: UN Human Rights Expert Says Saudi Arabia is Responsible for 'Premeditated Execution'*. OHCHR, June 19. https://www.ohchr.org/en/press-releases/2019/06/khashoggi-killing-un-human-rights-expert-says-saudi-arabia-responsible.

5
THE DOUBLE-EDGED SWORD OF HUMAN RIGHTS NEWS

Matthew Powers

Introduction

For decades, researchers have found that non-governmental organisations (NGOs) struggle to capture media attention on issues pertaining to human rights (Ramos, Ron and Thoms 2007; Thrall, Stecula and Sweet 2014). Recent transformations in journalism, advocacy, politics, and technology, though, raise questions about whether this might be changing. Diminished revenues and increased profitability expectations make news organisations less likely to commit time and resources to human rights coverage, especially when it entails costly travel. At the same time, the growth and diversification of an advocacy sector dedicated to human rights issues – as well as its legitimation in political circles – present the possibility that NGOs might enjoy a newfound power to drive news coverage, whether in legacy news media or through their own online channels and networks. Do these transformations diversify human rights news by incorporating long-excluded topics and voices? Or do they threaten to turn journalism into a platform for both advocacy and fundraising? And for NGOs, is news coverage a useful tool for pursuing their objectives – or ultimately a distraction from the core issues to which they are dedicated?

In this chapter, I argue that available evidence suggests that the cumulative effect of these transformations can be interpreted as a "double-edged sword" for news organisations, NGOs, and the public more broadly. On the one hand, NGOs are more likely to appear in the news today than in the past, and their presence helps to diversify coverage by exposing audiences to a wider range of institutional voices and by using digital tools to maximise their organisational objectives. On the other hand, journalists, mediated through their enduring reliance on government officials, retain the upper hand in defining what counts as human rights news. As a result, NGOs, in part due to fundraising needs and reputation-building efforts of their own, tend to appear in the news when speaking about topics and issues already on the media agenda – even though their own work extends far beyond those areas. The mixed effects of these developments, I suggest, have analytical and practical implications for understanding the determinants of human rights news coverage, and the extent to which transformations within and beyond journalism provide new opportunities to shape public understanding, and potentially political action, of human rights issues.

In what follows, I begin by summarising extant research on the relationship between NGOs, journalism, and human rights news, and highlight the transformations among them that raise questions about the validity of prior research that emphasises the difficulty NGOs face in trying to capture news attention. Then, I draw on more recent research, some of it my own, to substantiate the claim that these transformations can be best grasped as a "double-edged sword" for NGOs, journalism, and the news-consuming public. Finally, I discuss the implications of these findings, both for researchers and practitioners, and I suggest some areas where further research is warranted. Throughout, I aim to include an internationally diverse set of empirical examples while stressing the imbalance in research – an important task for future scholarship to collectively redress – towards news media and advocacy groups based in the Global North.

Journalism, NGOs, and human rights news

Scholars have long argued that human rights reporting is not a direct reflection of realities on the ground (International Council on Human Rights Policy 2002; Maier 2021). Partly, this derives from the contested meaning of human rights themselves – that is, whether they pertain strictly to political rights or ought to include economic concerns, how they should be measured, and so forth. But it also stems from the fact that human rights news, however human rights are defined, is the product of professional and economic considerations on the part of journalists. Professionally, news professionals have long tended to emphasise the actions of public officials to the relative exclusion of activists (Hall et al. 1978); economically, news organisations lack the time and resources to produce news without the aid of sources, which leads them to turn to official sources for what Gandy (1982) terms 'information subsidies'. Together, this skews coverage towards government officials and geographic locations already in the media spotlight.

In this context, NGOs have long faced an uphill battle for publicity. Scholars have documented this struggle in contexts as varied as Europe (Lang 2013), Latin America (Waisbord 2011), Africa (Wright 2018), and North America (Ramos, Ron and Thoms 2007). In all these places, human rights groups are rarely included in the news. When they do appear in the news, it tends to be in relation to topics and on issues that already capture the news agenda. What's more, their inclusion is skewed heavily towards a few well-known organisations. One study examining more than 250 human rights organisations in more than 600 news outlets found that just 10 percent of all groups garner 90 percent of all media citations (Thrall, Stecula and Sweet 2014). Other research finds that human rights groups of any size tend to receive coverage 'only if there is valorised input from government representatives' (Lang 2013, 127). Because the work of many human rights groups, especially those with fewer resources, only sometimes aligns with either media interest or extant government opinions, they have historically been at a disadvantage in their quest for publicity.

Transformations in journalism, advocacy, politics, and technology raise questions about the validity of these prior findings. Adverse economic conditions – specifically, reduced revenues and declining audience sizes – have led many news organisations to slash the resources they commit to human rights coverage (Sambrook 2010). As a result, many organisations find it difficult to monitor human rights situations with their own staff, or even using freelancers and so-called 'parachute' journalists; this is especially true for human rights issues whose occurrence are not geographically proximate to the news organisations covering them. At the same time, the proliferation of different types of news organisations (e.g., partisan outlets, digital upstarts, regional/global channels linked to a country's geopolitical ambitions) arguably expands the ways journalists report on human rights issues, with at least some outlets decentering government voices as primary definers in human rights stories (Chadwick 2013).

During this period of retrenchment for news organisations, which has lasted at least since the early 2000s, NGOs have expanded considerably (Lang 2013). No longer run primarily by volunteers, many human rights groups – and not just the largest ones – are durable organisations with paid professional staff, including more than a few former journalists, that produce information for a variety of stakeholders (Lang 2013). This information ranges from reports and policy statements to press releases and multimedia features; their cumulative effect is to widen the supply of potential sources of human rights news (Powers 2018). And as this organised advocacy sector has grown, it has also been characterised by a heightened sense of competitiveness. Part of this competition pertains to a search for funding and attention, which ensures that each group must take considerable interest in managing its brand by seeking ways to maximise its potential for favourable publicity while minimising the risks of unfavourable media exposure (Scurlock, Dolsack and Prakash 2020). All of this means that NGOs produce more – and more types of – information for a wider range of audiences than they ever did in the past.

The political contexts in which both the news media and advocacy groups operate are likewise characterised by transformation – and with implications for human rights reporting. Notions of citizenship have changed from a dominant understanding that emphasised infrequent participation via elections to one that emphasizes quasi-regular, if highly uneven, participation in efforts to hold governments and others accountable for their actions (Keane 2009). This shift has led governments to interact on a quasi-regular basis with a range of social groups – one of which is NGOs, who increasingly find themselves included in summits, conferences, and other fora. At the same time, amidst a growing and generalised public scepticism towards organised politics to act as a force for improving social life, NGOs are also viewed as more trusted sources of information and potential organisers of collective action (Tarrow 2022). These shifts in the world of politics thus have the effect of both legitimating NGOs – that is, incorporating them into the range of accepted viewpoints – while potentially decentering government officials as the dominant authority on human rights topics.

Finally, in a change that cuts very broadly across the others, digital technologies have the potential to reshape human rights reporting by diversifying the tools associated with producing and circulating information. Comparatively low production costs make it possible for many advocacy groups – not just the best-resourced – to produce their own media materials and monitor issues of interest online, sometimes relying not only on their own staff but on citizen activists. As McPherson (2015) has shown, NGOs increasingly rely on such activists to aid in their information gathering, especially in cases where they do not have their own staff on the ground to investigate. For those organisations with substantial resources, more costly technologies can be and are integrated to produce powerful new forms of human rights reporting and evidence (Herscher 2014): this is the case, for example, in the use of satellite imaging by human rights groups to verify claims about human rights abuses, which groups like Amnesty Internal and Human Rights Watch have deployed in Syria and Ukraine, among other places. Thus, rather than being inherently dependent on the news media for visibility, human rights organisations can conceivably see legacy news coverage as one of many potential options in their longstanding quest for public attention (Bennett and Segerberg 2013; Chadwick 2013). This fact itself raises basic questions about the potential for advocacy groups to simply bypass the news media entirely, or at least utilise it in a highly strategic fashion, in order to best achieve their organisational objectives. It also raises questions about how both journalists and advocacy groups sift through online information in an effort to verify or refute claims of human rights violations (Ristovska 2021).

The mixed effects on human rights news

What are the effects of these transformations on NGOs, news organisations, and audiences of human rights reporting? The available evidence is mixed on this question. The resources that human rights organisations have dedicated to publicity have indeed translated into greater media presence (Powers 2016). Large organisations like Amnesty International and Human Rights Watch, for example, appear far more today in the news than in the past; this finding is consistent across media systems in North America and Western Europe and presumably elsewhere, though systematic studies are necessary to confirm, modify, or refute these inferences (see, e.g., Thrall, Stecula and Sweet 2014 for one effort in this regard). The growing inclusion of these and other groups in the media far outpaces their visibility in other settings (e.g., their presence via testimony or mentions in parliamentary debates and multinational dialogues). Furthermore, human rights groups are cited not only for their factual reporting on issues of interest, itself an important issue for journalists concerned with stamping out misleading and false claims; they are also included for their advocacy statements that attempt to define the problem and propose solutions. Sometimes, these statements introduce human rights frames into news items that otherwise deal with seemingly unrelated topics (e.g. trade pacts between governments, labor disputes with multinational companies). As a result, news audiences overall are privy to a wider range of at least occasionally dissenting institutional voices than they were in the past.

Additionally, human rights NGOs can and do utilise digital technologies to strategically shape news coverage in ways that maximise their advocacy aims. Seeing the digital environment as inherently chaotic leads also them to perceive it as potentially permeable. These groups therefore have staff that monitor news coverage carefully with the hopes that they can graft their perspectives onto news stories already on the media agenda (Hall, Schmitz and Dedmon 2020). By many groups' own admission, their overall success rate is low; nonetheless, when success does occur it fosters the belief that such efforts, even if statistical outliers, are worthwhile precisely because their success cannot be predicted in advance (Powers 2018). Moreover, human rights groups increasingly see online settings as a place to verify the content produced by other groups and individually, especially information circulating on social media; to stir publicity around their chosen causes; to promote their organisations and raise the funds necessary for their work; and even to use advanced technology (e.g., satellite imagery) to conduct original research (McPherson 2015). In all these ways, human rights groups use digital tools to diversify the news agenda and sometimes insert advocacy frames into news coverage (e.g., by discussing 'hot' news topics like elections or sporting events from the vantage point of human rights, even when those topics are unrelated to human rights). As such, it represents an expanded understanding of both the providers and content of contemporary human rights news.

At the same time, these efforts involve costs and compromises, and these have impacts not only on NGOs but also on the types of human rights news that audiences do and do not get to consume. In their efforts to garner media attention, human rights groups adopt news norms (i.e., expectations regarding what types of reports are newsworthy) that give both journalists and public officials the advantage in defining what 'counts' as human rights news (Wright 2018). This norm adoption takes place even though human rights groups produce coverage about a far wider range of topics and issues than is covered in the news. For the most part, their most cited work tends to occur on themes already present in the news (Powers 2018). Limited victories in pushing the news agenda towards topics and issues outside the dominant spotlight also generate a sense of quasi-inevitability that such efforts are not worthwhile. Arguably even more concerning is the fact that the incorporation of comparatively well-funded international NGOs like Amnesty International and Human Rights Watch does not displace the long-standing dominance of government sources. Rather, they tend to stand in for – and speak in the place of – less well-resourced groups and individuals, often those from the Global South. This dovetails uneasily with a longstanding tendency in the politics of human rights representation wherein audiences in the Global North conceive of themselves as 'saviors' for problems whose sources are typically attributed to local causes (e.g. corruption, violence) rather than broader systemic forces that might implicate actors in the Global North, a tendency which some authors (e.g., Dogra 2014) see the largest human rights NGOs as contributing to rather than challenging (e.g., by focusing on local corruption as the primary cause of human rights violations rather than the outcome of geopolitics and global capitalism).

In principle, digital media can be used to bypass legacy news outlets and directly target specific audiences (e.g., policymakers that might take action on a specific human rights issue). Nonetheless, extant research suggests that human rights groups for the most part use such tools to both monitor media professionals and promote and protect their own organisational identities (Cottle and Nolan 2007; Harness 2022). Ethnographic research finds that the communication staff employed at human rights groups spend much of their time discussing what issues are already on the media agenda and exploring ways to tailor their work to align with those issues (Powers 2018). Even when utilising the work of citizen activitists, advocacy groups tend to focus on contributions that can satisfy the existing news agenda (i.e., stories already of interest to media professionals). They also rely overwhelmingly on a subset of citizen activists – particularly those with large online followings and established reputations, which minimises the potential risks of utilising their work (McPherson 2015).

What's more, the very visibility that digital tools provide also makes it possible for critics to assail human rights groups and challenge their legitimacy as information providers. Responding to this criticism can be extremely costly and time-consuming for such groups, especially when the veracity of their work is called into question and forces them to redo prior analyses – as happened to Human Rights Watch several times over the past decade (Powers 2018). As a result, many organisations have over time taken a relatively conservative approach to the affordances of interactive tools online (i.e. minimising their interactions with members of the public, requiring verification of other activists that can sometimes be difficult for less well-resourced groups to attain) (McPherson 2017). Overall, this gives the public engagement of many groups a relatively superficial form, and one that tends to lay emphasis on brand management and organisational identity over alternative considerations like engagement and interaction with a wider range of audiences.

Cumulatively, the available research therefore paints a mixed portrait of the effects of political, professional, and technological transformations on human rights news making. These findings, which I interpret as a "double-edged sword", nuance both overly positive or excessively negative views on human rights news. Journalism is not, at least in the cases scholars have studied thus far, best characterised as becoming a mere platform for the aims of advocacy groups. "Churnalism" – i.e. news that is copied and pasted wholesale from the press releases of advocacy groups and others (Lewis, Williams and Franklin 2008) – no doubt exists both in general and in the case of human rights reporting; however, it hardly describes the major tendencies observed with respect to news production on these issues. Instead, most human rights news is still shaped by journalists, who themselves rely overwhelmingly on government officials. And while human rights groups no doubt mimic news norms, it is misleading to claim that NGOs merely "clone" the news (Fenton 2010). At least sometimes, their work does contribute to diversification in the sources and, less often, the topics of news coverage. Just as importantly, the very processes that lead NGOs to engage in these practices are less the direct effect of a pervasive media logic and more the outcome of these organisation's own histories and aims. In other words, NGOs turn to media first and foremost because doing so fits with their historically developed strategies for addressing human rights violations. These include everything from using public opprobrium to press human rights violators into changing their behaviours to seeing media attention as a way to ensure that donors view advocacy groups' work as effective. It is these factors, rather than some external media logic, that induce organisations to seek out publicity for their work.

These descriptive findings raise a series of analytical questions in turn. Why, for instance, should human rights organisations spend so much energy seeking out media coverage, especially when they seem to have many of the tools to bypass them? Part of the answer has to do with the political economy of the advocacy sector (Powers 2018). Donors want to see "impact", but this impact can be difficult to substantiate in many human rights crises. Rarely is it easy to say that an organisation succeeded in stopping a specific human rights violation – a point that human rights advocates themselves readily concede when asked about the efficacy of their campaigns (Powers 2018). In such a context, being cited in the news is one measure of organisational effectiveness. Related research also finds that political officials continue to turn to news organisations, especially elite agenda-setting ones, to efficiently learn about advocacy demands. This makes media attention an important route for capturing the attention of policymakers, even if the remainder of the audience – which is to say the overwhelming bulk of it – is not directly relevant to such concerns. Staff at human rights organisations, moreover, tend to be socially proximate to journalists. They share similar social circles, often have similar educational backgrounds, and share a broadly comparable vision of the social world (de Waal 1997; Powers 2018). As a result, human rights groups are led to see news media as a sort of natural ally in their efforts to redress human rights violations.

With respect to journalism, a distinct but related question arises: Why, despite reasonable expectations to the contrary, should news norms – which give journalists the upper-hand in defining what counts as human rights news, and which are based on longstanding ideas regarding newsworthiness that emphasise the actions of government officials – endure amidst the many upheavals confronting the profession? One reason is that reporters seek out human rights sources to fulfil well-defined tasks. These include asking them to provide responses to government statements and offer eyewitness reports of events on the ground (Sampaio-Dias 2016). This slots human rights perspectives into stories driven largely by other sources, with advocacy groups being turned to either to offer criticism of government positions or to help verify claims regarding human rights violations. What's more, advocacy organisations' own hiring strategies – namely, hiring former journalists – help to incorporate these norms within the organisations themselves (Jones 2017). This fosters a sense of what coverage is – and, crucially, is not – possible for advocacy groups to aspire for. Thus, while human rights groups conduct research in nearly all countries around the world, they know that their likelihood of garnering attention is limited to countries already of interest to the news media. This point is well captured by an Amnesty International official: 'You can work all you like on Mauritania', he says, 'but the press couldn't give a rat's ass' (quoted in Ron, Ramos and Rodgers 2005, 576). They 'don't want a press release' on issues related to events in such countries, as they are unlikely to ever cover events in those countries.

Evaluations regarding the persistence of news norms depend for the most part on what one expects from journalism and advocacy groups, respectively. Normative aspirations for a journalism that produces its own original reporting and maintains a distance from all its sources find cause for concern in these developments. Newsroom reductions make it hard to produce original reports and lead journalists to rely increasingly on both government officials and advocacy groups to create human rights news. What's more, the organised advocacy sector, given its remarkable growth over time, is not only a potential source but a sector ripe for investigation as well, as some of the largest organisations have budgets that rival those of small governments, thus creating an opportunity to explore how effectively that money is utilised. The fact that a growing number of freelancers move quasi-seamlessly between assignments for human rights groups and news organisations arguably makes these investigations less likely (Conrad 2015). By contrast, those who desire journalists to engage with civil society groups to better understand the world and address human rights violations will likely find the growing role played by NGOs salutary. Advocacy groups provide critical information about human rights issues that would otherwise almost certainly go unreported in the news media. These groups' occasional use of citizen activists, moreover, helps to incorporate voices otherwise ignored by journalists. In this way, human rights news represents a space where journalists interface more regularly with civil society groups – and, in doing so, present audiences with their voices and perspectives with greater frequency.

Evaluations of advocacy groups' role in the production of human rights news are similarly varied. Those who hold out hope for the inclusion of a greater number of human rights groups in news are likely to be frustrated. The best known and most generously funded groups continue to far outpace smaller organisations as sources in the news. Similarly, the relatively conservative use of digital technologies by many advocacy groups is likely to disappoint those who see potential in them (e.g., to bypass news media, to facilitate greater dialogue; see Bennett and Segerberg 2013). Yet those who aim for human rights groups to be viewed by journalists as reliable sources of information are no doubt pleased by their growing inclusion in news coverage – a reminder that evaluations of both journalists and advocacy groups depend on the expectations placed on them.

Conclusion

Research examining the factors involved in human rights reporting has grown tremendously in the past two decades. Collectively, this research paints of mixed portrait of the effects of these developments on journalism, advocacy, and public understanding. Human rights groups' investment in reporting expands the supply of human rights information and diversifies who speaks on human rights topics. Yet in their efforts to attract journalists to cover these issues, human rights groups often take as given which types of issues will be of interest to the news media. Both advocates and journalists get something useful from these interactions: NGOs get more publicity than they could achieve on their own; journalists get credible information from places they can no longer afford to visit. Yet each party also finds cause for concern in these developments: NGOs worry about the extent to which investing in media coverage is the best use of their limited funds; journalists worry about becoming overly dependent on a source.

Ample opportunities exist for further inquiry. Ideally, such research would serve to remedy some of the extant biases found in the available research. Probably the most glaring bias remains the tendency to focus on newsmakers (both journalism and human rights groups) located in the Global North. The orientation is to study newsmakers in the Global North looking at human rights issues in the Global South rather than within their own societies. It risks creating a scholarly understanding that not only lets a few newsmakers – namely, the best-known journalists and NGOs in the Global North – stand in for the whole; it also remains open to criticisms that human rights frameworks are applied selectively in ways that reinforce global inequalities (Williams 2010).

The factors that lead to this situation are probably easier to recognise than to remedy. News organisations and human rights groups in the Global North enjoy comparatively greater recognition among many scholars. Probably even more importantly, and given the dominance of Anglophone institutions in global academic knowledge production, researchers tend to possess a greater awareness of the histories and trajectories of these actors and social contexts. Thus, the issue is not merely identifying groups or issues to examine outside the Global North. They also require grasping the linguistic, cultural, and social histories that produce them. This context is only acquired over relatively time-intensive periods – a situation that the publishing demands of contemporary academic life tend to disincentivise, and that is exacerbated by the Anglophone dominance of communication scholarship more generally.

Beyond geographic imbalances, scholarship on human rights news also tends to be heavily focused on issues of production. The reception and interpretation of such news are far less examined (but see Kyriakidou 2015; Bruna Seu 2010). This should seem odd, given how much discussion of human rights news talks about "raising awareness" or facilitating empathy among audiences across distances, as well as reverse concerns about "compassion fatigue". What types of awareness do different styles of human rights reporting elicit? What are the meanings that audiences assign to such news? How do these meanings differ according to various social factors like race, class, or gender? And what impact does human rights news have on their political and moral views? These and other questions are important and largely unexamined components of a more holistic understanding of human rights news.

There are practical reasons for posing and answering such questions. Human rights practitioners and journalists alike ask themselves, or are asked by others, about the most effective ways of communicating human rights issues. Are some ways of framing human rights issues more effective at inducing audience interest, or getting perpetrators to cease their abuses? At least sometimes, there seems to be a tension between short-term needs (e.g. raising funds, cessation of abuses) and longer-term considerations (e.g. protecting organisational reputations, ensuring long-term flourishing; see Cohen and Green 2012). Being able to identify these trade-offs and explain what they imply for basic factors like organisational funding, strategic success, and audience awareness are all important concerns. Such work can also foster tacit theories carried by human rights organisations and news professionals about the 'types' of stories that elicit interest among audiences.

Whether focused on production or reception, most scholarship to date draws primarily from news texts. Human rights news, though, contains important visual dimensions. How we know about the human beings associated with human rights issues depends in part on visual understanding. What kinds of people are presented in human rights news? Are they, for example, seen as suffering masses or citizens with a voice? Relatedly, how do visual producers think about the varied uses their work can be used for, which potentially range from legal proceedings to inducing audience empathies? While scholars have done much to analyse the discourse of human rights, much less work has explored its visual grammars (but see Ristovska 2021 for an important example). Studies of these visual dimensions – whether on the imagery itself, or the factors shaping its production or reception – are therefore another useful avenue for future research.

Analytically, one avenue for continued exploration lay in the varied logics that characterise the production and reception of human rights news. Claims of an all-encompassing 'media logic' that ensnares activist organisations capture a general trend; however, they are too sweeping to make sense of the heterogeneity of both journalists and activists involved in producing human rights news, as well as the audiences that consume them. The news media are hardly unitary. And to the extent that advocacy groups do adapt, it is often less the result of any direct media effect and instead the outcome of a series of interdependencies in which organisations are themselves caught (e.g., donor demands, political officials' attention). Said otherwise, scholars might move from asking whether human rights news is characterised by a 'media logic' or an advocacy influence and instead ask about the conditions under which such logics might be more or less dominant.

Discussion questions

1. Why, according to the author, do recent developments in journalism and advocacy amount to a "double-edged sword" for human rights news? Do you agree with this evaluation? Why or why not?
2. Find a recent human rights story in the news. To what extent does the story reflect the trends identified in this chapter? For example, are NGOs used to respond to the statements of government officials and offer first-hand reporting? Are they tasked with any other functions? If so, what are those functions?
3. Check out the social media account of a human rights group. What sorts of information are they posting? Is it news, calls for action, requests for

donations – or something else entirely? Why, in your view, are they using their accounts in these ways?
4. What standards should citizens use to evaluate human rights news? How important, for example, is it for such news to include voices and topics that are otherwise absent from news coverage? Why?

Further reading

Clark, Ann Marie. 2001. *Diplomacy of Conscience: Amnesty International and Changing Human Rights Norms.* Princeton: Princeton University Press.

Hopgood, Stephen. 2006. *Keepers of the Flame: Understanding Amnesty International.* Ithaca: Cornell University Press.

Keck, Margaret, and Kathryn Sikkink. 1998. *Activists Beyond Borders: Advocacy Networks in International Politics.* Ithaca: Cornell University Press.

Moyn, Samuel. 2010. *The Last Utopia: Human Rights in History.* Cambridge, MA: Harvard University Press.

Snyder, Jack. 2022. *Human Rights for Pragmatists: Social Power in Modern Times.* Princeton: Princeton University Press.

References

Bennett, W. Lance, and Alexandra Segerberg. 2013. *The Logic of Connective Action: Digital Media and the Personalization of Contentious Politics.* New York: Cambridge University Press.

Bruna Seu, Irene. 2010. "Doing Denial: Audience Reaction to Human Rights Appeals." *Discourse & Society* 21 (4): 438–57. https://doi.org/10.1177/0957926510366199.

Chadwick, Andrew. 2013. *The Hybrid Media System: Politics and Power.* New York: Oxford University Press.

Cohen, Dara Kay, and Amelia Hoover Green. 2012. "Dueling Incentives: Sexual Violence in Liberia and the Politics of Human Rights Advocacy." *Journal of Peace Research* 49 (3): 445–58. https://doi.org/10.1177/0022343312436769.

Conrad, David. 2015. "The Freelancer-NGO Alliance: What a Story About Kenyan Waste Reveals About Contemporary Foreign News Production." *Journalism Studies* 16 (2): 275–88. https://doi.org/10.1080/1461670X.2013.872418.

Cottle, Simon, and David Nolan. 2007. "Global Humanitarianism and the Changing Aid-Media Field." *Journalism Studies* 8 (6): 862–78. https://doi.org/10.1080/14616700701556104.

De Waal, Alex. 1997. *Famine Crimes: Politics and the Disaster Relief Industry in Africa.* Bloomington: Indiana University Press.

Dogra, Nandita. 2014. *Representations of Global Poverty: Aid, Development and International NGOs.* London: IB Tauris.

Fenton, Natalie. 2010. "NGOs, New Media, and the Mainstream News: News From Everywhere." In *New Media, Old News: Journalism and Democracy in the Digital Age*, edited by Natalie Fenton, 153–68. London: Sage.

Gandy, Oscar. 1982. *Beyond Agenda Setting: Information Subsidies and Public Policy.* Norwood, New Jersey: Ablex Publishing.

Hall, Nina, Hans Peter Schmitz, and J. Michael Dedmon. 2020. "Transnational Advocacy and NGOs in the Digital Era: New Forms of Networked Power." *International Studies Quarterly* 64 (1): 159–67. https://doi.org/10.1093/isq/sqz052.

Hall, Stuart, Chas Critcher, Tony Jefferson, John Clarke, and Brian Roberts. (1978). *Policing the Crisis: Mugging, the State, and Law and Order*. London: Macmillan Press.
Harness, Delaney. 2022. "The Strategy of NGO Journalism in the Fight for Refugee Rights." In *Global Perspectives on NGO Communication for Social Change*, edited by Guiliana Sorce, 49–72. New York: Routledge.
Herscher, Andrew. 2014. "Surveillant Witnessing: Satellite Imagery and the Visual Politics of Human Rights." *Public Culture* 36 (3): 469–500. https://doi.org/10.1215/08992363-2683639.
International Council on Human Rights Policy. 2002. *Journalism, Media and the Challenge of Human Rights Reporting*. Geneva: ICHRP.
Jones, Ben. 2017. "Looking Good: Mediatisation and International NGOs." *European Journal of Development Research* 29: 176–91. https://doi.org/10.1057/ejdr.2015.87.
Keane, John. 2009. *The Life and Death of Democracy*. London: Simon & Schuster.
Kyriakidou, Maria. 2015. "Media Witnessing: Exploring the Audience of Distant Suffering." *Media, Culture & Society* 37 (2): 215–31. https://doi.org/10.1177/0163443714557981
Lang, Sabine. 2013. *NGOs, Civil Society, and the Public Sphere*. New York: Cambridge University Press.
Lewis, Justin, Andrew Williams, and Bob Franklin. 2008. "A Compromised Fourth Estate? UK News Journalism, Public Relations, and News Sources." *Journalism Studies* 9 (1): 1–20. https://doi.org/10.1080/14616700701767974.
Maier, Scott. 2021. "News Coverage of Human Rights: Investigating Determinants of Media Attention." *Journalism: Theory, Practice & Criticism* 22 (7): 1612–28. https://doi.org/10.1177/1464884919832722.
McPherson, Ella. 2015. "Advocacy Organizations' Evaluation of Social Media Information for NGO Journalism: The Evidence and Engagement Models." *American Behavioral Scientist* 59 (1): 124–48. https://doi.org/10.1177/0002764214540508.
McPherson, Ella. 2017. "Social Media and Human Rights Advocacy." In *The Routledge Companion to Media and Human Rights*, edited by Howard Tumber and Silvio Waisbord, 279–88. New York: Routledge.
Powers, Matthew. 2016. "Opening the News Gates? Humanitarian and Human Rights NGOs in the US News Media, 1990–2010." *Media, Culture & Society* 38 (3): 315–31. https://doi.org/10.1177/0163443715594868.
Powers, Matthew. 2018. *NGOs as Newsmakers: The Changing Landscape of International News*. New York: Columbia University Press.
Ramos, Howard, James Ron, and Oskar N. T. Thoms. 2007. "Shaping the Northern Media's Human Rights Coverage, 1986–2000." *Journal of Peace Research* 44 (4): 385–406. https://doi.org/10.1177/0022343307078943.
Ristovska, Sandra. 2021. *Seeing Human Rights: Video Activism as a Proxy Profession*. Cambridge: The MIT Press.
Ron, James, Howard Ramos, and Rodgers Kathleen. 2005. "Transnational Information Politics: NGO Human Rights Reporting, 1986–2000." *International Studies Quarterly* 49 (3): 557–87. https://doi.org/10.1111/j.1468-2478.2005.00377.x.
Sambrook, Richard. 2010. *Are Foreign Correspondents Redundant? The Changing Face of International News*. Oxford: Reuters Institute for the Study of Journalism.
Sampaio-Dias, Susana. 2016. *Reporting Human Rights*. New York: Peter Lang.
Scurlock, Rebecca, Neves Dolsack, and Akseem Prakash. 2020. "Recovering From Scandals: Twitter Coverage of Oxfam and Save the Children Scandals." *Voluntas* 31: 94–110.
Tarrow, Sydney. 2022. *Power in Movement*. New York: Cambridge University Press.

Thrall, Trevor, Dominik Stecula, and Diana Sweet. 2014. "May We Have Your Attention Please? Human-Rights NGOs and the Problem of Global Communication." *International Journal of Press/Politics* 19 (2): 135–59. https://doi.org/10.1177/1940161213519132.

Waisbord, Silvio. 2011. "Can NGOs Change the News?" *International Journal of Communication* 5: 142–65. https://doi.org/1932–8036/20110142.

Williams, Randall. 2010. *The Divided World: Human Rights and Its Violence*. Minneapolis: University of Minnesota Press.

Wright, Kate. 2018. *Who's Reporting Africa Now? Non-Governmental Organizations, Journalists and Multimedia*. London: Peter Lang.

PART II

6

WOMEN JOURNALISTS AND ONLINE HARASSMENT

A human rights approach

Susana Sampaio-Dias, Maria João Silveirinha and João Miranda

Introduction

In democratic societies, journalism plays a critical role in providing information to the public. Freedom of the press is a human rights matter codified in human rights instruments, namely in Article 19 of the Universal Declaration of Human Rights (UDHR). This right is essential for realising other fundamental human rights, including the right to seek, receive, and share information.

Despite the recognition of these rights by most countries, persecution and violence against journalists have been an instrument of control, particularly for authoritarian regimes. However, hateful harassment of these professionals is now also part of democratic contexts, facilitated by increased usage and exposure to online technologies (see, for example, Löfgren Nilsson and Örnebring 2016; Rees 2023). Online violence is now one of the most prevalent forms of aggression against journalists, representing a step backwards in their rights (IFJ 2023). Online harassment, intimidation, and defamation campaigns are among the new threats that add to old strategies of silencing journalists – such as detentions, physical attacks, arrests, and murders – bringing critical challenges to freedom of expression for journalists worldwide. Although journalists' working conditions and safety are considerably different across regions (Westlund, Krøvel and Skare Orgeret 2022), they are not immune to this global online trend.

In this context, and as abundant statistical data shows, women journalists are preferential targets of discrimination and abuse in the course of their work (Posetti and Shabbir 2022a; Ferrier and Garud-Patkar 2018; Miller 2022; RSF 2021). Both as women and as journalists, they are subjected to sexist comments and sexual violence threats as well as different shaming tactics, threats of

DOI: 10.4324/9781032662589-8

physical violence, rape, kidnapping, doxing, and racist, sexist, and misogynistic abuse (Binns 2017).

Journalists' organisations such as the International Federation of Journalists (IFJ) (2023, 2018) have long been calling for internationally binding standards to create safeguards for journalists and media professionals, denouncing precisely the growing gender-based abuses of women journalists. Following a decade of work on the safety of journalists, the UN Human Rights Council (2022), for example, recognised that 'online attacks against women journalists, including through targeted unlawful or arbitrary digital surveillance, are one of the serious contemporary threats to their safety' and it 'condemns unequivocally the specific attacks on women journalists and media workers in relation to their work, such as gender-based discrimination, sexual and gender-based violence, threats, intimidation and harassment, online and offline' (*Idem*). Yet, despite these significant advances, there is still much to accomplish in establishing efficient accountability systems and preventing impunity for individuals who target journalists for their work, gender, or identities while acknowledging the gender disparity of online violence.

In this chapter, we examine the issues concerning press freedom and online violence against women journalists as a violation of human rights. We look into them as a vulnerable category of journalists exposed to online violence. We explore how the protection and application of human rights legislation for women journalists in online contexts is consequently affected, namely in the scope of their rights and the corresponding obligations from various actors, including states, platforms, and news organisations. We finally take a broad view of the role of regulation mechanisms in fostering freedom of the press. In the conclusion, we highlight the main issues emerging from the need to protect journalists in ways that consider women's challenges when they do not work in a safe environment.

Gendered harassment and intimidation of women journalists

In 2021, Maria Ressa was awarded the Nobel Peace Prize (jointly with Dmitry Muratov) for safeguarding freedom of expression in the Philippines. In her acceptance speech, she said:

> As only the 18th woman to receive this prize, I need to tell you how gendered disinformation is a new threat and is taking a significant toll on the mental health and physical safety of women, girls, trans, and LGBTQ+ people all over the world. Women journalists are at the epicentre of risk. This pandemic of misogyny and hatred needs to be tackled now.
>
> *(Ressa 2021)*

Ressa is one of the many women journalists targeted with a contemporary manifestation of an old phenomenon as an attempt to silence them. Research has shown that while suffering retaliation for news content is familiar to all journalists, women journalists experience a unique set of risks: threats against them are often highly sexualised, emphasising their physical appearance, ethnicity, or cultural background, rather than on the content of their work (OSCE 2021; Chen et al. 2020; Martin 2018).

For Høiby (2020), violence against women journalists is a result of three interrelated factors: who they are (women), what they do (journalism), and the context they are operating within (online space/regulation), arguing that these issues are 'dependent on systematic antipress violence, persisting patriarchal social structures and that the conditions of online space allow harassment to thrive' (109). Together, the three factors put women journalists on a 'continuum of violence' (Kelly 1988), of which online abuse is just the latest aspect in an interconnected spectrum of manifestations of violence that not only overlap but also inform and reinforce one another. Online violence is just the tip of the iceberg, with a broad range of other violent behaviours and attitudes hidden below the waterline where contextual factors that legitimise the logic of misogyny reside. Sofia Strid (2018, 71) calls this a regime of violence: 'Though online manifestations of violence are ostensibly individual expressions of violence, they co-constitute a system of linked events and ideologies, a regime of violence. In the regime's most empirical form, the events are linked via hashtags'.

Perpetrators may be lone stalkers or snowballing mobs. Still, they are part of a 'networked misogyny' (Banet-Weiser and Miltner 2016) that affects women and girls. The simple, direct and anonymous way in which attacks can be carried out on digital platforms makes online violence a ubiquitous phenomenon in contemporary digital environments, ranging from organised forms of violence (such as mobbing) to broader, pervasive, and usually more subtle forms of violence.

Although there is no agreement over how or whether to distinguish forms of gender-based violence such as hate speech, sexual harassment, or gendered disinformation (Radsch 2022), gender-based online violence is acknowledged as a form of gender discrimination and prejudice that involves digitally-enabled forms of harassment and abuse. As one of the most widespread violations of human rights that takes place in online spaces, the gendered nature of the harm it causes – often involving sexualisation and objectification – should be recognised as affecting women in particular. Furthermore, although the damage online violence causes is psychological and emotional, it is no less real or destructive than offline violence.

Adding to the misogynistic aspect of online violence, women journalists also suffer because of their profession. In that respect, as their male colleagues, they are vulnerable to relentless digital harassment by individual citizens or by organised actors aiming to demonise, dehumanise, and persecute journalists:

> Trolls use degrading language to express their sense of (gender, racial, sexual, ethnic, religious) superiority. Their purpose is to cow journalists into

silence by using language that marks them as different, lesser human beings based on their perceived social identity.

(Waisbord 2020, 1036)

Online harassment of journalists can take different forms, such as acute harassment (e.g., generalised verbal abuse), chronic harassment (e.g., repeatedly occurring over time), and escalatory harassment (e.g., more personalised and threatening forms) (Holton et al. 2021). It has, therefore, become 'journalism safety's new frontline – and women journalists sit at the epicentre of risk' (Posetti and Shabbir 2022a, 17).

Research has gathered evidence of the gendered nature of harassment, and its disproportionate impact on women is now well-established (Barão da Silva et al. 2023; Claesson 2023; Jamil and Appiah-Adjei 2021; Miller and Lewis 2022; Sampaio-Dias et al. 2024; Stahel and Schoen 2019). In a survey of US journalists, Lewis, Zamith and Coddington (2020) found that online harassment is pervasive among journalists but does not affect them all equally, with women journalists taking most of the abuse. Miller and Lewis (2022) used qualitative interviews with broadcasters, finding that women face gender-specific online abuse, including disruptive in-person harassment, physical in-person harassment, unwanted online sexual advances, and online threats and criticism. In this same line, Chen et al. (2020) documented that most of the abuse women journalists experienced was sexual and based on misogynistic ideals, leading to their 'rampant online gendered harassment that influences how they do their jobs' (877-8).

Also, research has documented that attacks are more intense for women of colour, minorities, or other intersecting identities. For example, a 2020 global survey found that 64% of white women journalists and 80 to 90% of Black, Indigenous, and Jewish women journalists experienced online violence (Posetti et al. 2020). This research, published by UNESCO and the International Center for Journalists, summed up the global problem: three quarters (73%) of 714 international female journalists surveyed claimed having experienced online violence during their work. In addition, gender as a topic of news is a trigger for attacks: almost half of women journalists who covered gender issues – feminism, domestic violence, sexual assaults, femicide, abortion, or transgender questions. This tendency reinforces the gendered character of the phenomenon. Moreover, 20% of the respondents indicated that they had experienced offline attacks and abuse that they believed had been seeded online. Across this body of research, the features of violence against female journalists can be devised: it is generally sexist and misogynistic, and its patterns vary from large-scale attacks or extreme threats to the slow burn of networked gaslighting, which involves constant lower-level abuse. Furthermore, 'gender-based online violence against journalists could be a predictor of physical violence, including murder with impunity' (Posetti, Maynard and

Shabbir 2022), suggesting a clear need for more systematic monitoring and reporting of online violations against female journalists, adopting a human rights-based approach.

Journalists' protection, equality, and human rights

Taking a naturalistic approach to journalism and press freedom as human rights, Cruft (2022, 373) argues that the journalist's role-based rights to communicate are not only distinct from ordinary human rights of communication but also are of high importance given their protective relationship to the universally held human rights to education, legitimate authority, and voice. Harrison and Torsner (2022) explain a two-dimensional basis for journalists' protection under international human rights law. First, they argue that not only are states obligated to safeguard fundamental rights attached to any individual journalist (such as the right to freedom of expression and opinion), but journalists also have the right to life and a person's dignity. Secondly, protecting journalism is essential to inform the public and enable citizens to address collective concerns through interpersonal exchange. International human rights law also establishes that the protection of journalists includes provisions to prevent all forms of discrimination, such as race, colour, sex, language, or other status, applying to every person without distinction. Because women journalists are often targeted for their identity as women, this provision against discrimination also applies.

The international non-governmental organisation Article 19 (2009) recalls the UDHR linking equality and dignity to all human rights, including freedom of speech and communication:

> freedom of expression and equality are foundational rights, whose realisation is essential for the enjoyment and protection of all human rights. They are also mutually supporting and reinforcing human rights. It is only when coordinated and focused action is taken to promote both freedom of expression and equality that either can effectively be realised

Countering the idea that freedom of expression and equality are in conflict, the organisation argues that promoting freedom of expression and equality is necessary to tackle the kind of discrimination and prejudice which underlines gender-based violence, namely against women. Women's right to freedom of expression requires them to be equally able to share their ideas or work without censorship or fear of retaliation.

Other vital conventions, recommendations, and resolutions, together with national and international laws, enshrine freedom of expression and women's rights. These include 'soft law' or non-binding instruments developed by UN human rights bodies – including the authoritative interpretation of the

Human Rights Committee, the resolutions of the Human Rights Council, and the Special Rapporteur's recommendations on freedom of opinion and expression.

The United Nations (UN) and several other institutions have increasingly drawn attention to gender-related dimensions of human rights. Two instruments are worth recalling in the context of this chapter: Section J of the UN Beijing Women's Conference in 1995 called for 'increasing the participation and access of women to expression and decision-making in and through the media and new technologies of communication' (United Nations 1995), and the Convention on the Elimination of All Forms of Discrimination against Women (Council of Europe 2011) defines gender-based violence against women as 'violence that is directed against a woman because she is a woman, or violence that affects women disproportionately'. Since adopting these resolutions, the UN has continued getting actors and stakeholders to agree on fundamental principles and define priorities for action.

Although many countries have enacted laws based on these treaties and legislation, and almost all UN member states have enshrined freedom of speech, equality, and non-discrimination, none has been fully implemented:

> The resistance of governments and national authorities, deregulation, and lack of media accountability mechanisms, a global economic model that has privileged profit over respect for human rights and dignity, and a weakening of the multilateral system with the United Nations at its core, have all played a part in the implementation deficit.
>
> *(Ran 2023, 143)*

Padovani (2023, 19) also notes that in the latest UN *Global Acceleration Plan*, communication is not conceptualised as the foundation of all social organisation 'nor as a human right that would underpin the enjoyment of women's other rights, but rather as infrastructure or technology'.

Online violence against journalists: self-censorship and management of trauma

Despite the prevalence of online harassment, there is a tendency to normalise these attacks against journalists as 'part of the job', something expected as 'the price to pay' to be in journalism today (Adams 2018; Chen et al. 2020; Deavours et al. 2022; Gardiner 2018; Kantola and Harju 2023; Lewis, Zamith and Coddington 2020; Miller and Lewis 2022; Miranda et al. 2023). Nevertheless, this hostility impairs media work, causes emotional and psychological damage to journalists, discourages their active participation in public debate, and leads to reduced public visibility. Normalising violence causes desensitisation to common forms of online harassment, like insults, and journalists tend to undervalue and underreport such incidents (Lewis, Zamith and Coddington 2020). Research on women journalists who suffered online harassment has shown that they tend not to report such incidents, deeming them as 'not important enough' or believing that nothing would be done (Ferrier and Garud-Patkar 2018).

In defiance of the sector's pressure to connect with the public and use personal branding (Molyneux 2019), women journalists are more prone to limit their engagement with audiences and try to reduce their visibility on social media platforms or fully disconnect. One way of becoming less visible is to disguise their gender and name or publish anonymously (Adams 2018; Miller 2023). Another typical response is to block harassing users and delete abusive posts on social media platforms (Deavours et al. 2022; Miller and Lewis 2022). While these responses address the interactions between journalists and trolls, other common responses have more profound implications for personal and professional freedom. Often, women journalists change their reporting, self-censor, or even consider leaving the journalism sector (Stahel and Schoen 2019). The thought of leaving the profession is not only gendered (Miller 2023) but also connected to age and career longevity, as young journalists are almost twice as likely to consider it than older colleagues (Ferrier and Garud-Patkar 2018), as they feel age is a factor of increased exposure to violence (Sampaio-Dias et al. 2024). Self-censorship is an emotion management strategy used by journalists as a response to hostility from sources or audiences that is often unrecognised and even collectively unperceived (Himma-Kadakas and Ivask 2022). Reporters often avoid publishing stories that antagonise online trolls or choose to frame controversial topics differently (Binns 2017; Rees 2023; Waisbord 2020). The impact of harassment is usually avoidance, denial, or leaving the profession. It rarely ends with a confrontation with the abuser (Parker et al. 2014).

Online violence has a further impact on news content and, consequently, on democracy. Upon experiences of online harassment, journalists, particularly women journalists, admit to changing the way they research, dropping stories, or avoiding topics altogether (Löfgren Nilsson and Örnebring 2016). By conceding to the pressure, journalists are gagged, and diversity and pluralism are threatened, particularly the voices of women and other marginalised groups (OSCE 2021). The report by Posetti and Shabbir (2022a), which results from research carried out in 16 countries, describes the impact of online abuse as having a 'chilling effect' on women journalists' 'active participation (along with that of their sources, colleagues, and audiences) in public debates' (6). Fear of losing their jobs, shame, stigma, further abuse, or normalisation have kept many women silent. Irene Khan, UN Rapporteur on freedom of expression, emphasised the impact of gendered violence online and offline. In her 2021 report on gender justice and freedom of expression, she describes silencing women's expression as a form of 'gendered censorship' (UN Human Rights 2021).

When platforms, law enforcement, and news organisations fail to deal with the problem structurally, journalists face the added challenge of dealing with the abuse with increased emotional labour. The problem of online harassment is then managed individually rather than collectively, adding a burden to journalists' work and highlighting the need for a systemic approach to the problem. As OSCE (2021, 8) writes,

> there is still prevalent thinking of law enforcement that 'online is not real', which leads to a lack of institutional support and reinforces impunity for perpetrators. This can lead to a lack of willingness to report online attacks, which, in turn, further reinforces impunity, creating a vicious circle.

In this sense, experiences of online harassment must then be accounted for when capturing the full range of emotional work performed in journalism (Pantti and Wahl-Jorgensen 2021). Journalists increasingly mention online harassment as a common feature of their working lives, becoming a new normal (Waisbord 2020) and an invisible burden that contributes to experiences of fatigue, anxiety, and disconnection from social media as well as their profession (Holton et al. 2021). To women, in particular, as preferential targets, online harassment and misogyny induce an emotional and psychological price they feel they must pay to do their job (Chadha et al. 2020; Kantola and Harju 2023). In their research with broadcast journalists, Miller and Lewis (2022) explain that women perform significant unpaid emotional labour when dealing with, mitigating, and preventing further harassment. As digital security is perceived as an individual issue, media organisations are reluctant to adopt security-related mechanisms, viewing these as a low priority (Henrichsen 2022). The lack of institutional responses and the virtually absent discussion within the sector leads women journalists to manage this burden of harassment at work as an individual responsibility, an invisible burden of emotional labour added to the already-stressful job.

The role of regulators and self-regulation mechanisms in fostering freedom of the press

These online violence phenomena undermine the freedoms of the press and information in ways that go beyond the effects of insecurity and censorship they might have on journalists. They also affect how society perceives the media, the quality of the news produced by journalists, and the very role of journalism in the functioning of democracy. In democratic societies, the goals of media regulation, in its broadest sense, are often linked with ensuring the freedom of journalism to serve the public interest and to fulfil its role in democracy. This entails legally recognising journalists' right to expression and citizens' right to be informed. However, it also comprehends, for instance, fostering journalism's public credibility and responsibility, preventing political or economic control of the media and ensuring journalists' editorial autonomy, or stimulating pluralism and diversity and tackling media concentration (Freedman 2013; McQuail 2007). Considering the risk of political capture of these normative processes, co- and self-regulatory solutions can also be instrumental in guaranteeing the conditions for press freedom. However, these mechanisms, such as Press Councils, Ethics Committees, or Ombudspersons, are not limited to overseeing the media's compliance with ethical and professional standards but also act as liaison with the general public, highlighting requirements and conditions for the media's freedom to inform, drawing attention to infringements and abuses of those freedoms or, ultimately, fostering media literacy and sensitising audiences to the role and relevance of the news media in society (Bertrand 2018).

More recently, particular attention has been drawn to the role of legislators and media regulators in ensuring the protection and safety of journalists, which involves not only further and more specific efforts in designing and deploying effective instruments to prevent and address attacks against journalists and journalism (European Commission 2021), but also to make the digital platforms in which many of these attacks take place accountable for combating online violence against journalists (Posetti and Bontcheva 2022). While defending journalists is commonly credited to their professional associations and unions, professional self-regulatory bodies can also actively contribute to addressing and repelling attacks on journalists. Simultaneously, they can facilitate access to channels for reporting violence against journalists for newsmakers and audiences, take on an advocacy role (Fierens et al. 2023), document and publicly denounce cases involving attacks on journalists, and raise awareness of the issue. Although progress has been made in implementing some of these instruments, there is still a relative lack of effective measures to guarantee conditions of protection and equality (Posetti, Maynard and Shabbir 2022).

News organisations not only have to ensure effective comment moderation on their own websites but must also develop preventive and responsive strategies that recognise that the primary site of online attacks against women journalists is social media. Although their preventive actions are limited given that online attacks primarily occur on social media platforms and not their websites, media companies at least have to navigate different dimensions that include a need to shift the responsibility for managing gendered online violence 'from the individual journalists under attack to the news organisations that hire them, the political actors who frequently instigate and fuel attacks, and the digital services that act as vectors for abuse' (Posetti and Shabbir 2022b, 5).

While there is a lack of structural responses by social media platforms, legislation, and media organisations (with a few exceptions), a more concerted effort to support journalists, and women journalists in particular, to prevent and deal with online harassment is, in recent years, fostered by international organisations and philanthropic bodies who manage platforms and reports with solutions for online violence, collective support, and lobbying of news media employers. For example, the UN Plan of Action on the Safety of Journalists and the Issue of Impunity, developed in 2010, was updated in recent years to include new challenges to safety, including online harassment. Other sources recommend gender-specific responses, such as the OSCE Guidelines for monitoring online violence against female journalists, the Coalition Against Online Violence's Violence Response Hub, which maps incidents, offers resources and advocates for women journalists, or Trollbusters, led by scholar and former journalist Michelle Ferrier, offering support resources to women journalists, including digital defence courses (for references, see Further Reading). Other more spontaneous actions documented include creating support networks as coping mechanisms for journalists. These networks can be organised in WhatsApp groups (see, for example, research in Latin America by Harlow, Wallace and Cueva Chacón 2023) or include other agents, such as lawyers and media allies, who assist reporters pro-bono with filing criminal cases and complaints and provide legal advice (see Bhat 2024, about the case of the Digital Patrakar Defense Clinic in India). Finally, the weaknesses in UN and regional human rights instruments and current international law led to the lack of a precise set of obligations towards journalists and the recognition of specific risks associated with the profession (Draghici and Woods 2019). Since no binding treaty norms contain safeguards for journalists, consolidated legal frameworks for their protection, for example as proposed by the draft International Convention on the Safety and Independence of Journalists and Other Media Professionals, are much needed (IFJ 2018).

Conclusion

Throughout the chapter, we have developed three key ideas. Firstly, gender-based online violence is a form of gender discrimination and prejudice that involves digitally enabled forms of harassment and abuse. This form of violence is a widespread violation of women's human rights. In this context, women journalists are at the epicentre of a global crisis of attacks on freedom of the press and on the activities of journalists that have intensified in recent years. Furthermore, given that perpetrators target women journalists both offline and online in ways that can be easily defined as violations of universal human rights, it should also be acknowledged that these attacks are not only restricting access to knowledge but also women's participation in the digital realm.

Secondly, while the freedom of the press is primarily acknowledged because of its crucial role in fulfilling the right of the people to be informed, it is also essential to recognise journalists' role-based rights to communicate as distinct from ordinary human rights of communication. These rights are of high priority, given their protective relationship to the universally held human rights and their enabling access to knowledge, information, and truth.

Thirdly, the generic nature of the all-important human rights provisions on the protection of freedom of expression often fails to acknowledge journalists' distinctiveness and the gendered aspects of the attacks. While international human rights laws are becoming more gender-sensitive, there are still issues regarding the subjects of liability and the gendered nature of rights relating to online offences. Furthermore,

> pre-existing issues in international human rights law – concerning the gendered regulation, content and hierarchy of rights – are also exacerbated by the Internet, with gender-cased online harm often falling outside the scope of regulation or overridden in conflicts with the freedom of expression.
> *(Sjöholm 2022, 346)*

A critical theoretical approach to these issues needs to untangle different forms of online gendered violence requiring specific responses and solutions. Broad-based gendered abuse, such as online misogyny, is well-known, whereas other phenomena like gendered and sexualised disinformation are less explored. This may affect the responses to more specific issues, such as the attacks on women journalists as coordinated disinformation campaigns (Posetti, Maynard and Shabbir 2022).

Research should also look into specific aspects of governance and regulation. For example, determining the gender and identity composition of state and self-regulation councils/mechanisms and the identity bias in the AI that controls some of the detection mechanisms for hate speech and harassment would introduce the much-needed intersectional dimension on regulation and legal provisions concerning the protection of journalists. Only this intersectional perspective can better capture 'how violence against women journalists is compounded by stereotypes and prejudice related to ethnicity, religion, and sexual orientation/gender identity' (Harrison and Torsner 2022, 15). To combat online harassment, legislators, social media platforms, and media organisations must, therefore, adopt a gender-sensitive and intersectional approach as established, for example, in recommendations of Article 19 (2022, 2009) relating to the challenges and violence women face in their private and public spheres. International laws can also be further developed, as Sjöholm (2022, 344) suggests, by using the legal method of asking the 'woman question', 'which involves assessing whether law . . . is inclusive of women's distinct life experiences, values, and biological differences'.

To protect journalists in ways that consider the challenges women face to work in a safe environment is to provide for their communicative rights, for better journalism, and to safeguard a healthy democracy. After all,

> if you don't have women covering the news, you're only getting half the story. And if only white women are covering the news, you're not getting

genuine coverage of diverse perspectives, nor are you achieving true balance, accuracy, and fairness in reporting across all demographic communities and groups.

(Pulfer 2020, 8)

Discussion questions

1. Journalism is one of the cornerstones of democracy, and many professionals are women who are preferential targets of online harassment and attacks. Without reliable information to shape good decision-making and an informed citizenry, society loses its transparency and freedom of speech. As you read this chapter, please consider the following: What mechanisms and protection of journalists does your country hold, and how gender-specific are they?
2. News organisations have an obligation to provide guidance and support for journalist safety. Consider how female reporters should operate in hostile environments. Are they well-equipped to face the danger that online contact with the public poses to them both as journalists and as women? What specific protections do they need to work in a safe virtual world?
3. The UDHR sets out all human beings' fundamental rights and freedoms, regardless of race, colour, sex, language, religion, political or other opinion, ethnicity, and national background. Yet, women journalists worldwide face increasing online attacks and are subject to disproportional and specific threats. Please consider: how does the protection of the rights of women journalists align with broader efforts to promote human rights, equality, and dignity for all?

Further reading

"Coalition Against Online Violence: Online Violence Response Hub." https://onlineviolenceresponsehub.org/.

Lu, A., J. Posetti, and N. Shabbir. 2022. *Legal and Normative Frameworks for Combatting Online Violence Against Women Journalists*. UNESCO. https://unesdoc.unesco.org/ark:/48223/pf0000383789.

OSCE. 2023. "Countering Online Violence: Guidelines for Monitoring Online Violence Against Female Journalists." https://www.osce.org/representative-on-freedom-of-media/553951.

RSF. 2020. "Obligations for Digital Platforms to Safeguard the Information Space." https://rsf.org/sites/default/files/2020-10-recommendations-rsf-dsa-en.pdf.

Trollbusters. 2018. "Attacks and Harassment: The Impact on Female Journalists and Their Reporting." https://www.iwmf.org/wp-content/uploads/2018/09/Attacks-and-Harassment.pdf.

References

Adams, Catherine. 2018. "They Go for Gender First." *Journalism Practice* 12 (7): 850–69. https://doi.org/10.1080/17512786.2017.1350115.

Article 19. 2009. "Camden Principles on Freedom of Expression and Equality." https://www.article19.org/resources/camden-principles-freedom-expression-equality/.

Article 19. 2022. "Equally Safe: Towards a Feminist Approach to the Safety of Journalists. https://www.article19.org/wp-content/uploads/2022/12/Equally-Safe-FemSoj_08.12.22.pdf.

Banet-Weiser, Sarah, and Kate M. Miltner. 2016. "#MasculinitySoFragile: Culture, Structure, and Networked Misogyny." *Feminist Media Studies* 16 (1): 171–74. https://doi.org/10.1080/14680777.2016.1120490.

Barão da Silva, Gisele, Giulia Sbaraini Fontes, Francisco Marques, and Paulo Jamil. 2023. "Risks and Resilience in the Case of Brazilian Female Journalists: How Women Perceive Violence Against Media Professionals and Cope With Its Effects." *Journalism Studies* 24 (7): 956–75. https://doi.org/10.1080/1461670X.2022.2150873.

Bertrand, Claude Jean. 2018. *Media Ethics and Accountability Systems.* London: Routledge.

Bhat, Prashanth. 2024. "Coping With Hate: Exploring Indian Journalists' Responses to Online Harassment." *Journalism Practice* 18 (2): 337–55. https://doi.org/10.1080/17512786.2023.2250761.

Binns, Amy. 2017. "Fair Game? Journalist's Experiences of Online Abuse." *Journal of Applied Journalism & Media Studies* 6 (2): 183–206. https://doi.org/10.1386/ajms.6.2.183_1.

Chadha, Kalyani, Linda Steiner, Jessica Vitak, and Zahra Ashktorab. 2020. "Women's Responses to Online Harassment." *International Journal of Communication* 14: 239–57.

Chen, Gina Masullo, Paromita Pain, Victoria Y. Chen, Madlin Mekelburg, Nina Springer, and Franziska Troger. 2020. "'You Really Have to Have a Thick Skin': A Cross-Cultural Perspective on How Online Harassment Influences Female Journalists." *Journalism* 21 (7): 877–95. https://doi.org/10.1177/1464884918768500.

Claesson, Annina. 2023. "'I Really Wanted Them to Have My Back, But They Didn't': Structural Barriers to Addressing Gendered Online Violence Against Journalists." *Digital Journalism* 11 (10): 1809–28. https://doi.org/10.1080/21670811.2022.2110509.

Council of Europe. 2011. *Convention on Preventing and Combating Violence Against Women and Domestic Violence.* Council of Europe Treaty Series, No. 210. https://rm.coe.int/168008482e.

Cruft, Rowan. 2022. "Journalism and Press Freedom as Human Rights." *Journal of Applied Philosophy* 39 (3): 359–76. https://doi.org/10.1111/japp.12566.

Deavours, Danielle, Will Heath, Kaitlin Miller, Misha Viehouser, Sandra Palacios-Plugge, and Ryan Broussard. 2022. "Reciprocal Journalism's Double-Edged Sword: How Journalists Resolve Cognitive Dissonance After Experiencing Harassment From Audiences on Social Media." *Journalism* 24 (11): 2454–73. https://doi.org/10.1177/14648849221109654.

Draghici, Carmen, and Lorna M. Woods. 2019. "Killing Journalists is Not Media Regulation: Private Rights, Collective Wrongs and the Impact of Impunity." *Transnational Law & Contemporary Problems* 29 (1): 263–307.

European Commission. 2021. "Commission Recommendation of 16.9.2021 on Ensuring the Protection, Safety and Empowerment of Journalists and Other Media Professionals in the European Union (C(2021) 6650 Final." https://ec.europa.eu/newsroom/dae/redirection/document/79357.

Ferrier, Michelle, and Nisha Garud-Patkar. 2018. "TrollBusters: Fighting Online Harassment of Women Journalists." In *Mediating Misogyny: Gender, Technology, and*

Harassment, edited by Jacqueline Ryan Vickery and Tracy Everbach, 311–32. Cham: Springer International Publishing.

Fierens, Marie, Florence Le Cam, David Domingo, and Simone Benazzo. 2023. "SLAPPs Against Journalists in Europe: Exploring the Role of Self-Regulatory Bodies." *European Journal of Communication* 39 (2): 161–76. https://doi.org/10.1177/02673231231213539.

Freedman, Des. 2013. *The Politics of Media Policy*. Cambridge: Polity.

Gardiner, Becky. 2018. "'It's a Terrible Way to Go to Work:' What 70 Million Readers' Comments on the Guardian Revealed About Hostility to Women and Minorities Online." *Feminist Media Studies* 18 (4): 592–608. https://doi.org/10.1080/14680777.2018.1447334.

Harlow, Summer, Ryan Wallace, and Lourdes Cueva Chacón. 2023. "Digital (In)Security in Latin America: The Dimensions of Social Media Violence Against the Press and Journalists' Coping Strategies." *Digital Journalism* 11 (10): 1829–47. https://doi.org/10.1080/21670811.2022.2128390.

Harrison, Jackie, and Sara Torsner. 2022. *Safety of Journalists and Media Freedom: Trends in Non-EU Countries From a Human Rights Perspective*. Brussels: European Union. https://www.ila-americanbranch.org/wp-content/uploads/2023/09/JHARRI1.pdf.

Henrichsen, Jennifer R. 2022. "Understanding Nascent Newsroom Security and Safety Cultures: The Emergence of the 'Security Champion'." *Journalism Practice* 16 (9): 1829–48. https://doi.org/10.1080/17512786.2021.1927802.

Himma-Kadakas, Marju, and Signe Ivask. 2022. "Journalists Under Attack: Self-Censorship as an Unperceived Method for Avoiding Hostility." *Central European Journal of Communication* 15 (3(32)): 359–78. https://doi.org/10.51480/1899-5101.15.3(32).2.

Høiby, Marte. 2020. "The 'Triple Effect' Silencing Female Journalists Online: A Theoretical Exploration." In *Journalist Safety and Self-Censorship*, 100–13. Routledge.

Holton, Avery E., Valérie Bélair-Gagnon, Diana Bossio, and Logan Molyneux. 2021. "'Not Their Fault, But Their Problem': Organizational Responses to the Online Harassment of Journalists." *Journalism Practice* 1–16. https://doi.org/10.1080/17512786.2021.1946417.

IFJ. 2018. "International Convention on the Safety and Independence of Journalists and Other Media Professionals." https://www.ifj.org/fileadmin/user_upload/Draft_Convention_Journalists_E.pdf.

IFJ. 2023. "Press Freedom: Another Step Backwards, Says IFJ." https://www.ifj.org/media-centre/news/detail/category/press-releases/article/press-freedom-another-step-backwards-says-ifj.

Jamil, Sadia, and G. Gifty Appiah-Adjei. 2021. "Discrimination, Gender Disparity, and Safety Risks in Journalism: An Introduction." In *Handbook of Research on Discrimination, Gender Disparity, and Safety Risks in Journalism*, 1–7. IGI Global.

Kantola, Anu, and Anu A. Harju. 2023. "Tackling the Emotional Toll Together: How Journalists Address Harassment With Connective Practices." *Journalism* 24 (3): 494–512. https://doi.org/10.1177/14648849211055293.

Kelly, Liz. 1988. *Surviving Sexual Violence*. Oxford: Polity Press.

Lewis, Seth C., Rodrigo Zamith, and Mark Coddington. 2020. "Online Harassment and Its Implications for the Journalist–Audience Relationship." *Digital Journalism* 8 (8): 1047–67. https://doi.org/10.1080/21670811.2020.1811743.

Löfgren Nilsson, Monica, and Henrik Örnebring. 2016. "Journalism Under Threat: Intimidation and Harassment of Swedish Journalists." *Journalism Practice* 10 (7): 880–90. https://doi.org/10.1080/17512786.2016.1164614.

Martin, Fiona. 2018. "Tackling Gendered Violence Online: Evaluating Digital Safety Strategies for Women Journalists." *Australian Journalism Review* 40 (2): 73–89.

McQuail, Denis. 2007. "Media, Regulation of." In *The Blackwell Encyclopedia of Sociology*, edited by G. Ritzer. Blackwell Publishing. https://doi.org/10.1002/9781405165518.wbeosm069.

Miller, Kaitlin C. 2022. "The 'Price You Pay' and the 'Badge of Honor': Journalists, Gender, and Harassment." *Journalism & Mass Communication Quarterly* 100 (1): 193–213. https://doi.org/10.1177/10776990221088761.

Miller, Kaitlin C. 2023. "Harassment's Toll on Democracy: The Effects of Harassment Towards US Journalists." *Journalism Practice* 17 (8): 1607–26. https://doi.org/10.1080/17512786.2021.2008809.

Miller, Kaitlin C., and Seth C. Lewis. 2022. "Journalists, Harassment, and Emotional Labor: The Case of Women in On-Air Roles at US Local Television Stations." *Journalism* 23 (1): 79–97. https://doi.org/10.1177/1464884919899016.

Miranda, João, Maria João Silveirinha, Susana Sampaio-Dias, Bruno Dias, Bibiana Garcez, and Mateus Noronha. 2023. "'It Comes With the Job': How Journalists Navigate Experiences and Perceptions of Gendered Online Harassment." *International Journal of Communication* 17.

Molyneux, Logan. 2019. "A Personalized Self-Image: Gender and Branding Practices Among Journalists." *Social Media + Society* 5 (3): 1–10. https://doi.org/10.1177/2056305119872950.

OSCE. 2021. *The 2021 Annual Report of the OSCE PA Special Representative on Gender Issues*. Organization for Security and Co-operation in Europe. https://www.oscepa.org/en/documents/special-representatives/gender-issues/report-17/4247-2021-report-by-the-special-representative-on-gender-issues-violence-against-women-journalists-and-politicians-a-growing-crisis/file.

Padovani, Claudia. 2023. "Gender Dimensions of Communication Governance. Perspectives, Principles, and Practices." In *The Handbook of Gender, Communication, and Women's Human Rights*, edited by Margaret Gallagher and Aimée Vega Montiel, 17–33. John Wiley and Sons.

Pantti, Mervi, and Karin Wahl-Jorgensen. 2021. "Journalism and Emotional Work." *Journalism Studies* 22 (12): 1567–73. https://doi.org/10.1080/1461670X.2021.1977168.

Parker, Kelsey, Susan Drevo, Nigel Cook, Autumn Slaughter, and Elana Newman. 2014. "Journalists and Harassment: Dart Center for Journalism and Trauma." https://dartcenter.org/content/journalists-and-harassment.

Posetti, Julie, Diana Maynard, and Nabeelah Shabbir. 2022. *Guidelines for Monitoring Online Violence Against Female Journalists*. OSCE. https://www.osce.org/files/f/documents/b/0/554098_1.pdf.

Posetti, Julie, and Kalina Bontcheva. 2022. *The Chilling: Recommendations for Action Responding to Online Violence Against Women Journalists*. UNESCO. https://unesdoc.unesco.org/ark:/48223/pf0000383788.

Posetti, Julie, and Nabeelah Shabbir. 2022a. *The Chilling: A Global Study of Online Violence Against Women Journalists*. UNESCO. https://unesdoc.unesco.org/ark:/48223/pf0000383788.

Posetti, Julie, and Nabeelah Shabbir. 2022b. *The Chilling: What More Can News Organisations Do to Combat Gendered Online Violence?* UNESCO. https://unesdoc.unesco.org/ark:/48223/pf0000383043#:~:text=Accordingly%2C%20there%20is%20a%20need,abuse.%20News%20organisations%20at%20least.

Posetti, Julie, Nermine Aboulez, Kalina Bontcheva, Jackie Harrison, and Silvio Waisbord. 2020. *Online Violence Against Women Journalists: A Global Snapshot of Incidence and Impacts*. UNESCO. https://unesdoc.unesco.org/ark:/48223/pf0000375136.

Pulfer, Rachel. 2020. *Half the Story is Never Enough: Threats Facing Women Journalists*. Canadian Commission for UNESCO. https://jhr.ca/wp-content/uploads/2020/11/HalfOfTheStoryIsNeverEnough.pdf.

Radsch, Courtney. 2022. *Artificial Intelligence and Disinformation: State-Aligned Information Operations and the Distortion of the Public Sphere*. Office of the OSCE Representative on Freedom of the Media. https://www.osce.org/representative-on-freedom-of-media/522166.

Ran, Mindy. 2023. "Challenges for Women Journalists in the Age of Covid, and Union and Media Repression." In *The Handbook of Gender, Communication, and Women's Human Rights*, edited by M. Gallagher and A. V. Montiel, 141–58. Wiley & Sons.

Rees, Yann P. M. 2023. "Free Press Under Pressure? Experiences and Consequences of Hateful Harassment on Journalists in Germany." *Media and Communication* 11 (4): 13. https://doi.org/10.17645/mac.v11i4.7179.

Ressa, Maria. 2021. *Nobel Lecture*. Stockholm: The Nobel Foundation. https://www.nobelprize.org/prizes/peace/2021/ressa/lecture/.

RSF. 2021. "Reporters Without Borders: Sexism's Toll on Journalism." https://rsf.org/sites/default/files/sexisms_toll_on_journalism.pdf.

Sampaio-Dias, Susana, Maria João Silveirinha, Bibiana Garcez, Filipa Subtil, João Miranda, and Carla Cerqueira. 2024. "'Journalists Are Prepared for Critical Situations . . . But We Are Not Prepared for This': Empirical and Structural Dimensions of Gendered Online Harassment." *Journalism Practice* 18 (2): 301–18. https://doi.org/10.1080/17512786.2023.2250755.

Sjöholm, Maria. 2022. *International Human Rights Law and Protection Against Gender-Based Harm on the Internet*. Springer Nature.

Stahel, Lea, and Constantin Schoen. 2019. "Female Journalists Under Attack? Explaining Gender Differences in Reactions to Audiences' Attacks." *New Media & Society* 22 (10): 1849–67. https://doi.org/10.1177/1461444819885333.

Strid, Sofia. 2018. "Patriarchy Fights Back: Violent Opposition to Gender Equality in Online Contexts." In *Varieties of Opposition to Gender Equality in Europe*, edited by M. Verloo, 57–76. Abingdon: Routledge.

UN Human Rights. 2021. "Statement by Irene Khan, Special Rapporteur on the Promotion and Protection of Freedom of Opinion and Expression." https://digitallibrary.un.org/record/3925306?v=pdf.

UN Human Rights Council. 2022. "On the Safety of Journalists (A/HRC/RES/51/9)." https://digitallibrary.un.org/record/3992428?ln=en.

United Nations. 1995. *The Beijing Declaration and the Platform for Action: Fourth World Conference on Women*. New York. https://www.unwomen.org/sites/default/files/Headquarters/Attachments/Sections/CSW/PFA_E_Final_WEB.pdf.

Waisbord, Silvio. 2020. "Mob Censorship: Online Harassment of US Journalists in Times of Digital Hate and Populism." *Digital Journalism* 8 (8): 1030–46. https://doi.org/10.1080/21670811.2020.1818111.

Westlund, Oscar, Roy Krøvel, and Kristin Skare Orgeret. 2022. "Newsafety: Infrastructures, Practices and Consequences." *Journalism Practice* 16 (9): 1811–28.

7
FORCED DISPLACEMENT OF JOURNALISTS AND HUMAN RIGHTS

Sanem Şahin

Introduction

Journalists flee their home countries for various reasons: Some escape war, while others seek refuge from threats of imprisonment, torture, or death resulting from their journalistic activities. The repression of media freedom and concerted efforts to silence journalists expose them to harassment, intimidation, and threats from authorities, militias, and organised crime groups. Journalists are compelled to relocate when independent and safe work conditions become untenable (Reporters Without Borders 2023; Schönert 2022; Yeğinsu 2020). However, even in their new locations, some continue to be targets of physical and online violence, living in fear of reprisals.

The predicament of forcibly displaced journalists intersects two significant human rights crises: one is the forced displacement of people and the other is violence against journalists and news organisations. The latter not only infringes on individual journalists' human rights by endangering their right to life and dignity but also impacts their community's right to information. Journalism is essential for a healthy public sphere and the protection of human rights. It can safeguard fundamental rights such as the right to freedom of expression by informing citizens, checking the legitimacy of power, and giving voices to different views in public debate (Harrison and Torsner 2022). In an era where real and fake information is increasingly difficult to distinguish, journalists assist citizens by sifting through vast amounts of information and providing context to make sense of it (Lamer 2016, 2018). However, when journalists are compelled to flee their countries due to persecution and violence, these responsibilities become compromised. Their displacement also weakens the mechanisms that scrutinize power and provide citizens with essential information. The

DOI: 10.4324/9781032662589-9

media and communities left behind are often intimidated into self-censorship, and dissent is silenced, threatening communities' right to information.

The safety of journalists is a precondition for effective media freedom (Harrison and Torsner 2022), but as threats against journalists escalate, media freedom continues to decline globally (UNESCO 2022). The experiences of displaced journalists are not isolated incidents but are indications of emerging trends of risks and challenges journalism faces globally. The relocation of journalists does not always guarantee safety and solutions, but it presents additional problems. They encounter numerous hardships in the host country, making them vulnerable and unable to practice the profession they worked hard to build over the years.

This chapter examines the experiences of refugee journalists from the human rights perspective to understand the impact of displacement on them. It uses data from research interviews with 10 journalists who have found refuge in the UK to provide insights into the challenges they have encountered since their displacement. These journalists have myriad reasons for leaving their countries and to capture them all, they will be referred to as refugee, exiled, or displaced journalists to encapsulate their shared experiences of displacement.

Forced displacement

People become refugees for various reasons such as conflict, violence, persecution, human rights violations, or disasters caused by humans or nature. Unlike migrants, who choose to move for work, education, family, or other reasons, refugees flee because of risks and dangers to their lives. They are compelled to leave their homes as a result of 'the culmination of a long chain of deteriorating circumstances' (Henningsen 2023) and seek safety in other places for fear of being persecuted in their home countries.

Exile, resonant with forced displacement, involves the banishment of individuals or groups due to a political action that forces them to leave their country (Baumann 2010; Barbour 2007; Vasanthakumar 2021). Vasanthakumar (2021, 31) conceptualizes exiles as both political refugees and those fleeing generalised disorder. 'What unites this category is that exiles' flight is prompted by defective political institutions and practices'. People usually go into exile to escape persecution and are usually considered transitional as exiles often have 'an enduring longing to remigrate to the place of origin' (Baumann 2010, 19). While living and working in a host country, their attention, identification, and efforts are mainly focused on their home countries and hope to return home when the political conditions change (Vasanthakumar 2021).

Exiled journalists

Journalists who are forced to displace are usually examined within diaspora media studies. They are part of the diaspora media but, unlike those who leave their countries for a better life and work opportunities, they are compelled to leave their home countries due to imminent threats. Their forced exile significantly impacts their professional roles, identities, and practices. Research in various diaspora communities, such as Syrian, Tibetan, and Ukrainian, (Arafat 2021; Badran and Smets 2021; Balasundaram 2019; Crete-Nishihata and Tsui 2023; O'Loughlin and Schafraad 2016; Porlezza and Arafat 2022; Skjerdal 2010, 2011; Voronova 2020) show how journalists who continue practising their profession in their new locations regard themselves to be on a mission motivated by a commitment to truth, justice, and protection of human rights in their home countries. They serve as alternative sources of information to counterbalance the reports in government-controlled media to inform international, diasporic, and local audiences in their country of origin. As they work for change, their journalism is a combination of professional, advocacy, and activism (Arafat 2021; Porlezza and Arafat 2022; Skjerdal 2010, 2011). Advocacy journalism 'actively supports or argues for specific causes, policies, or issues' and combines traditional reporting with a standpoint (Bachmann Cáceres 2019). Activist journalism, on the other hand, is 'motivated by a strong sense of justice and a passion to make a significant change' (Ginosar and Reich 2022, 660). Activist journalists cover issues they care for in their professional capacity but are also personally involved in activities such as lobbying and consulting politicians or providing personal assistance to individuals and groups in need (Ginosar and Reich 2022).

Exiled journalists are caught between two worlds: While physically residing in their host countries, their minds and efforts remain focused on their homelands. Exile is often considered a temporary phase or a transitional state (Baumann 2010). However, the duration of exile varies based on individual circumstances: Some journalists can return home once threats subside, while others face a more extended period of displacement. Regardless of its length, the experience of displacement significantly impacts these journalists personally and professionally. As refugees, they grapple with numerous challenges, including uncertainties regarding their residency status, separation from loved ones, difficulties in securing accommodation, the process of integrating into the host country and dealing with trauma.

As journalists, they experience further difficulties. The concept of serving the public and protecting its interests is at the centre of professional ideals and performances for journalists (Christians et al. 2009; Deuze 2005; Hanitzsch and Vos 2018). But it is difficult to fulfil these roles in exile. They are dislocated from their positions in society, and their contact and communication networks with audiences, sources, and institutions that support them are disrupted. They can also no longer attend firsthand and witness unfolding situations, both of which are fundamental to journalistic authority (Zelizer 2017). Instead, they must rely on other sources acting as eyewitnesses. The transition to a new country brings about shifts in living and working conditions, cultural integration, language acquisition, and job opportunities, all of which can pose threats to their careers. While some manage to continue practising journalism, others are compelled to seek alternative employment.

Professional identity is an essential resource for identification. Research shows not continuing with their profession can erode the personal and professional identity of professional refugees (Zikic and Richardson 2016; Wehrle et al. 2018). It can lead to mental health problems such as despair, loss of self-value, and isolation (Nieto-Brizio and Márquez-Ramírez 2023; O'Donnell et al. 2016) and disrupt 'their fundamental human needs for a sense of worth, distinctiveness, continuity, and control over who they are in general and in their vocation in particular' (Wehrle et al. 2018, 98).

Not all journalists who are at risk cross an international border and go into exile or become refugees. Some become internally displaced: they flee their homes but stay within their own country's borders. Studies on internally displaced journalists (Nieto-Brizio and Márquez-Ramírez 2023; Voronova 2020; Ashraf and Brooten 2017) indicate that journalists who are forcibly displaced because of occupational violence are also vulnerable and suffer from profession-related challenges in addition to the hardships experienced by other displaced populations.

Human rights

Journalists voluntarily or involuntarily leave their countries to seek safety in exile. An exiled journalist is 'someone who publishes something that leads them to be driven out of a country' (Schönert 2022, 4). These journalists are persecuted for exercising their freedom of expression, a right that extends to all individuals, irrespective of the reach of their messages. This right also underpins media freedom, an essential element in the safeguarding of freedom of expression and other human rights. Some argue that the right to freedom of expression is not sufficient to protect independent media and journalists and propose press freedom to be recognized as a human right to guarantee their protection (Cruft 2022; Lamer 2016, 2018; Oster 2015). They point to the important role journalists play in public life and suggest it should be an institutional right to protect media and journalists in their editorial, newsgathering, and dissemination efforts (Oster 2015). What sets press freedom apart from freedom of expression is the ability of journalists to reach a mass audience. As Lamer (2018, 85) notes, 'journalists are more prominent precisely because they have more power as a result of reaching a bigger audience than regular citizens, making them the first ones to be arrested or killed'. Therefore, Cruft (2022, 364) makes a case for the prominence of 'the human rights to journalism and press freedom' within the human rights framework to offer greater protection for journalists from the mistreatment they receive for serving the public and holding the government accountable. Their work, after all, is in the public interest and vital for the protection of other human rights.

Some exiled journalists continue informing the public back home of their government's abuses of power and human rights. Their journalism from afar can be essential for the exercise of democratic rights, especially in countries where human rights, including freedom of expression, are restricted. However, they require protection and support to continue with their journalism without fear. Some are victims of transnational repression and continue to face harassment and attacks and need protection even in the safety of a host country. A Freedom House report (White et al. 2023) documents transnational attacks, including assault, detention, kidnapping, unlawful deportation, intimidation of journalists' family members, digital harassment, smear campaigns, doxing, and other attempts to prevent truthful reporting, silencing journalists and having damaging impacts on their careers and well-being.

Studying displaced journalists

Refugee journalists have unique experiences as displaced people, journalists, and individuals, and they present a good study of the impact of displacement on professional refugees. This chapter, using a multi-level analysis by studying macro, meso, and micro factors, explores the common structures, problems, and processes shaping the experiences of exiled journalists. Macro-level influences are the structural factors that define the conditions in which they live as displaced people. Meso-level factors include occupational elements that shape their professional experiences. Micro-level analysis looks into the personal impact of displacement on these journalists. It is important to note that these factors are not separate from each other but interconnected with structural elements affecting personal lives and professional practices.

The chapter uses data from semi-structured interviews conducted with 10 refugee journalists in the United Kingdom (UK) to explain their experiences. Interview questions explored a wide range of issues such as their identity definitions, their perception of professional roles, and the professional challenges and constraints they experienced in the UK.

Macro-level – journalists as displaced people

Integration into a host society is crucial for refugees to build their lives successfully. It happens when refugees have economic and social opportunities and resources to integrate and participate in their new community (Hynie 2018; Harder et al. 2018). However, they must navigate many challenges that range from finding accommodation to securing residency permits and accessing services such as health and education. Separated from their family and friends and without their support networks, they deal with problems, including health-related ones, like trauma, alone. Employment barriers due to insufficient language skills, lack of professional networks, cultural differences, or limited understanding of the job market in the host country further complicate their situation (Breaking Barriers no date).

Journalists, as displaced persons, also struggle with these challenges. For those seeking asylum, the process of establishing their right to remain and work can be a lengthy one with economic, professional, and emotional impacts (Wehrle et al. 2018). In the UK, delays in processing applications can lead asylum-seeking journalists to live in temporary accommodations, such as hotels, unsuitable for long-term housing. A journalist interviewed for this project, at the time of the interview, had been living in a hotel for over a year. He described his experience as isolating and exhausting (Personal Interview, 2023).

These journalists' problems do not end with the approval of their asylum applications. When they gain refugee status, they lose their asylum support within 28 days. They must leave the accommodation they are provided, find their own place to stay, access mainstream benefits, and secure employment (GOV.UK 2021). The transition can be disorienting without proper support and guidance, leaving some refugees homeless. Furthermore, navigating services, such as healthcare or banking, can be difficult if they don't have the required documentation which some refugees lack due to hasty departures from their homes. Delays in accessing healthcare can have serious repercussions, especially for those dealing with trauma or other mental health issues requiring immediate medical attention.

Finding employment poses another significant challenge for asylum-seeking journalists. Legal restrictions prevent them from working in the UK while their applications are under consideration (GOV.UK n.d.). The length of this process can range from months to years, barring asylum seekers from entering the labour market. The waiting period can be frustrating and demoralising, as an asylum-seeking journalist expressed during the interview. He had been waiting for a work permit at the time of the interview and found the process not just depressing but also affecting his future job prospects (Personal Interview, 2023).

Even when they obtain the right to work, these journalists face numerous barriers to re-entering their profession. Journalism, being a language-dependent profession, requires a sufficient command of English, which many lack. Additionally, they often don't have the social networks that could aid their job search. Financial pressures and unemployment often push these journalists towards 'survival jobs' (Zikic and Richardson 2016, 153), typically in low-skilled roles, to earn a living rather than perform their profession.

Journalists also confront discrimination and the stigma associated with being refugees (Baranik et al. 2018). Their new status as refugees imposes 'new, stigmatized, and threatening identities upon them (e.g., being unemployed, foreign, and a potential threat to the host country's real and/or symbolic resources)' (Wehrle et al. 2018, 84). They become targets of hostility when political and media discourses position refugees' human rights with concerns about 'our' safety and pressures on welfare, education, health, and other social resources (Moore 2017). This contributes to the public's negative perception and discrimination of refugees.

Meso-level: professional challenges

In addition to navigating a new country and comprehending its governance and support systems, displaced journalists face professional challenges. The most significant one is finding employment in the UK. Employment is a vital element of integration into a host country as through work, refugees can become independent, establish social networks, and connect and participate in society (Campion 2018; Smyth and Kum 2010; Willott and Stevenson 2013). However, even when the restrictions on their right to work are lifted, finding jobs in journalism can be hard. Insufficient English proficiency to work as a journalist, a lack of networks of contacts and sources, and unfamiliarity with the labour market can hinder refugee journalists from getting employment in the media. Even those with good English language skills find themselves competing with British journalists who have the advantage of established social networks and an understanding of the media in a competitive job market. Refugee journalists, particularly newcomers, struggle to approach news organisations for jobs or work placements due to their experience in different media systems and journalism cultures. The absence of social networks means they lack the necessary support and guidance they need to find their way in the job market.

Refugee journalists also struggle to get recognition for their professional experience, knowledge, and skills, especially by those who gatekeep potential media jobs in the UK. Unlike professions such as medicine and education, qualifications are not required for entry into journalism, making it hard for displaced journalists to demonstrate their professional competencies. It frustrates those whose abilities and knowledge are not accepted and creates tensions between their perception of their status and skills and the recognition of others (Pietka-Nykaza 2015). Even those who manage to secure employment may find their roles unsatisfying. For instance, a Ukrainian journalist who worked as a freelancer after fleeing to the UK felt that her assignments were limited to topics related to refugees or the war in Ukraine, rather than reflecting her professional background and experience.

> I want to work on other interesting stories, not just about Ukrainian refugees . . . I am not given any other story to work on. . . . What else can I say about them (refugees)? . . . In Ukraine, I covered stories about the Middle East and am very good at it. Nobody here understands that I can write other stories.
>
> *(Personal Interview, 2023)*

Similarly, another journalist, despite possessing journalism experience, proficiency in Kurdish, Turkish, and Arabic, and a deep understanding of Middle Eastern international relations, believed his skills would not be valued, hindering his employment prospects.

Safety is another concern for journalists, especially for those who fled their countries due to harassment or threats linked to their journalism. Authoritarian governments continue targeting journalists beyond their borders, using overt or covert methods to silence or discredit their work. According to a report by Freedom House (Gorokhovskaia et al. 2023, 1), 'tactics of transnational repression – including assassinations, unlawful deportations, detentions, renditions, physical and digital threats, and coercion by proxy – are used by governments to stamp out dissent among diasporas and exiles living beyond their borders'. For example, in 2021, Belarusian authorities forced a passenger plane to land in Belarus to arrest a dissident journalist, Raman Pratasevich, travelling on board (BBC 2021). Journalists who continue to report or comment on their home country's situation can encounter violence, physical attacks, or online threats and harassment even in exile. Another report by Freedom House (White et al. 2023) shows that more states are employing tactics, such as assassination, physical attacks, digital harassment, detentions, kidnapping, smear campaigns, and intimidation of family members, to silence journalists abroad. The assassination of Washington Post columnist Jamal Khashoggi by Saudi Arabian authorities in 2018 (Harris et al. 2018) and the poisoning of exiled Russian journalists in 2023 are some examples of physical attacks on journalists (Escritt 2023). Online violence, including death threats, smear campaigns, and even rape threats for female journalists, are used to intimidate and discredit them (Posetti et al. 2021).

These attacks are to hinder journalists from continuing to report on their countries. Journalists in exile often lack the resources to investigate and verify information, and being away from their information sources and support networks impedes their work. Physical and digital attacks and harassment against them and their families impact their well-being, often causing them to avoid reporting on certain issues or to remain silent (White et al. 2023). For instance, a journalist interviewed for this chapter chose to keep a low profile after his social media posts drew criticism from his home country's authorities and he received a threatening message concerning his partner's safety. He now refrains from writing about sensitive political topics (Personal Interview, 2023). Criminal investigations and accusations in their countries, such as being labelled terrorists, create a chilling effect that severs their relationship with their sources and support networks. These accusations also present obstacles in the host country during background checks for matters such as immigration issues, banking, or housing as they must prove they are not a threat to society. Their concerns for their own safety and that of their families not only heighten their sense of insecurity but also incur additional costs as they are compelled to enhance their physical and digital security (White et al. 2023).

Micro-level: personal challenges

Displaced journalists, once central figures in their societies due to their professional, economic, or social status, find themselves removed from these roles in their new locations. The unemployment resulting from displacement can lead to a loss of self-worth and potentially an identity crisis (Zikic and Richardson 2016; Mackenzie Davey and Jones 2020). A professional identity is vital for coping with and adapting to new situations and its loss, and the barriers to resuming it, threaten

> some of the last resources these people bring with them: Their identities, and with that, their fundamental human needs for a sense of worth, distinctiveness, continuity, and control over who they are in general and in their vocation in particular.
>
> *(Wehrle et al. 2018, 98)*

Research indicates that the attitudes of professional refugees towards employment vary: some are willing to work in any job, some strive to return to their profession, and others retrain or adapt their skills to find alternative work (Willott and Stevenson 2013; Pietka-Nykaza 2015). The inability to secure jobs in the media sector, coupled with financial concerns, pressures journalists to abandon their professional aspirations and seek work that does not utilize their skills and knowledge. For instance, financial needs compelled a refugee journalist to accept a low-skilled job: 'I washed dishes in a pub. I am an experienced journalist. I had a good career at home. Here, I washed dishes. I found it very hard to accept' (Personal Interview, 2023). Engaging in 'survival jobs' (Zikic and Richardson 2016, 153) can disillusion journalists about the prospect of returning to their careers and can undermine their self-esteem. For those who believe they will never be able to practice journalism again, the effect can be akin to emotional trauma (O'Donnell et al. 2016). One exiled journalist, who feared his journalism career had ended when he left his country, expressed his sadness at this loss: 'I feel really bad. As if they killed me . . . I feel like I'm dead' (Personal Interview, 2023).

Their immigration status becomes another facet of their identity, and they reconstruct it in a hybrid form. For example, they may identify themselves as a Syrian journalist seeking asylum or a refugee journalist from Ethiopia. As one journalist stated,

> I used to be a journalist. Now, I'm only an asylum seeker. That is what I tell people because I don't have any other identity. I'm a journalist. But I am not writing or reporting. It means I'm not a journalist at the moment.
>
> *(Personal Interview, 2023)*

Despite reflecting the journalist's disillusionment with the situation, the statement also demonstrates a strong attachment to the professional identity, which, despite barriers to practising it, can serve as a link between their past and present and can be both sustaining and limiting for professionals.

Forced displacement significantly impacts the mental well-being of asylum seekers and refugees. Their experiences, pre-migratory (in their home country), in transit (while travelling), and post-migratory (in the host country), such as war, persecution, violence, loss, hardships, and uncertainty about the future, impact their mental health (Ali-Naqvi et al. 2023; Vaghefi 2024; Trueba et al. 2023; Rowley et al. 2020). The World Health Organisation (WHO) describes asylum seekers and refugees as 'the most vulnerable members of society faced often with xenophobia; discrimination; poor living, housing, and working conditions; and inadequate access to health services, despite frequently occurring physical and mental health problems' (World Health Organization 2023). Like other asylum seekers and refugees, journalists' experiences before and during their escape from their countries, coupled with the physical and emotional hardships they face in the host country, contribute to their stress and anxiety, making them susceptible to mental health disorders. They grapple with issues such as isolation, trauma, depression, loss of self-value, and insecurity. The absence of family and friends and the lack of established support networks can exacerbate their problems (Ali Naqvi et al. 2023). Difficulties with asylum procedures and concerns about finance, housing, and employment add to their mental distress. Journalists who were victims of persecution in their countries due to their work also have safety concerns, adding to their sense of insecurity. They also worry about family and friends left behind, fearing reprisals as retaliation. The overall impact is not only on their health and morale but also on their journalism, as these factors may discourage them from reporting on issues that should be highlighted.

Mental health support is available for asylum seekers and refugees in the UK. However, barriers such as lack of awareness of the available support, language, fear of disclosing personal information, or lack of trust hinder them from accessing it (Royal College of Psychiatrists n.d.). Cultural differences in understanding mental health issues also influence how individuals cope with problems such as anxiety, stress, and depression. One participant from Ukraine believed she was suffering from post-traumatic stress disorder (PTSD) when she arrived in the UK, stating, 'I lost my connections, relatives, friends. I didn't want to speak to anyone; just wanted to be left alone'. In contrast, another participant from Iraq was dismissive about the effects of the traumatic events he had experienced:

> I was kidnapped and threatened. I watched people beheaded many times. The first time I watched it, it affected me badly. After many times, I stopped reacting. In Iraq, we got used to bombs exploding. Bombs exploded but we carried on with our lives as if nothing happened.
>
> *(Personal Interview, 2023)*

Conclusion

This chapter explored the profound impact of displacement on journalists, examining their experiences as refugees, professionals, and individuals. Forced to leave their homelands, these journalists' plights not only affect their personal and professional lives, their human rights and dignity but also their societies by undermining the media's role in upholding human rights, including freedom of expression. The safety of journalists is a vital prerequisite for effective media freedom and human rights protection (Harrison and Torsner 2022). Media freedom is untenable if journalists cannot safely inform the public about collective concerns. Attacks aimed at intimidating and silencing journalists also infringe upon their human rights, sometimes leaving them with no alternative but to flee their countries.

Refugee journalists have diverse experiences in the host country. They deal with challenges common to displaced individuals, such as economic hardship, integration difficulties, unemployment, and mental health issues. However, they also face professional obstacles. Insufficient English proficiency, lack of supportive networks, and limited understanding of the media and job market act as barriers to their employment and continuation of their profession. Some wrestle with questions about their identity, sense of belonging, and self-worth. The notion of a hyphenated identity emerges as they exist in a state of dual orientation: they are drawn towards their homeland, with some continuing to address their home public, while simultaneously needing to establish a life in their host country. Their actions towards their home country can make them targets of transnational repression, even within the safety of the host country. Threats to their own and their families' security intensify their mental distress. Many struggle with mental health issues alone in the absence of support from family and friends, and their lack of awareness about available services hinders them from accessing necessary help.

Understanding the impact of displacement is essential for supporting professional journalists during their transition. Refugee journalists need assistance and support from the host countries, civil society groups, and professional organisations to integrate. They require help with residency status, accommodation, and access to essential services such as healthcare. Additionally, they need professional training and language courses to continue with their careers. In the absence of such support, these journalists may become vulnerable and hesitant to report on sensitive issues or continue their journalistic endeavours. Professional groups or ancillary organisations, such as professional membership associations, trade groups, and professional training centres, can play a pivotal role in providing this much-needed support (Lowrey et al. 2019). Similarly, diaspora journalists and networks can offer mentorship and protection to journalists back in their home country and when they arrive in the UK (Porlezza and Arafat 2022). Such assistance is particularly crucial for those who have recently arrived and are seeking employment or internships. It helps them understand the media landscape and journalism practices in the

UK, enabling them to align their skills with the job market demands. Understanding the expectations and prerequisites of the professional labour market aids these journalists when making decisions about their future career paths. Like other professional refugees, journalists want to find employment within their professional field. However, if unsuccessful, they consider retraining or seeking employment outside the media profession.

Recognizing the challenges journalists experience can help better address their unique needs and foster resilience. In a world where media freedom is increasingly under threat, it is imperative to protect and support journalists forced to leave their countries. This enables them to continue reporting accurate information in a safe environment.

Discussion questions

1. What are the main obstacles displaced journalists encounter when trying to continue their profession in a new country? What strategies can be implemented to support their professional reintegration?
2. How does the displacement of journalists affect media freedom both in their countries of origin and in the countries they relocate to?
3. In what ways does transnational repression affect exiled journalists? How can international communities protect and support these journalists?

Further reading

Reuters Institute for the Study of Journalism. 2021. "Journalism in Exile: A Plea for Better Support of Refugee Journalists." Journalist Fellowship Paper, Reuters Institute for the Study of Journalism, September 2021. Accessed July 12, 2024. https://reutersinstitute.politics.ox.ac.uk/sites/default/files/2021-12/RISJ_Final%20Report_Alaa_2020_FINAL.pdf.

Romero, Laura Dulce. 2024. "Hundreds of Journalists Go into Exile Every Year. These Are the Problems They Face and How to Tackle Them." Reuters Institute for the Study of Journalism, March 27. Accessed July 12, 2024. https://reutersinstitute.politics.ox.ac.uk/news/hundreds-journalists-go-exile-every-year-these-are-problems-they-face-and-how-tackle-them.

Westcott, Lucy. 2024. "Forced to Flee: Exiled Journalists Face Unsafe Passage and Transnational Repression." Committee to Protect Journalists. Accessed July 12, 2024. https://cpj.org/?p=396654.

References

Ali-Naqvi, Ozaay, Tariq A. Alburak, Kavin Selvan, Hana Abdelmeguid, and Monali S. Malvankar-Mehta. 2023. "Exploring the Impact of Family Separation on Refugee Mental Health: A Systematic Review and Meta-Narrative Analysis." *Psychiatric Quarterly* 94 (1): 61–77.

Arafat, Rana. 2021. "Examining Diaspora Journalists' Digital Networks and Role Perceptions: A Case Study of Syrian Post-Conflict Advocacy Journalism." *Journalism Studies* 22 (16): 2174–96.

Ashraf, Syed Irfan, and Lisa Brooten. 2017. "Tribal Journalists Under Fire. Threats, Impunity and Decision Making in Reporting on Conflict in Pakistan." In *The Assault on Journalism: Building Knowledge to Protect Freedom of Expression*, edited by Ulla Carlsson and Reeta Pöyhtäri. Göteborg: Nordicom.

Bachmann Cáceres, Ingrid. 2019. "Advocacy Journalism." In *Oxford Research Encyclopedia of Communication*, June 25. https://oxfordre-com.proxy.library.lincoln.ac.uk/communication/view/10.1093/acrefore/9780190228613.001.0001/acrefore-9780190228613-e-776.

Badran, Yazan, and Kevin Smets. 2021. "Anatomy of a Precarious Newsroom: Precarity and Agency in Syrian Exiled Journalism in Turkey." *Media, Culture and Society* 43 (8): 1377–94.

Balasundaram, Nirmanusan. 2019. "Exiled Journalists as Active Agents of Change: Understanding Their Journalistic Practices." In *Reporting Human Rights, Conflicts, and Peacebuilding*, edited by Ibrahim Seaga Shaw and Senthan Selvarajah, 265–80. Palgrave Macmillan.

Baranik, Lisa E., Carrie S. Hurst, and Lillian T. Eby. 2018. "The Stigma of Being a Refugee: A Mixed-Method Study of Refugees' Experiences of Vocational Stress." *Journal of Vocational Behavior* 105: 116–30.

Barbour, John D. 2007. "Edward Said and the Space of Exile." *Literature and Theology* 21 (3): 293–301.

Baumann, Martin. 2010. "Exile." In *Diasporas: Concepts, Intersections, Identities*, edited by Kim Knott and Sean McLoughlin, 19–23. London: Zed Books.

BBC. 2021. "Roman Protasevich: Belarus Dissident Seized From Ryanair Plane." *The BBC News*, June 25. https://www.bbc.co.uk/news/world-europe-57229635.

Campion, Emily D. 2018. "The Career Adaptive Refugee: Exploring the Structural and Personal Barriers to Refugee Resettlement." *Journal of Vocational Behavior* 105: 6–16.

Christians, Clifford G., Theodore L. Glasser, Denis McQuail, Kaarle Nordenstreng, and Robert A. White. 2009. *Normative Theories of the Media: Journalism in Democratic Societies*. Urbana: University of Illinois Press.

Crete-Nishihata, Masashi, and Lokman Tsui. 2023. "The Truth of What's Happening: How Tibetan Exile Media Develop and Maintain Journalistic Authority." *Journalism* 24 (2): 295–312.

Cruft, Rowan. 2022. "Journalism and Press Freedom as Human Rights." *Journal of Applied Philosophy* 39 (3): 359–76.

Deuze, Mark. 2005. "What is Journalism?: Professional Identity and Ideology of Journalists Reconsidered." *Journalism* 6: 442–64.

Escritt, Thomas. 2023. "Exiled Russian Journalist Describes 'Poisoning' Ordeal on German Train." *Reuters*, August 28. Accessed March 22, 2024. https://www.reuters.com/world/europe/exiled-russian-journalist-describes-poisoning-ordeal-german-train-2023-08-26/.

Ginosar, Avshalom, and Zvi Reich. 2022. "Obsessive–Activist Journalists: A New Model of Journalism?" *Journalism Practice* 16 (4): 660–80.

Gorokhovskaia, Yana, Nate Schenkkan, and Grady Vaughan. 2023. "Still Not Safe: Transnational Repression in 2022." *Freedom House*, April. https://freedomhouse.org/sites/default/files/2023-04/FH_TransnationalRepression2023_0.pdf.

GOV.UK. n.d. "Claim Asylum in the UK." Accessed March 22, 2024. https://www.gov.uk/claim-asylum.

GOV.UK. 2021. "Welcome a Guide for New Refugees." Accessed March 22, 2024. https://assets.publishing.service.gov.uk/media/602e3783d3bf7f7221aad81d/English_only_-_web_accessible.pdf.

Hanitzsch, Thomas, and Tim P. Vos. 2018. "Journalism Beyond Democracy: A New Look into Journalistic Roles in Political and Everyday Life." *Journalism* 19 (2): 146–64.

Harder, Niklas, Lucila Figueroa, Rachel M. Gillum, Dominik Hangartner, David D. Laitin, and Jens Hainmueller. 2018. "Multidimensional Measure of Immigrant Integration." *Proceedings of the National Academy of Sciences of the United States of America* 115 (45): 11483–88.

Harris, Shane, Greg Miller and Josh Dawsey. 2018. "CIA Concludes Saudi Crown Prince Ordered Jamal Khashoggi's Assassination." *The Washington Post*, November 16. https://www.washingtonpost.com/world/national-security/cia-concludes-saudi-crown-prince-ordered-jamal-khashoggis-assassination/2018/11/16/98c89fe6-e9b2-11e8-a939-9469f1166f9d_story.html.

Harrison, Jackie, and Sara Torsner. 2022. *Safety of Journalists and Media Freedom: Trends in Non-EU Countries From a Human Rights Perspective.* Brussels: European Union.

Henningsen, Geraldine. 2023. "Big Data for the Prediction of Forced Displacement." *International Migration Review.* https://doi.org/10.1177/01979183231195296.

Hynie, Michaela. 2018. "Refugee Integration: Research and Policy." *Peace and Conflict: Journal of Peace Psychology* 24 (3): 265–76.

Lamer, Wiebke. 2016. "Promoting the People's Surrogate: The Case for Press Freedom as a Distinct Human Right." *Journal of Human Rights* 15 (3): 361–82.

Lamer, Wiebke. 2018. *Press Freedom as an International Human Right.* Palgrave Pivot.

Lowrey, Wilson, Lindsey Sherrill, and Ryan Broussard. 2019. "Field and Ecology Approaches to Journalism Innovation: The Role of Ancillary Organizations." *Journalism Studies* 20 (15): 2131–49. https://doi.org/10.1080/1461670X.2019.1568904.

Mackenzie Davey, Kate, and Catherine Jones. 2020. "Refugees' Narratives of Career Barriers and Professional Identity." *Career Development International* 25 (1): 49–66. https://doi.org/10.1108/CDI-12-2018-0315.

Moore, Kerry. 2017. "Media and Human Rights." In *The Routledge Companion to Media and Human Rights*, edited by H. Tumber and S. Waisbord, 446–55. London: Routledge.

Nieto-Brizio, Marcelino, and Mireya Márquez-Ramírez. 2023. "Fleeing Danger for a Better Life? A Social-Ecological Study of Internally Displaced Journalists in Mexico." *Journalism Studies* 24 (7): 990–1007. https://doi.org/10.1080/1461670X.2022.2150874.

O'Donnell, Penny, Lawrie Zion, and Merryn Sherwood. 2016. "Where Do Journalists Go After Newsroom Job Cuts?" *Journalism Practice* 10 (1): 35–51. https://doi.org/10.1080/17512786.2015.1017400.

O'Loughlin, Conor, and Pytrik Schafraad. 2016. "News on the Move: Towards a Typology of Journalists in Exile." *Observatorio (OBS*)* 10 (1): 45–66. https://doi.org/10.15847/obsobs1012016869.

Oster, Jan. 2015. *Media Freedom as a Fundamental Right.* New York: Cambridge University Press.

Pietka-Nykaza, Emilia. 2015. "I Want to Do Anything Which is Decent and Relates to My Profession: Refugee Doctors' and Teachers' Strategies of Re-Entering Their Professions in the UK." *Journal of Refugee Studies* 28 (4): 523–43.

Porlezza, Colin, and Rana Arafat. 2022. "Promoting Newsafety From the Exile: The Emergence of New Journalistic Roles in Diaspora Journalists' Networks." *Journalism Practice* 16 (9): 1867–89. https://doi.org/10.1080/17512786.2021.1925947.

Posetti, Julie, Nabeelah Shabbir, Diana Maynard, Kalina Bontcheva, and Nermine Aboulez. 2021. *The Chilling: Global Trends in Online Violence Against Women Journalists.* Paris: UNESCO.

Reporters Without Borders (RSF). 2023. *Exile Journalists Map: Fleeing to Europe and North America*. RSF. Accessed July 12, 2024. https://rsf.org/en/exile-journalists-map-fleeing-europe-and-north-america.

Rowley, Lauren, Nicola Morant, and Cornelius Katona. 2020. "Refugees Who Have Experienced Extreme Cruelty: A Qualitative Study of Mental Health and Wellbeing After Being Granted Leave to Remain in the UK." *Journal of Immigrant & Refugee Studies* 18 (4): 357–74. https://doi.org/10.1080/15562948.2019.1677974.

Royal College of Psychiatrists. n.d. "Asylum Seeker and Refugee Mental Health." Accessed March 15, 2024. https://www.rcpsych.ac.uk/international/humanitarian-resources/asylum-seeker-and-refugee-mental-health.

Schönert, U. 2022. *Exile Journalism in Europe: Current Challenges and Support Programmes*. Hamburg: Körber-Stiftung.

Skjerdal, Terje S. 2010. "How Reliable Are Journalists in Exile?" *British Journalism Review* 21 (3): 46–52.

Skjerdal, Terje S. 2011. "Journalists or Activists? Self-Identity in the Ethiopian Diaspora Online Community." *Journalism* 12 (6): 727–44.

Smyth, Geri, and Henry Kum. 2010. "When They Don't Use It They Will Lose It: Professionals, Deprofessionalization and Reprofessionalization: The Case of Refugee Teachers in Scotland." *Journal of Refugee Studies* 23 (4): 503–22.

Trueba, Mei L., Tessa Axelrod, and Sonja Ayeb-Karlsson. 2023. "Are Asylum Seekers and Refugees Provided with Appropriate Mental Health Support in the United Kingdom?" *Journal of Ethnic and Migration Studies* 49 (13): 3163–83.

UNESCO. 2022. *Journalism is a Public Good: World Trends in Freedom of Expression and Media Development*. Paris: United Nations Educational, Scientific and Cultural Organization.

Vaghefi, Sanam. 2024. "Refugee Mental Health during the Asylum Waiting Process: A Qualitative Study of Turkish and Canadian Contexts." *Journal of Identity & Migration Studies* 18 (2): 33–45.

Vasanthakumar, Ashwini. 2021. *The Ethics of Exile: A Political Theory of Diaspora*. Oxford: Oxford University Press.

Voronova, Liudmila. 2020. "Conflict as a Point of No Return: Immigrant and Internally Displaced Journalists in Ukraine." *European Journal of Cultural Studies* 23 (5): 817–35.

Wehrle, Katja, Ute-Christine Klehe, Mari Kira, and Jelena Zikic. 2018. "Can I Come as I Am? Refugees' Vocational Identity Threats, Coping, and Growth." *Journal of Vocational Behavior* 105 (April): 83–101. https://doi.org/10.1016/j.jvb.2017.10.010.

White, Jessica, Grady Vaughan, and Yana Gorokhovskaia. 2023. *A Light That Cannot Be Extinguished: Exiled Journalism and Transnational Repression*. Washington: Freedom House.

Willott, John, and Jacqueline Stevenson. 2013. "Attitudes to Employment of Professionally Qualified Refugees in the United Kingdom." *International Migration* 51 (5): 120–32. https://doi.org/10.1111/imig.12038.

World Health Organization. 2023. *Mental Health of Refugees and Migrants: Risk and Protective Factors and Access to Care*. Geneva: World Health Organization. https://www.who.int/publications/i/item/9789240081840.

Yeğinsu, Can. 2020. *The High Level Panel of Legal Experts on Media Freedom: Report on Providing Safe Refuge to Journalists at Risk*. International Bar Association Human Rights Institute. https://www.ibanet.org/Safe-Refuge-report-launch-2020.

Zelizer, Barbie. 2017. *What Journalism Could Be*. Cambridge: Polity.

Zikic, Jelena, and Julia Richardson. 2016. "What Happens When You Can't Be Who You Are: Professional Identity at the Institutional Periphery." *Human Relations* 69 (1): 139–68. https://doi.org/10.1177/0018726715580865.

8
MEDIA'S RESPONSIBILITY TO REPORT (R2R)

The case for an international legal obligation

Lorenzo Fiorito and Senthan Selvarajah

Introduction

On 3 December 2003, the International Criminal Tribunal for Rwanda (ICTR) convicted a journalist named Hassan Ngeze of genocide, alongside private Rwandan news media directors Ferdinand Nahimana and Jean-Bosco Barayagwiza. In this trial, dubbed 'the Media Trial', Ngeze was shown to have used his journalistic platform to call on Hutus to murder Tutsis for their ethnicity. The Tribunal found Ngeze guilty not only of inciting genocide but also of directly committing genocide and crimes against humanity (such as persecution and extermination). Ngeze was sentenced to life in prison. Paragraph 1101 of the ICTR's sentence on Ngeze (ICTR 2003, 359) included the following words (emphasis added):

> Hassan Ngeze, as owner and editor of a well-known newspaper in Rwanda, was **in a position to inform the public and shape public opinion towards achieving democracy and peace** for all Rwandans. Instead of using the media to promote human rights, he used it to attack and destroy human rights. He has had significant media networking skills and attracted support earlier in his career from international human rights organizations who perceived his commitment to freedom of expression. However, Ngeze **did not respect the responsibility that comes with that freedom**. He abused the trust of the public by using his newspaper to instigate genocide. . . . The Chamber notes that Ngeze saved Tutsi civilians from death by transporting them across the border out of Rwanda. His power to save was more than matched by his power to kill. He poisoned the minds of his readers, and by words and deeds caused the death of thousands of innocent civilians.

DOI: 10.4324/9781032662589-10

Journalists can and should understand their 'responsibility to report' (hereafter, R2R) as an ethical obligation. A humanitarian outlook – in the common humanity of all people, in the human interest that no one should commit atrocities, and in the belief that when powerful people and states do inflict atrocities, everyone has a responsibility to stop them – is enough for most journalists to exercise their profession responsibly. However, journalists should also be aware that hiding evidence of crimes or downplaying their significance to avoid the resulting public outcry could make them just as complicit in international crimes as those irresponsible journalists who have sometimes encouraged people to commit these acts. In such extreme cases, only legal remedies will suffice. Understanding and exercising their R2R could keep journalists safe from criminal charges and safeguard their media institutions from lawsuits based on international humanitarian and human rights law.

As the previous quote showed, the ICTR has described R2R as a 'responsibility that comes with the freedom' of being a journalist. In its definition, the ICTR identifies R2R as the journalists' obligation to promote democracy and peace within public opinion. Media's influence on the public could accelerate, or help prevent, a society's regression towards war and genocide. In law, journalists have a positive obligation to help uphold the global society's respect for human rights. Journalists have the obligation to report on mass atrocities and violations of human rights, regardless of where they occur. They also have the legal responsibility to promote the democratic and egalitarian values that prevent a society from descending into conflict, by encouraging people to treat each other with dignity and respect.

Cole (2010) points out that in a country where human rights are violated, the media can hold rulers accountable when they reveal accurate and reliable information about them, thus helping to reverse the situation, which is called the 'information paradox'. Cole (2010, 306) states,

> Lack of information regarding a country's practices can distort its human rights record, producing a more anodyne perception than is warranted. As the availability and accuracy of information increases, abuses that were once concealed come to light; consequently, evaluations of a country's human rights practices can worsen even if actual levels of repression and abuse remain constant.

R2R is not merely a moral or ethical issue, but also an obligation in international law: to report in ways that protect the victims of human rights violations. Using the wording that the ICTR provided in Ngeze's sentence, this is a requirement to 'inform the public and shape public opinion towards achieving democracy and peace'. Especially in volatile and sensitive contexts, such as covering conflict zones, members of the profession should be aware that they are legally required to use that power to promote democracy and peace (especially in times when those values are under threat), just as they are obliged to refrain from inciting hatred and violence.

Journalists' R2R and the media's role in states' responsibility to protect

In 'The Responsibility to Report: A New Journalistic Paradigm', Thompson (2007) outlined several lessons learned from the role of media in the Rwandan genocide. He held that the media sometimes has the power to raise awareness of atrocity crimes, disseminating information among the concerned public. This spread of information could, at times, result in pressure on political decision-makers to act to stop these atrocities from taking place. Thompson (2007, 444) argued that journalists thus have an ethical responsibility to ensure that such reporting takes place: both as individual reporters and in their roles as members of media institutions. He concluded by asking journalists to 'do your job, use the power that this profession affords and take up your responsibilities, starting with the responsibility to report'. Thompson thus introduced the concept of R2R into journalistic discourse. The wording of Thompson's concept – a 'responsibility to report' – derives from the existence of the doctrine of a 'responsibility to protect' (hereafter, R2P) in international law. This chapter presents R2R as an integral support for the three pillars of R2P, described in the following.

R2P was also first recognised in the aftermath of the Rwanda genocide. It is a liberal, holistic notion that promotes a sense of obligation among individual states (and the international community) to prevent violence, promote peace-making, and rebuild societies during and after mass atrocities. Such atrocities include genocide, war crimes, crimes against humanity, and ethnic cleansing (Global Centre for the Responsibility to Protect 2001, 2021).

The ICISS report emphasises that 'universal human rights' and 'common humanity' are the sources of responsibility for R2P actions (Welsh and Banda 2010, 283). This is the foundation upon which the three R2P pillars have been constructed:

1. The state is primarily in charge of protecting populations against crimes against humanity, war crimes, genocide, ethnic cleansing, and their provocation.
2. The international community must support and encourage governments in carrying out this obligation.
3. The international community must protect populations against these crimes by employing appropriate diplomatic, humanitarian, and other measures. Under the United Nations Charter, the international community must be ready to act collectively to safeguard civilians when a state blatantly fails (Global Centre for the Responsibility to Protect, 2021).

R2P not only respectfully recognises states' responsibility to protect their citizens, but also offers the possibility of international intervention when a state fails in its obligation to protect its citizens' rights despite the international community's assistance. Military intervention is also permitted as a method of international intervention as a last resort.

The media have an important role in the realisation of R2P. Cottle (2019, 172–74) emphasises that the media can reinforce the 3-pillar basis of R2P for its fair implementation:

1. The media may support the first pillar by informing the public about the risks and dangers. It pressures them to perform their responsibilities, and inform society about the increasingly violent conditions.
2. With support from international responsibility-holders, which are primarily states exercising their R2P, the media may draw attention to conflict situations and warn of the imminent dangers of deadly violence. It can facilitate appropriate interventions, remind the general public and international authorities of their duties to support such interventions, and aid states in carrying out their responsibilities to protect their own citizens.
3. The media has the power to create public discourse regarding the obligation of the international community to take prompt action if a state fails to execute its obligations and disputes escalate into mass atrocity crimes.

While explaining how journalists can report human rights violations following the three pillars of R2P, Cottle (2017) argues that journalists act as duty-bearers of the internationally shared responsibility to protect people facing genocide and crimes against humanity under R2P, and thus they deserve increased international recognition and protection for doing their duty. He says institutional and legal frameworks under international law should be more effectively and robustly enforced to establish recognition and safeguarding for journalists working in dangerous situations to prevent gross human rights violations. Cottle (2017, 29) argues that the 'recognition' and 'responsibility to report' of journalists who expose human suffering and human rights violations in and from dangerous places cannot be 'simply seen as a matter to do with "journalists" or, even more broadly, as simply being about "journalism"'.

Various alternative journalism theories have been proposed in recent decades, due to the deficiencies in the objectivity concept in conventional journalism to prevent human rights violations, protect human rights, and establish peace in times of conflict such as journalism of attachment (Bell 1998), peace journalism (Galtung 2002), and Human Rights Journalism (HRJ) (Shaw 2012). Particularly, HRJ supports the idea that journalism also has obligations under R2P. HRJ, as introduced by Shaw (2012, 2), is based on the reporting of 'physical, structural and cultural violence within the context of humanitarian intervention' with the aims of promoting: (1) 'the understanding of the human-rights based approach to journalism', (2) the journalistic role that entails informing and connecting people all over the world, (3) 'public knowledge' of human rights, and (4) the journalistic 'moral responsibility' and 'duty' to 'educate the public, increase awareness in its members of their rights and monitor, investigate and report all human rights violations'.

Journalists' legal responsibility to protect human rights

Ngeze's conviction was obtained for a 'crime of commission' (for having done something that he was legally obliged not to do). Although there does not yet appear to have been a prosecution for a journalistic 'crime of omission' (failure to do something one is legally obliged to do), international criminal law is still evolving. Legal advocacy could foreseeably bring many perpetrators of recent and ongoing conflicts to international courts, with accompanying charges of war crimes, crimes against humanity, genocide, ethnic cleansing, or aggression. In recent conflicts where charges of genocide have actually been brought to the International Criminal Court or the International Court of Justice, like the Russia–Ukraine war (Selvarajah and Fiorito 2023) and the Israel–Gaza conflict (Khouri 2023), media reporting (or, potentially, the lack thereof) has arguably played a significant role. Quite positively, in the past, several journalists played a key role in exposing genocide in Bosnia and Herzegovina, enabling the work of the International Criminal Tribunal on the Former Yugoslavia (Daly 2017).

The ICTR's definition of a legally binding R2R that exists for journalists, on matters of international human rights and humanitarian law, begins in Article 19(3) and Article 20 of the International Covenant on Civil and Political Rights (ICCPR) (Office of the High Commissioner on Human Rights 1966). Article 19(3) states that freedom of expression 'carries with it **special duties and responsibilities**' (emphasis added). Article 20 prohibits war propaganda, advocacy of hatred, and incitement to violence, so journalists (like all other members of society) may not engage in these activities.

During future legal proceedings, journalists and directors of media institutions who knowingly fail to report on acts of genocide might, for example, have their omissions assessed by the Genocide Convention, which lists 'complicity in genocide' as a crime punishable under the Convention (UN General Assembly, Convention on the Prevention and Punishment of the Crime of Genocide, Article III[e]).

R2R as an *'erga omnes'* obligation in international law

Journalists' R2R is an aspect of R2P, which is considered an *'erga omnes'* (or universally applicable) legal obligation. This means that states have the responsibility to prevent atrocity crimes, no matter where they occur, and journalists have the obligation to report on atrocities, no matter where they take place. As Thompson (2007), Shaw (2012), and Selvarajah (2020) all showed, when journalists uphold their duty to report on atrocities, this can result in public pressure on governments to act in ways that prevent, halt, and punish those crimes. States are legally bound by their R2P, and as members of the wider international community, journalists are legally bound by their R2R. Cruft (2022, 365) has approached these themes of journalistic responsibility from the standpoint of moral philosophy, to define it this way:

> when something of public importance is taking place of which I should be aware (perhaps corruption or evil, or events constituting strong evidence of corruption or evil), then I have interests of sufficient importance to ground moral duties that I be told about it, and, to a lesser extent, that others also be told about it. This constitutes a 'natural' moral 'positive' right against the world that I and the relevant others be told. . . . By calling it 'natural', I mean that it exists as the person's right whether or not anyone recognises this. Journalism . . . involves taking on the job of fulfilling the moral duties correlative to this form of human right, duties borne initially by the world at large.

Cruft's concept of journalists' moral obligation coincides exactly with this chapter's presentation of R2R as an *erga omnes* legal obligation. In Cruft's moral framework, states and civil society have the right to be informed about atrocities taking place (or that could emerge soon), so that they can act to prevent and halt these atrocities. Cruft states that this human right to information implies a corresponding moral duty (borne by those who possess this information) to disseminate it. At the outset, Cruft says that this duty to inform is 'borne by the world at large', and this is precisely what international law calls an '*erga omnes* obligation'. In other words, anyone who knows about a potential atrocity is obliged to draw attention to it, so that the international community can help to stop or prevent the crime. Eventually, this information makes its way to journalists. This 'duty to inform', when placed in the hands of journalists, becomes the 'responsibility to report'. This responsibility is not simply moral: the ICTR's sentence on Ngeze shows that courts of law can enforce it too. R2R is universally applicable because there are no exceptions to the responsibility to uphold the rule of law, democracy, and peace; and because this responsibility applies everywhere in the world, to every context.

R2P is an *erga omnes* obligation under several instruments of international humanitarian law. As the first and third pillars of R2P summarise this obligation, all states must uphold the rule of international law and human rights, no matter where these violations may be taking place. In R2P's second and third pillars, since journalists and media are part of 'the wider international community' that assists states, R2R similarly obliges members of the journalistic profession to protect human rights across borders. To uphold their responsibilities under R2P, states must rely on journalists to carry out their profession responsibly, in all cases. Because it is part of R2P, R2R is therefore also an *erga omnes* obligation, and it specifically applies to journalists. Journalists may not pick and choose which atrocities they will report on and which they might wish to downplay. In the worst case, such a journalistic omission would be part of an intentional cover-up for such violations.

The same argument applies from the standpoint of universal human rights. As a 'universal declaration', the Universal Declaration on Human Rights (UN 1948) recognises the basic rights of everyone, across the world; and it recognises that these rights impose corresponding duties on everyone, across the world, to respect these rights. As similarly shown previously, Article 19 of the ICCPR expects the media to protect and uphold human rights; while Article 20 prohibits war propaganda and the incitement of hatred (Office of the High Commissioner on Human Rights 1966). The UDHR and ICCPR are universally applicable instruments and therefore have an *erga omnes* character. As Balabanova (2015) points out, both the UDHR and the ICCPR form the basis of expectations about the media's role in human rights and humanitarian law.

R2R as a means of protecting peremptory norms of international law

When a principle of law is so fundamental that without it the entire legal system would break down, this is known as a '*jus cogens*' or 'peremptory' norm. The UN International Law Commission (ILC) writes (2001, 85): 'Those peremptory norms that are clearly accepted and recognized include the prohibitions of aggression, genocide, slavery, racial discrimination, crimes against humanity and torture, and the right of self-determination'. Reporting on any violations of this list of peremptory norms can be one way to indicate to states when they should invoke R2P and conduct a humanitarian intervention.

In international law, human rights are enjoyed by individuals. Under the UDHR, individual journalists share the same rights and freedoms that all individual persons hold in their private capacity. These include liberty of conscience (Article 18 UDHR) and freedom of expression (Article 19 UDHR). The main right that 'peoples' hold in international law is the right of self-determination: the right to be free from foreign attack, military occupation, colonisation, and other forms of collective subjugation; and thus the right to determine their own political futures freely. The UN Human Rights Committee's (HRC's) General Comment 12 on the International Covenant on Civil and Political Rights (ICCPR) Article 1 notes:

> The right of self-determination is of particular importance because its realization is an essential condition for the effective guarantee and observance of

individual human rights and for the promotion and strengthening of those rights. It is for that reason that States set forth the right of self-determination in a provision of positive law in both Covenants [the ICCPR and the International Covenant on Economic, Social, and Cultural Rights (ICESCR)] and placed this provision as article 1 apart from and before all of the other rights in the two Covenants.

(HRC 1984. Emphasis added)

Of the ILC's list of seven peremptory norms, without which the international legal order would cease to exist, five of them can, by definition, only apply to peoples as a collective group (rather than to individuals). Journalists' enjoyment of their individual human rights derives, therefore, from their membership in collective groups that international law recognises as 'peoples'. Thus, international law shows a relationship between protecting the rights of groups, and those of individuals such as journalists. If groups are subject to aggression or genocide, individual journalists belonging to those groups cannot be fully free to report. This places an obligation on journalists from other parts of the world to help them do the job, even though this is likely to be dangerous. Because Article 19 of the UDHR is worded broadly enough to encompass all members of society, it is possible to argue that there is no specific legal protection for journalists. Elaborating on the meaning of Article 19, specifying that it protects journalists, would likely require written aids on how to interpret and clarify Article 19, drafted by UN member states. In practice, however, the work of the Special Rapporteur on Freedom of Opinion and Expression often appears to specifically focus on the protection of journalists, as a specific case of the rights granted to all people by Article 19 (Office of the High Commissioner on Human Rights 2024).

During times of armed conflict, journalists are generally regarded as non-combatants and may not be attacked. Implied within provisions like Article 3 of the Hague Regulations, and Article 43(2) of Additional Protocol I to the Geneva Conventions, journalists are accredited to but not affiliated with the military. They are not members of the armed forces but remain eligible for prisoner of war status in the event of their capture. Nevertheless, these safeguards are forfeited by journalists who actively take part in conflicts such as by transmitting military messages (Heyns and Srinivasan 2013, 314–25; UN 2010, para 19).

The United Nations Security Council has brought attention to the targeting of journalists during armed conflict and the associated impunity in two resolutions: 1738 (2006) and 2222 (2015). There are numerous other dedicated 'soft law' instruments on journalist safety and impunity in non-conflict situations, dating back to the 1970s (Berger 2017, 38). Nevertheless, according to the Committee to Protect Journalists, 1715 journalists have been killed between 1992 and 2024 (Committee to Protect Journalists n.d.). If journalists wish to have the freedom to report, they share a mutual obligation with other journalists worldwide to report violations of that right.

The HRC's Comment shows that, at times when an aggressor violates a people's right of self-determination or commits atrocity crimes (like genocide) against them, individual rights like the journalistic 'right to impart information' cannot be exercised freely either. Hence, just as states not specifically affected by a situation still have an R2P towards states or people who cannot protect themselves, so journalists who may not be directly affected by the situation still have an R2R: taking up the work that more vulnerable journalists, belonging to the group or state under attack, cannot carry out. This is the meaning of the *erga omnes* obligations that international law provides under R2P, as it applies to journalists and media institutions.

As the ICTR pointed out when sentencing Ngeze, journalists' enjoyment of the 'right to impart information' implies corresponding duties to use their media platforms to fulfil their *erga omnes* legal obligations. The ICTR identified such duties as promoting peace and democracy. From the standpoint of peremptory norms in international law, this chapter argues that another such duty is the journalistic responsibility to report on unjust wars, genocides, crimes against humanity, and ethnic cleansing, and to expose the crimes of aggressor states against peoples under attack and occupation. Thus, corresponding to their own individual freedom to impart information, journalists have a responsibility to report in ways that preserve the freedom of all peoples. By upholding their R2R in situations where peremptory norms are being violated, journalists participate in, and help to preserve, the international legal order.

R2R as a concept of natural law

The roots of R2P lie in a natural law. The 'natural law' perspective emphasises that concepts of right and wrong are common to all peoples and equivalent to the status of law. Natural law is also the foundation of inalienable 'human rights', which exist independently of whether any state enforces them, as a concept. Rights are deemed to exist independently of a positivist lawmaker to confer them. Positive law cannot take them away – this is what their 'inalienable' status means.

Perspectives like those of Shaw, Selvarajah, Thompson, and Cruft demonstrate how practitioners within the field of journalism and media believe that their own deeply felt concepts of right and wrong have implications for the ways that they exercise their profession. The ICTR's 'Media Trial' shows that this moral and ethical sense of duty within the journalistic profession indeed has a legal meaning. It would be legally wrong to knowingly fail to report on atrocity crimes, even if there were no judicial consequences for such an omission. Thus, those consequences might emerge in the future, with full legal justification, if new courts were set up or new governments came to power that had such interests in mind.

Journalistic work underlies the moral and legal justifications of R2P. In a globally interlinked society, where news media plays a key role in disseminating information, journalists have a legal responsibility to report and inform the public of atrocities. This enables the public to pressure governments to act and to protect the victims of such violations.

HRJ and R2R

Human rights journalism (HRJ) supports the idea that journalism also has obligations under R2P. HRJ is a more proactive practice, which is based on critical, diagnostic, and intervention-centric methods, built around five frames: empathy/critical frame; diagnostic reporting; proactive; interventionist; and peace journalism. Its approach is to challenge the status quo of power politics against marginalised minorities, to promote and protect human rights and peace (Shaw 2012, 46). It encourages journalists to structure news articles around the five frames which are interconnected across various aspects of human rights and conflict transformation. It aims to reflect social reality through information and sharing of knowledge about direct and indirect causes of violence, in order to safeguard and foster human rights by prompting the public to care for and act to end the suffering (Selvarajah 2020, 68). HRJ provides substantial content to the journalistic practices that facilitate R2R, by establishing *prima facie* evidence of a crime, and by constructing narratives informed by social, political, cultural, ethical, and moral foundations (Shaw and Selvarajah 2019). Selvarajah (2020, 109–14) identifies five key elements that define the nexus and establish a functional relationship between HRJ and R2P.

1. Just cause and global justice advocacy.
2. Just peace, peace building, and conflict prevention.
3. Empowering, mobilising, and intervening.
4. Human rights-based approach.
5. Monitoring and accountability.

Both R2P and HRJ unequivocally advocate for preventing human rights violations, including mass atrocity crimes, and protecting civilians in times of crisis, thereby contributing to creating the conditions for sustainable peace. This relates to the 'just cause' theory, which argues for interventions, including restricted recourse to force when there is cause. Thus, the 'just cause and global justice advocacy' element helps identify potentially serious situations that could escalate into mass atrocity.

Such HRJ can put the international community 'on alert' that state actors should implement pre-emptive, diplomatic interventions to prevent a conflict situation (or other serious human rights violations) from emerging. HRJ demonstrates a political function by bringing people's suffering, human rights abuses, and their underlying causes, to the world's attention. This enables the international community to act as a cosmopolitan community of humanity and invoke R2P within just peace, peace building and conflict prevention principles.

The five frames of HRJ emphasise addressing power imbalance in society to achieve positive social change by empowering, mobilising, and intervening, which go hand in hand with the three responsibilities and three pillars of R2P. A human rights-based approach reinforced by constructive epistemology allows the HRJ to analyse all factors that influence a conflict at the personal, institutional, and structural-cultural level, as well as power relations within a socio-cultural and political context. Thus, the HRJ constructs a social reality and aids in designing human rights and peace-building strategies within the R2P framework. HRJ, through its monitoring and accountability function, watches and assesses the implementation of R2P at all stages to ensure and strengthen the transparency and accountability of its operations and actions, particularly those who intervene in the crisis (Selvarajah 2020).

These five elements of the nexus between HRJ and R2P define how the news media can uphold its legal obligations under R2R. They also emphasise the media's moral obligations as a vital part of global civil society, and a 'Fourth Estate', to focus on and protect human rights by exposing human rights violations and their underlying causes wherever they occur.

Conclusion

This chapter opened with the ICTR's verdict against Ngeze, a journalist who had used his platform to incite ethnic slaughter, for genocide. When sentencing Ngeze, the ICTR emphasised his responsibilities as a journalist: to inform the public and shape public opinion towards democracy and peace, to accept the responsibilities that came with journalistic freedom of expression, and to use that freedom to promote these positive values. While Ngeze was sentenced for a crime of commission, it is possible that concealing or knowingly failing to report on grave atrocities could also be recognised as crimes of omission (or complicity) that would apply to journalists. There is, therefore, a legal 'responsibility to report' in international law, which this chapter terms 'R2R'.

Where previous scholarship (Thompson 2007; Selvarajah 2020) has examined the media's R2R in terms of ethical duty, this chapter argues that R2R is also a legal duty. It has defined the concept using the ICTR's sentence on Ngeze, and Articles 19 and 20 of the ICCPR. This chapter went on to show R2R's grounding in natural law, and that it is an *erga omnes* rule – without any exceptions based on the location or identity of the victims or perpetrators.

Journalists who have neglected their R2R might thus be held accountable later when a court or government emerges that has the jurisdiction and political will to act on these omissions.

The chapter has also shown that Shaw's and Selvarajah's identification of a nexus between HRJ and R2P provides the substantive content of R2R. When HRJ is carried out with a sense of ethical responsibility, it also fulfils a legal obligation to expose abuses against vulnerable populations and help stop them from happening.

Just as the ICTR punished Ngeze for committing genocide through his irresponsible journalistic practices, his sentencing implicitly showed that he had the responsibility – a positive obligation under international criminal law – to use his media platform to promote peace and democracy during a time of ethnic tension. This chapter has shown that this obligation of R2R is contained within the concept of R2P.

Discussion questions

1. This chapter has focused on journalists' R2R. What does the concept of R2R mean for large media companies, who often make editorial decisions for their journalists? What does it mean for individual journalists, who work for media companies that might act to suppress or downplay evidence of human rights violations and war crimes?
2. What role does citizen journalism, where ordinary people gather evidence of war crimes and broadcast it on social media, have within the concept of R2R? Do these principles only apply to official members of the press corps, do they apply to everyone with a mobile phone and an internet connection, or can a line of distinction be drawn where R2R does and does not apply?
3. Should portraying R2R as a legal concept change the way that journalists think about their responsibilities in conflict situations? How could journalists use the legal perspective on R2R to assist the work of international criminal inquiries (as done in the International Criminal Tribunal for the Former Yugoslavia)?

Further reading

Corredoira y Alfonso, L., I. Bel Mallen, and R. Cetina Presuel, eds. 2021. *The Handbook of Communication Rights, Law, and Ethics: Seeking Universality, Equality, Freedom and Dignity*. Wiley.

Hilsum, Lindsey. 2018. *In Extremis: The Life and Death of the War Correspondent Marie Colvin*. Farrar. Straus and Giroux.

Tumber, Howard. 2008. "Journalists, War Crimes and International Justice." *Media, War & Conflict* 1 (3): 261–69. https://doi.org/10.1177/1750635208097051.

References

Balabanova, Ekaterina. 2015. *The Media and Human Rights: The Cosmopolitan Promise*. London: Routledge.

Bell, Martin. 1998. "The Journalism of Attachment." In *Media Ethics*, edited by Matthew Kiernan, 16–22. London: Routledge.

Berger, Guy. 2017. "Why the World Became Concerned with Journalistic Safety, and Why the Issue Will Continue to Attract Attention." In *The Assault on Journalism: Building Knowledge to Protect Freedom of Expression*, edited by Ulla Carlsson and Reeta Pöyhtäri, 33–34. Gothenburg: Nordicom.

Cole, Wade M. 2010. "No News is Good News: Human Rights Coverage in the American Print Media, 1980–2000." *Journal of Human Rights* 9 (3): 303–25.

Committee to Protect Journalists. n.d. "1715 Journalists and Media Workers Killed." https://cpj.org/data/killed/all/?status=Killed&motiveConfirmed%5B%5D=Confirmed&type%5B%5D=Journalist&type%5B%5D=Media%20Worker&start_year=1992&end_year=2024&group_by=year.

Cottle, Simon. 2017. "Journalist Killings and the Responsibility to Report." In *The Assault on Journalism: Building Knowledge to Protect Freedom of Expression*, edited by Ulla Carlsson and Reeta Pöyhtäri, 129–41. Gothenburg: Nordicom.

Cottle, Simon. 2019. "Humanitarianism, Human Insecurity, and Communications: What's Changing in a Globalised World?" In *Humanitarianism, Communications and Change*, edited by Simon Cottle and Glenda Cooper, 19–38. New York: Peter Lang.

Cruft, Rowan. 2022. "Journalism and Press Freedom as Human Rights." *Journal of Applied Philosophy* 39 (3). Symposium on Media Ethics.

Daly, Emma. 2017. "Beyond Justice: How the Yugoslav Tribunal Made History." *Human Rights Watch*. https://www.hrw.org/news/2017/12/19/beyond-justice-how-yugoslav-tribunal-made-history.

Galtung, Johan. 2002. "Peace Journalism: A Challenge." In *Journalism and the New World Order: Studying War and the Media*, edited by Wilhelm Kempf and Heikki Luostarinen, 269–72. Gothenburg: Nordicom.

Global Centre for the Responsibility to Protect. 2001. "The Responsibility to Protect: Report of the International Commission on Intervention and State Sovereignty." https://www.globalr2p.org/resources/the-responsibility-to-protect-report-of-the-international-commission-on-intervention-and-state-sovereignty-2001/.

Global Centre for the Responsibility to Protect. 2021. "The Responsibility to Protect: A Background Briefing." January 14. https://www.globalr2p.org/publications/the-responsibility-to-protect-a-background-briefing/.

Heyns, Christof, and Sharath Srinivasan. 2013. "Protecting the Right to Life of Journalists: The Need for a Higher Level of Engagement." *Human Rights Quarterly* 35: 304–32.

International Criminal Tribunal for Rwanda. 2003. "The Prosecutor v. Ferdinand Nahimana, Jean-Bosco Barayagwiza, Hassan Ngeze (Judgement and Sentence). Case No. ICTR-99-52-T." *Refworld*. https://www.refworld.org/jurisprudence/caselaw/ictr/2003/en/91852.

International Law Commission. 2001. "Draft Articles on Responsibility of States for Internationally Wrongful Acts, With Commentaries." Commentary on Article 26. Vol. II, Part 2. Yearbook of the International Law Commission. https://legal.un.org/ilc/texts/instruments/english/commentaries/9_6_2001.pdf.

Khouri, Rami G. 2023. "Watching the Watchdogs: Media, Law, and Gaza Genocide." *Al-Jazeera*. https://www.aljazeera.com/opinions/2023/12/15/watching-the-watchdogs-media-law-and-gaza-genocide.

Office of the High Commissioner on Human Rights. 1966. "International Covenant on Civil and Political Rights." https://www.ohchr.org/en/instruments-mechanisms/instruments/international-covenant-civil-and-political-rights.

Office of the High Commissioner on Human Rights. 2024. "A/HRC/56/53: Journalists in Exile: Report of the Special Rapporteur on the Promotion and Protection of the Right to Freedom of Opinion and Expression." *Special Rapporteur on Freedom of Opinion and Expression.* https://www.ohchr.org/en/documents/thematic-reports/ahrc5653-journalists-exile-report-special-rapporteur-promotion-and.

Selvarajah, Senthan. 2020. *Human Rights Journalism and Its Nexus to Responsibility to Protect: How and Why the International Press Failed in Sri Lanka's Humanitarian Crisis.* London: Palgrave.

Selvarajah, Senthan, and Lorenzo Fiorito. 2023. "Media, Public Opinion, and the ICC in the Russia–Ukraine War." *Journalism and Media* 4 (3): 760–89.

Shaw, Ibrahim S. 2012. *Human Rights Journalism: Advances in Reporting Distant Humanitarian Interventions.* London: Palgrave Macmillan.

Shaw, Ibrahim S., and Senthan Selvarajah. 2019. "Human Rights Journalism: Towards a Critical Constructivist Epistemological Approach." In *Reporting Human Rights, Conflicts, and Peacebuilding: Critical and Global Perspectives*, edited by Ibrahim S. Shaw and Senthan Selvarajah, 13–29. Basingstoke: Palgrave.

Thompson, Allan. 2007. "The Responsibility to Report: A New Journalistic Paradigm." In *The Media and the Rwanda Genocide*, edited by Allan Thomson, 433–45. London: Pluto Press.

UN. 1948. "Universal Declaration of Human Rights." https://www.un.org/en/about-us/universal-declaration-of-human-rights.

UN General Assembly. 1948. "Convention on the Prevention and Punishment of the Crime of Genocide. Resolution 260 A (III)." *Office on Genocide Prevention and the Responsibility to Protect.* https://www.un.org/en/genocideprevention/documents/atrocity-crimes/Doc.1_Convention%20on%20the%20Prevention%20and%20Punishment%20of%20the%20Crime%20of%20Genocide.pdf.

UN General Assembly. 2010. "Report of the Special Rapporteur on the Situation of Human Rights Defenders (A/63/288)." *UN Department for General Assembly and Conference Management.* https://documents.un.org/doc/undoc/gen/n08/488/07/pdf/n0848807.pdf?token=5l3q8jai3PWdaROvd2&fe=true.

UN Human Rights Committee. 1984. "CCPR General Comment No. 12: Article 1 [Right of Self-Determination] The Right of Self-Determination of Peoples." *Refworld.* https://www.refworld.org/sites/default/files/legacy-pdf/en/1984-3/453883f822.pdf.

Welsh, Jennifer, and Maria Banda. 2010. "International Law and the Responsibility to Protect: Clarifying or Expanding States' Responsibilities?" *Global Responsibility to Protect* 2 (2): 213–31.

9
THE CHALLENGES OF REPORTING HUMAN RIGHTS IN CONFLICTS

Towards a human rights journalism approach

Ibrahim Seaga Shaw

Introduction

Protest movements are means by which citizens can register their collective disagreement and dissent, build public support and legitimacy for their aims, and influence government policy formation and even societal change. However, while there are apparently well-established mechanisms to express collective dissent against perceived unacceptable conditions, or policies, in established democracies, this is not the case in countries where democracy is either non-existent or relatively new. It is important to note that protest movements are more, or less, conflicts because they do not only disrupt public order but are normally seen as confrontations between the protesters and the state security apparatus, and by extension the state itself. The reporting of mass protest movements is largely similar in established and less established democracies. However, a plethora of research confirms that the media representation of protesters and the security personnel who try to stop them is not necessarily the same across the two democracies in question. For instance, as we will see in detail in this study, while in both democracies the focus on the dramatic physical and visible forms of violence over that of the invisible structural and cultural forms of violence is largely similar, in well-established democracies, there is a tendency for the media to demonise the protesters as the problem and present the security forces, especially the police, as the solution whereas in less established democracies such as Sierra Leone, it is the other way round since there is the tendency of the media to present the protesters as the good people and present the security forces as the problem.

This brings to mind two studies based on a detailed analysis of a major demonstration in London in 1968 and the 1960s student movement in the US, both protesting against American involvement in the Vietnam War. The first was published by Halloran, Elliott and Murdock (1970) and Murdock (1981). The second was published by Gitlin (1980/2003). The focus on these two protest movements in the 1960s is to provide proper context to the study in this chapter, which is about the newspaper reporting of the August 10 protests in Sierra Leone to determine the extent to which human wrongs journalism was evident. After all, going by the simple definition of conflict as a disagreement between two people, or groups of people, or within an individual, or a group of people, often manifested as visible or invisible forms of violence, protest movements are such as those we saw in Sierra Leone, the USA, and the UK.

Take for instance the media framing of the 1968 London demonstrations which speculated on anticipated violence and trouble. Murdock (1981) argued that by focusing on the 'expectation of violence' the media concentrated on the facts of the anticipated event and hence neglected their responsibility to investigate the underlying causes. The 'radical political content' of the protest march was relegated to the backburner in the media discourse and in its place was the criminalisation of the participants as 'violent extremists'. This problematic framing dominated the news media discourse of the event.

Todd Gitlin's study (1980/2003), for his part, examines how the media initially largely ignored the 1960s student movement in the US. The movement was not dramatic enough to catch media attention, but it became 'big news' following the Students for Democratic Society march on Washington in April 1965 and a series of student anti-war protests in the wake of the Vietnam War. Gitlin argues that the amplification was already selective as certain themes were emphasised while others were simply ignored. Frames such as 'civil disturbances', 'communists', and 'extremists' all rendering the participants as 'trouble makers' began to dominate the news media discourse.

There were protest movements in Sierra Leone on August 10, 2022, which were even more violent than those of the 60s in the UK and US discussed earlier. The Sierra Leone protests claimed 31 lives, including six policemen, with many others injured and hospitalised. The protesters largely pointed to the spiralling cost of living, among others, as the main cause of their action but this hardly featured in the news media. What dominated the news were the violent confrontations between the police and the protesters. While in both the UK and US protests the protesters were presented as the problem and security forces as the solution, in the case of the Sierra Leone protests, the media representation was largely skewed in favour of the protesters. Despite this difference, the media focus was more on the visible physical violence between the protesters and the police than on the invisible structural and cultural forms of violence that led to the protest movements. I have problematised it as human wrongs journalism and proposed human rights journalism as a counter-hegemonic model (Shaw 2012).

This chapter employs quantitative and qualitative studies of the local press reporting of the violent protests in Sierra Leone in 2022 to understand the extent to which challenges of reporting human rights violations in time of conflict were at play, or not. It will first examine the model of human rights journalism as the preferred alternative approach to reporting conflicts such as protest movements as opposed to the traditional human wrongs journalism approach and then embark on a quantitative and qualitative analysis of the reporting of the 2022 August 10 Protests in Sierra Leone by two local newspapers to determine the extent to which the four features of human wrongs journalism presented were evident, or not.

Human rights journalism as a counter-hegemonic model to mainstream human wrongs journalism

Perhaps the most important global development of the 20th century was the adoption of the Universal Declaration of Human Rights (UDHR) on 10 December 1948 in Paris. The first article in the Declaration asserts that all human beings 'are born free and equal in dignity and rights', and the significance of this is that these rights are thereby recognised regardless of any existing social division, whether of social class, status, ethnicity, gender, or religion. However, as I argue in my groundbreaking book, 'Human Rights Journalism: Advances in Reporting Distant Humanitarian Interventions' (Shaw 2012), there is a very big gap between the normative idea of this first article of the UDHR and what actually obtains on the ground, and I put the blame squarely on the doorsteps of mainstream journalists for their failure to practice human rights journalism. I argue that journalists have the moral responsibility as duty bearers to honestly monitor the promotion, protection, and/or abuse of these inalienable human rights which all human beings must enjoy. The failure of mainstream journalism to do this largely prompted me to develop human rights journalism as a counter-hegemonic model, and, by extension, to write this book. The purpose of this book is largely to serve as a moral benchmark to monitor the monitors – the journalists. According to a review of the book by the European Journal of Communication (2013), it critically examines the role of journalism in both promoting and protecting human rights and not just those deemed to be 'on our side' or in some way instrumental to 'our' interests.

Human rights journalism, as I argued, is not just about reporting the physical violations of people's human rights, for example, genocide, torture, rape, etc., but also violations of structural rights such as death by starvation or disease, poverty, forced migration, forced labour, human trafficking etc., and cultural rights such as racism, tribalism, regionalism, hate speech, xenophobia, etc. Thus, the human rights journalist is not only concerned about reporting human rights violations caused by direct physical violence in the sense of civil and political rights (negative rights/negative peace) but also, and perhaps more importantly, those violations caused by indirect structural and cultural violence in the sense of economic, social, and cultural rights (positive rights/positive peace). Direct physical violence is the type of violence that is visible and manifests clearly in the eyes of the public such as wounding, killing, torturing, etc., whereas structural violence is seen as an invisible or latent form of violence such as economic injustice, poverty, hunger, misery, etc. Cultural violence is also an invisible or latent form of violence such as inequality, racism, xenophobia, islamophobia, antisemitism, etc.

Human rights journalism is journalism with a human face, journalism that cares for people, journalism that prioritises them over the values and interests of capitalist ventures and concerns, and over the whims and caprices of political demagogues. It is a more proactive approach because it recognises the importance of critically addressing indirect structural and cultural violence as well as preventing or reducing direct physical violence (Shaw 2012). In his foreword to my book, Stuart Allan, Professor of Journalism at Cardiff University, had this to say:

> Shaw's challenge to us, then, is to identify and critique the often subtle ways in which journalism is implicated in the structural imperatives of militarism, which more often than not underpin human rights abuse. That is to say, to find new ways to disrupt the ideological purchase of official truth claims, not least where the waging of war by 'us' against 'them' is effectively normalised to the point that peace-centred alternatives are trivialised, marginalised or excluded altogether as being less than newsworthy.
> *(Allan 2012, xiii)*

Selvarajah (2020) also argues that the media's role is not limited to the protection of human rights but also involves investigating the causes of violations of these rights and conceiving ways of preventing such violations. He adds that the watchdog role of the journalist is relevant to the investigation of the causes of human rights violations.

> Media must analyse incidents and issues relating to human rights, disseminate information, including both violations and their causes to create a discourse of human rights education. In this way, media can help set up an acceptable standard of human rights practices within which the society has to operate.
> *(Selvarajah 2020, 52; Shaw and Selvarajah 2019)*

HRJ is a normative journalistic practice informed by the holistic human rights approach (negative and positive rights). It is inspired by Kant's ideas of enlightenment and cosmopolitanism. Kant believed in the existence of the cosmopolitan global society where every human being is valued. 'This is where', according to Selvarajah, 'HRJ becomes more important than conventional journalism, since the latter does not take into consideration the power imbalances in the society and thereby propagates the status quo, indirectly contributing to the human rights violations' (Selvarajah 2020, 67). The HRJ model is defined as a 'diagnostic style of journalism, which gives a critical reflection on the experiences and needs of the victims and perpetrators of human rights violations of all types – physical as well as cultural and structural – in order to stimulate understanding of the reasons for these violations, and to prevent, or solve, them in ways that would not produce more human rights imbalances, or violations, in the future' (Shaw 2012, 46). It employs a diagnostic approach aiming to analyse various factors causing a conflict; at various levels of a society, within a socio-cultural and political context (Shaw 2012, 99). 'In other words', according to Selvarajah (2020, 71), 'for human rights and peacebuilding strategies to be successful, actors should understand the true nature of events and their effects'. Selvarajah adds that 'HRJ, which focuses on holistic human rights, can play an important role in achieving this by establishing *prima facie* case within a critical constructivist epistemology'. It is a multidimensional approach to analysing various factors that lead to a given crisis (Selvarajah 2020, 71)

On the other hand, Human Wrongs Journalism (HWJ) is 'journalism that reinforces, rather than challenging, the problematic representational imbalances in society' that are mostly skewed in favour of the dominant classes of society (Shaw 2012, 47). I present Table 9.1, which provides a binary representation of HWJ and HRJ.

TABLE 9.1 Human Wrongs Journalism (HWJ) vs Human Rights Journalism (HRJ)

Human Wrongs Journalism (HWJ)	*Human Rights Journalism (HRJ)*
1. Competition orientated: Violence/visible/drama/evocative and reactive; solution after damage/business; profit or loss; some people come out happy and smiling while others come out sad and crying	1. Non-violence/invisible/structural/cultural violence orientated: diagnostic and proactive/preventing direct violence/triple win; everybody comes out happy and smiling
2. Expose "some" or "their" human wrongs; selective justice; communitarianism	2. Expose all human wrongs; global justice; cosmopolitanism
3. Demonisation-orientated: Focus on the human rights violations by "them", and on "our" friends, or "our friends'" victims	3. Demonisation of all human rights violators; people/human face-orientated/care for and empower all but biased in favour of vulnerable people
4. Partial solution-orientated: Focus on immediate physical needs only at the expense of long-term structural solutions	4. Holistic problem-solving orientated: now/tomorrow and surface/hidden problems

In HWJ, the focus of the media is on the direct, visible, manifest, and dramatic physical forms of human rights violations. For its opposite, HRJ, the focus is on the indirect, invisible, and latent structural and cultural forms of violence. While HWJ exposes some selected human rights violations, its opposite HRJ uncovers all human rights violations. HWJ in the media condemns the human rights violators against their friends, but HRJ condemns all human rights violators. Finally, while in HWJ the media looks for short-term solutions to solve the immediate physical needs, such as responding to healing the wounds of the victims, HRJ has long-term and sustainable approaches such as peacebuilding interventions that would prevent human rights violations in the future.

Newspaper reporting of the August 10, 2022 protests in Sierra Leone

The calm that Sierra Leone has enjoyed since the end of the civil war in 2002 was abruptly disrupted on the 10th of August 2022 by mass protest movements. The protesters pointed to the high cost of living caused by inflation and the rising prices of basic commodities for their collective action, although state authorities dismissed this claim as an alibi by some disgruntled elements of the main opposition party to stage a coup. They were resisted by state security forces, claiming about 31 lives, including six security personnel, while hundreds were injured and hospitalized. The rationale for choosing this case study to examine the challenges of reporting human rights violations from a human rights journalism lens is that it provides a unique opportunity to look at how these challenges are evident, or not, in less traditional conflict situations such as protest movements, especially in post-conflict developing countries such as Sierra Leone. This section of the chapter will undertake quantitative and qualitative content analyses of the news contents of two largely established independent newspapers in Sierra Leone: *Awoko* and *Politico*. The study uses quantitative analysis of the selected newspapers to understand their statistical representations of the four challenges of reporting human rights violations, or features of HWJ as indicated in Table 9.1, and qualitative analysis to understand how these four challenges or features of HWJ were visible, or not, in the narratives of the newspaper articles analysed. Both *Awoko* and *Politico* are published and edited by two highly respected journalists in Sierra Leone: Kevin Lewis of *Awoko* newspaper and Umaru Fofana of *Politico* newspaper. Both are widely and nationally circulated although there is no information available about their exact print runs. Both are former presidents of the Sierra Leone Association of Journalists and are also currently serving as correspondents for VOA and the BBC, respectively. These two newspapers were selected for this study because they are highly regarded as among the most neutral newspapers in a traditionally highly politically polarised media landscape in Sierra Leone. The media, especially the print media, in this small West African country with a population of about 8 million, is largely polarised along the two main parties in the country – the ruling Sierra Leone Peoples Party (SLPP) and the main opposition, All Peoples Congress (APC). As M'bayo (2013, 40) put it,

> With the state no longer the key mass communicator, party functionaries have resorted to creating non-state media outfits in the form of traditional newspapers and online portals. With party newspapers, party radio stations and privately owned media . . . the media environment in the country is polarised along party lines, and pro- and anti-state media organisations.

The other reason for choosing these two largely politically neutral newspapers *Awoko* and *Politico*, is first to put to the test their neutrality, and second whether their neutrality, or lack of it, was a factor in their choice of human rights journalism or human wrongs journalism frames in their reporting of the 10 August 2022, protest movements in Sierra Leone.

Sierra Leone has one of the most pluralistic media landscapes in the world with over 400 newspapers registered in the country, although only fewer than 100 are fully operational and regular. Despite a recent expansion of the liberal space of the media landscape with more media outlets joining the fray (www.imc.gov.sl), it is unclear whether journalists are adequately and proactively taking advantage of this new wind of liberalism and practising responsible journalism that serves the best interests of the public. This is partly why the study in this chapter is important.

Research methodology

The main objective of this chapter is to analyse the print media coverage of the 10 August 2022 protests to determine whether or not the challenges of human rights journalism which I problematise as human wrongs journalism were at play. Therefore, this chapter will explore the following research questions:

1. What was the volume and depth of dramatic/evocative/reactive/win-lose or proactive/diagnostic/structural/cultural/triple win frames?
2. What was the volume and depth of selective, or all, human rights violations frames?
3. What was the volume and depth of demonisation of 'our enemies', or all human rights violation frames?
4. What was the volume and depth of partial short-term, or holistic long-term, solutions frames?

The methodology is inspired by a combination of thematic and textual analysis of newspaper coverage of the protests, drawing on the quantitative content and qualitative frame analysis approaches of De Bonville (2000) and Entman (1993), respectively. The quantitative content analysis will look at the presence or absence of the four challenges, while the qualitative analysis will examine how the four challenges or HWJ features were dominant in the narratives of the articles analysed. For the quantitative analysis, I will examine the number of times the HRJ or HWJ frames in the research objectives and questions featured in the coverage, and for the qualitative frame analysis, I will take a closer look at some of the important HRJ or HWJ frames outlined in the research.

The unit of analysis is the coverage of the protests in the *Awoko* and *Politico* newspapers spanning the period of six months since the outbreak of the protests, that is the 10th of August 2022 to the 9th of February 2023. By using 'August 10 protests' as the key words when searching the web sites of both newspapers, a total of 19 articles, mostly news reports, were downloaded: nine from *Awoko* and 10 from *Politico*.

Quantitative content analysis of the four HRJ versus HWJ frames

Drawing on the De Bonville (2000) approach – looking at the presence and/or absence of the representations of HWJ or HRJ, the 19 articles downloaded from *Awoko* and *Politico* were analysed to determine how many of them foregrounded any of the four binary HRJ and HWJ frames. For this quantitative analysis, I am going to abbreviate the first binary HWJ frames (Evocative/dramatic/reactive/win-lose) as EDRWL and the HRJ frames (Proactive/diagnostic/structural/cultural/triple win) as PDSCTW; second binary HWJ frames (Selective Human Rights Violations) as SHRV and HRJ frames (All human rights violations) as AHRV; third binary HWJ frames (Demonisation of only our enemies' human rights violations) as DOOEHRV and HRJ frames (Demonisation of all human rights violators) as DAHRV; and fourth binary HWJ frames (Partial short-term solutions) as PSS and HRJ frames (Holistic long-term solutions) as HLS. Figures 9.1 and 9.2 present the findings of the quantitative analysis of the HWJ and HRJ frames.

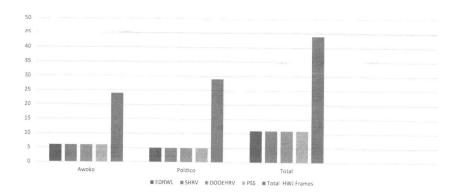

FIGURE 9.1 Human Wrongs Journalism frames

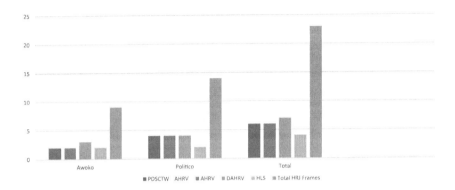

FIGURE 9.2   Human Rights Journalism frames

Discussion

As we can see in Figure 9.1, *Awoko* newspaper carried more human wrongs journalism (HWJ) frames (24 in total), six in each of the four categories of frames (EDRWL, SHRV, DOOEHRV, and PSS), than *Politico*, which carried 20 HWJ frames in total, five in each of the four categories of frames. This shows that the challenges of reporting the August 10 protests from a human rights journalism lens were more visible in the coverage by *Awoko* than that of *Politico*. Moreover, as we can see in Figure 9.2, the *Politico* newspaper carried more (HRJ) frames 14 in total, four in each of the first two categories (PDSCTW, AHRV), of four HRJ frames, and two in the fourth one (HLS) than that of *Awoko*, which had only nine HRJ frames. Out of the nine articles in the *Awoko* that featured the protests, only three were dominated by the HRJ frames, while the other six foregrounded the HWJ frames. On the other hand, out of 10 articles published by *Politico*, only four featured HRJ frames, while the other six foregrounded the HWJ frames. Thus, while both newspapers foregrounded HWJ frames more than HRJ frames, the analysis shows that *Awoko* relatively foregrounded more HWJ frames than *Politico*. This seems to suggest that the challenges of reporting the protests from a human rights journalism lens manifested in the *Awoko* coverage more than that of the *Politico*.

Overall, the HWJ framing of the August 10 protest was far more dominant, with a total of 44 frames than its binary HRJ framing with a total of 23 frames. One other interesting finding of this analysis is that the HWJ frames were consistently the same number: six (6) for each of the four categories of framing in the *Awoko*, and they were consistently the same number: five (5) for each of the four categories of framing in the *Politico*. However, this was not the same in the case of the HRJ frames where *Awoko* had two (2) consistent frames for three of the framing categories (PDSCTW, AHRV, and HLS), while *Politico* had four (4) consistent frames for three of the framing categories (PDSCTW, AHRV, and DAHRV). Thus, for the *Politico*, only two (2) of the HLS frames featured in its coverage, two (2) less than the other three frames, while for *Awoko* there were three (3) DAHRV frames, one (1) more compared to the three other frames. These inconsistencies further underscore the below-average performance of the two newspapers in the practice of human rights journalism in their reporting of the August 10 protest. However, despite the below-average performance of the two newspapers in HRJ, the findings show that *Awoko* was more vulnerable to the challenges of human rights journalism than *Politico*.

Qualitative content analysis of the four HRJ versus HWJ frames

Human rights journalism frames

A critical qualitative analysis of the texts and discourses in the coverage of the August 10 protests by *Politico* and *Awoko* newspapers shows very few HRJ frames compared to HWJ frames. Thus, the political story of the protests, which had to do with what actually caused them, either remotely or immediately, in the first place was largely lost in the reporting by these two newspapers. *Politico* did better than *Awoko* in reflecting the first HRJ frame of proactive and diagnostic invisible structural and cultural forms of violence. The *Politico* article where this was most evident was a feature by Mohamed Foday Conteh titled, 'The Indelible Scars of August 10 in Sierra Leone', in which he observed:

> Several nomenclatures have been attributed to the incident that occurred on the 10th of August this year. Proponents call it a protest and demonstration against the rising cost of living and suppression of free speech in the country. People opposed to the violent protests called it riot, a terrorist activity that was bent on removing the democratically elected administration of President Bio.
>
> *(Conteh 2022)*

Perhaps in keeping with its objectivity/neutrality conventional journalistic ethos, *Politico* provided two contrasting arguments to explain the protests, the first pointing fingers at the rising cost of living and dwindling free speech as justification, while the second blamed it on the action of desperate terrorists bent on removing the elected government by force. This has all the hallmarks of HRJ, as it provides two explanations to help readers make sense of what happened depending on which side of the divide they find themselves. The first explanation – the rising cost of living and lack of free speech caused by the state security refusal to allow public demonstrations – relates to 'economic structural violence'; and the second explanation – riotous conduct and terrorism to remove a democratically elected government – relates to cultural violence.

We also see two contrasting representations of those who carried out the mass protests, with the first explanation presenting them as the 'good guys' with a genuine public interest cause, while the second explanation presented them as the 'bad guys' with an ill-motivated self-interest cause reserved for terrorists. In the case of the 1960s protests in the UK and the US discussed earlier, the protesters were simply branded as the bad guys (terrorists), ignoring their political story of putting pressure on the US and the UK to pull out of the war in Vietnam. *Politico* got it right in terms of practising HRJ in this article because it brought into the reporting two diverse perspectives to explain the protests in keeping with the fine journalistic principle of objectivity.

Human rights reporting has been a highly contested and controversial paradigm, largely because it is seen as a threat to business as usual in journalistic practice. Small wonder that critics of HRJ often see it as a problem to some of the main standards of professional journalism, such as objectivity. What these critics fail to appreciate, however, is the fact that HRJ is the real panacea to the problems of mainstream reporting because it, among other many things, emphasizes both the 'news as it is' and the 'news as I see it' with special emphasis or bias towards marginalised and vulnerable voices who form the bulk of the victims of human rights abuses. This shows that HRJ can be said to be both objective, focusing on the facts as they are, and subjective, focusing on the individual interpretations of the facts.

However, there were some other narratives in the article that suggested that it was skewed more in favour of the second explanation of 'terrorism'. A case in point is the article's reference to President Bio, who described the August 10 protests as 'domestic terrorism' bent on illegally overthrowing him. He blamed politicians for using youths to carry out acts of terrorism in the country.

The 'rising cost' frame as the main cause of the protests was further reinforced in another *Politico* article, this time authored by publisher and editor Umaru Fofanah and titled, 'Sierra Leone Confirms 31 deaths in violent 10 August Protests', which observed that the protests were against the government because of the high cost of living with protesters chanting 'Bio Must go, we want peace' (Fofanah 29/8/2022).

For its part, the reporting of the August 10 protests by *Awoko* newspaper was more based on current affairs reporting of court proceedings and engagements of families of the victims of the protests; consequently, these had very little reflection of HRJ frames. For instance, the only reference to the first HRJ frame of proactive diagnostic structural and cultural forms of violence was reflected in the article by Alusine Rehme Wilson titled, 'Police Confirms Death of Evangelist Samson in Alleged Crossfire', in which he described Hassan Dumbuya aka Evangelist Samson as the "Voice of the Voiceless" and strong member of the Opposition APC party who was 'assassinated because of his political beliefs' (Wilson 17/8/2022).

The fourth HRJ frame, which is the Holistic Long-term Solution frame, was more dominant in almost all the articles in both *Awoko* and *Politico* that focused on the victims of the August 10 protests and their families. Take for example the *Awoko* article by Alusine Sesay titled 'Police Arrest(s) 24 Kids during Wednesday's Protests' (Sesay 17/8/2022), which presented the children arrested as both perpetrators and victims of the violent protestors: perpetrators because of their role in carrying out acts of violence during the protests, and victims because they were used and exploited by adults since they were under the age of consent. According to this article, the government, with the support of the Family Support Unit in the Sierra Leone Police and the Ministry of Social Welfare, ensured the protection of the fundamental rights of the detained children and eventually reunited them with their families. It reflects the HRJ third and fourth frames: demonisation of all human rights violators, adults or children, people human face-orientated/care for and empower all but biased in favour of vulnerable people – in this case 'protesting children' and Holistic problem-solving orientation: now/tomorrow and surface/hidden problems. It demonstrates caring for the vulnerable children who were forcefully conscripted to perpetrate violent conduct, as well as finding a more sustainable solution to their human rights violations.

Human wrongs journalism frames

A critical analysis of the texts and discourses of the coverage of the 10 August 2022 protests by the *Politico* and *Awoko* newspapers shows far more HWJ frames than HRJ. Here we see the dominance of dramatic evocative frames largely foregrounding the visible physical forms of violence associated with the protests and the pointing of fingers of blame at the protesters, and above all demonising only their own human rights violations with very little, if any, reflection on the underlying causes of the protest movements themselves. The *Awoko* newspaper had more of these HWJ frames compared to the *Politico* newspaper, which clearly shows that *Awoko* proved to be more vulnerable in succumbing to the challenges of HWJ. One *Awoko* article where this was clearly evident was a news report by Suliaman Sesay titled, '2 women jailed 5 months each for unlawful procession on August 10th' (Sesay 5/8/2022), in which he wrote: 'After they were found guilty of unlawful procession, Magistrate Marke Ngegba on Tuesday 4th October 2022, at the Pademba Road Court No.1 in Freetown slammed five months sentence on Adama Sesay and Simon Shimon Mansaray'.

In this article, we can see that the two women who 'allegedly illegally' marched with placards as part of the 10 August protest movement were found guilty and punished with five months' imprisonment, thus being presented as the problem (the bad guys), while the police officers who arrested and prosecuted them were presented as the solution (the good guys). Here, it was just the dramatic and evocative procession with placards and their subsequent arrest and prosecution that featured in the news discourse; what is noticeably missing is any kind of context to explain the decision and action of the women to take part in the procession that was deemed illegal. Moreover, even when the 'second prosecution witness Mr Issa Kamara, an Exhibit Clerk at the Criminal Investigation Department Headquarters tendered the placards taken from the accused persons', the protest messages inscribed on the placards could have provided some context to explain why the women processed never featured in the court proceedings or, by extension, in this news reporting. Moreover, there is no indication that the reporter or *Awoko* did follow up on the story after the court ruling by talking to relatives of the two women to find out anything that could have possibly motivated them to join the protest movement.

Politico for its part also carried a similar court story with HWJ frames titled: '3 More Sentenced over August 10 Protests in Sierra Leone' (Jalloh 26/10/2022). This also presented the three convicted protesters as 'the bad guys' who got an even harsher sentence of between 24 and 27 months with a fine of NLe 5,000. Here also they were convicted for 'unlawful processing with placards' without also providing any clue as to what was written on the placards, which was a lost opportunity to understand why they did it. We can see that for both the *Politico* and *Awoko* stories, it was a case of a zero-sum, win-lose, partial solution-orientated, and winner-takes-all kind of situation.

Conclusion

This study clearly shows that HWJ frames dominated the news media representation of the 10 August 2022 protests in some parts of Sierra Leone. Overall, the HWJ framing of the August 10 protest was far more dominant with a total of 44 frames than its binary HRJ framing with 23 frames. The analysis shows that *Politico* carried more HRJ frames than *Awoko*. Thus, while both newspapers foregrounded HWJ frames more than HRJ frames, the analysis shows that *Awoko* relatively foregrounded more HWJ frames than *Politico*. This seems to suggest that the challenges of reporting the August 10 protest from a human rights journalism lens manifested in the *Awoko* coverage more than that of the *Politico*.

Despite the dominance of HWJ in the reporting of the violent protests, the fact that HRJ frames were evident in the reporting, especially that of *Politico*, demonstrates that this journalistic practice is doable, and not just a utopian idea. The reporting of the protests in Sierra Leone provides us with a rare example of the test of human rights journalism and its opposite, human wrongs journalism, in the reporting of human rights violations in the context of protest movements. As we have seen in this case study, human rights journalism provides answers to address the challenges or limitations of the traditional reporting of human rights violations by not only looking at the physical direct forms of violence, such as beating, wounding, and killing, but also the hidden and invisible forms of violence, such as deprivation and discrimination that most often lead to the physical and direct forms of violence in the first place; by not only looking at selected but all human rights violations; by not only exposing some but all human rights violators; and finally by not only focusing on short-term but long-term solutions to human rights violations.

The results of this study demonstrate that it is not only in traditional conflict situations such as wars, civil wars, and acts of terrorism that we see the dominance of the practice of human wrongs journalism over the ideal human rights journalism. The challenges of human rights reporting are also evident in less traditional conflict situations, such as protest movements like those of August 10, 2022, in Sierra Leone. The findings of this study show that the two newspapers (*Awoko* and *Politico*) largely demonised the police who tried to calm the violent protesters in Sierra Leone as the problem and presented the protesters as the solution. This is in contrast to the demonisation of the protesters and glorification of the police in the protest movements in the 60s in the UK and the US which suggests that there is no one-size-fits-all in the reporting of protest movements. Finally, it is important to note the limited scope of this study which examined only two newspapers and a short period of time, making it difficult to draw conclusions on the challenges of reporting human rights violations under the lens of human wrongs journalism. However, it has the potential to serve as the basis for much a bigger research project in the future.

Discussion points

1. How do these differences impact the reporting of conflicts and human rights violations?
2. What are the main challenges journalists face when reporting human rights violations in conflict situations? How can the human rights journalism model address these challenges effectively?
3. How did the media in Sierra Leone report the August 10, 2022 protests compared to the 1960s protests in the UK and US?

Further reading

Ciftcioglu, Vasvi, and Ibrahim Seaga Shaw. 2021. "Peace Journalism in Times of 'War Risks': Coverage of the Hydrocarbons Conflict in Turkish Cypriot and Greek Cypriot Newspapers." *International Communication Gazette* 83 (6): 541–66. https://doi.org/10.1177/1748048520915668.

Shaw, Ibrahim Seaga. 2017. "Media, Culture and Human Rights: Towards an Intercultural Communication and Human Rights Journalism Nexus." In *Routledge Companion to Media and Human Rights*, edited by Howard Tumber and Julio Waisbord, 377–86. London: Routledge.

Shaw, Ibrahim Seaga. 2021. "The Prospects and Challenges of Mediating Peacebuilding in Africa: Towards a Human Rights Journalism Approach." In *Media, Conflicts and Peace building in Africa*, edited by Jacinta Maweu and Admire Mare. Routledge.

References

Allan, Stuart. 2012. "Foreword." In *Human Rights Journalism: Advances in Reporting Distant Humanitarian Interventions*, edited by Ibrahim Seaga Shaw. Basingstoke: Palgrave Macmillan.

Conteh, Mohamed Foday. 2022. "The Indelible Scars of August 10 in Sierra Leone." *Politico Newspaper*, August 29. Sierra Leone.

De Bonville, Jean. 2000. *Analyse de contenu des medias: de la problematique de traitment statistique*. Quebec, Canada: De Boek Université.

Entman, Robert. 1993. "Framing: Toward a Clarification of a Fractured Paradigm." *Journal of Communication* 43 (4): 51–58.

European Journal of Communication. 2013. "Distant Humanitarian Interventions." *European Journal of Communication* 28 (5): 603–4. https://doi.org/10.1177/0267323113494050d.

Fofanah, Umaru. 2022. "Sierra Leone Confirms 31 Deaths in Violent 10 August Protests." *Politico Newspaper*, September 4. Sierra Leone.

Gitlin, Todd. 1980. *The Whole World Is Watching*. Berkeley, CA: University of California Press.

Halloran, James D., Philip Elliott, and Graham Murdock. 1970. *Demonstrations and Communication: A Case Study*. Harmondsworth: Penguin Books.

Jalloh, Abass. 2022. "3 More Sentenced Over August 10 Protests in Sierra Leone." *Politico Newspaper*, October 26. Sierra Leone.

M'bayo, Ritchard Tamba. 2013. "Media and State Governance in a Post-Conflict Society: The Case of Sierra Leone." *Ecquid Novi: African Journalism Studies* 34 (2): 35–53. https://doi.org/10.1080/02560054.2013.772530.

Murdock, Graham. 1981. "Political Deviance: The Press Presentation of a Militant Mass Demonstration." In *The Manufacture of News: Deviance, Social Problems and the Mass Media*, edited by Jock Young and Stanley Cohen, 206–25. London: Constable.

Selvarajah, Senthan. 2020. *Human Rights Journalism and Its Nexus to Responsibility to Protect: How and Why the International Press Failed in Sri Lanka's Humanitarian Crisis*. Basingstoke: Palgrave Macmillan.

Sesay, Alusine. 2022. "Police Arrest 24 Kids During Wednesday's Protests." *Awoko Newspaper*, August 17. Sierra Leone.

Sesay, Suliaman. 2022. "2 Women Jailed 5 Months Each for Unlawful Procession on August 10." *Awoko Newspaper*, August 5. Sierra Leone.

Shaw, Ibrahim Seaga. 2012. *Human Rights Journalism: Advances in Reporting Humanitarian Interventions*. Basingstoke: Palgrave Macmillan.

Shaw, Ibrahim Seaga, and Senthan Selvarajah. 2019. "Human Rights Journalism: Towards a Critical Constructivism Epistemological Approach." In *Reporting Human Rights, Conflicts, and Peacebuilding: Critical and Global Perspectives*, edited by Ibrahim Seaga Shaw and Senthan Selvarajah. Basingstoke: Palgrave Macmillan.

Wilson, Alusine Rehme. 2022. "Police Confirms Death of Evangelist Samson in Alleged Crossfire." *Awoko Newspaper*, August 17. Sierra Leone.

PART III

10
REPORTING ASYMMETRICAL CONFLICT IN THE MEDIA

How poorly written stories impact the right to know

Barry Turner

Introduction

The very lifeblood of a free society is the ability of those living in it to be informed. In pluralistic democracies this is enshrined in rights and underpinned by legislation, and any erosion of this is resisted in the press, in the constitutional courts and at the ballot box in elections. It is a certainty that the absence of free expression is the hallmark of autocracy and that every other right is underpinned by democratic transparency via the free press. This chapter will challenge the role of the media in keeping people informed by studying its coverage of a perceived threat to democracy and freedom itself: that of terrorism. By examining the too-often poor quality of that content, the chapter will seek to investigate the extent to which terrorism, government, and law enforcement's counter-terrorism represent a threat to our rights to free expression and the press and media's failings in their reporting of terrorism, terrorists and the political context in which they are found.

Defining terrorism

While it is not the purpose here to redefine terrorism, some overview of the definition is required as a baseline against which we can measure the effect of the language of terrorism in the press.

Terrorism has been with us for a very long time. Historical records thousands of years old describe events we can recognise as terrorism even where the word itself is not used. A very good example is the case of the Sicarii. Following the Roman annexation of the province of Judea in 6 AD, a number of Messianic movements emerged with the aim of undermining the occupation.

The most violent, and some might argue effective, of these were the Sicarii (Silke 2014). Their targets were Roman soldiers, tax collectors, Jewish women who fraternised with Romans, Jews who worked for the Romans, Jewish shopkeepers or merchants who sold produce to the Romans – in short, anyone who in any way could be seen as supporting the occupation (Gearty 1991). Their tactics were simple. Individual terrorists would mingle with crowds at festivals and markets. Concealed in their clothing they carried daggers and without warning would strike their victims before disappearing back into the crowd. Two thousand years later, we experience the same threat. The seemingly senseless and brutal random attack on innocent victims is the very essence of terror itself.

The word 'terrorist' was first used in English by Anglo-Irish philosopher and parliamentarian Edmund Burke in 1795. It was used in denouncement of the appalling brutality that had taken place during a period in the French Revolution actually called the terror (la Terreur) in the immediate aftermath of the deposing of the absolute monarchy. Interestingly in its first use, it referred to a phenomenon that was later distinguished as state terrorism. In an almost counter-intuitive position, Burke actually approved of and supported the grievances of the American colonies in the run-up to the outbreak of the Revolutionary Wars, stating, "If that sovereignty and their freedom cannot be reconciled, which will they take? They will cast your sovereignty in your face. No body of men will be argued into slavery" (1774). Edmund Burke seemed to appreciate the distinction between a terrorist and a freedom fighter.

The Federal Bureau of Investigation (FBI) defines terrorism as "the unlawful use of force or violence against persons or property to intimidate or coerce a government or civilian population in furtherance of political or social objectives" (Pomerantz 1987). This somewhat clinical definition is in stark contrast to the wild hyperbole of the media, who talk in terms of existential threats. By contrast, "intimidate or coerce" seems more descriptive of transactional than a threat to the very existence of our society. The whole definition turns on the one word, 'unlawful', since force and even violence are frequently and legitimately used by society's agents in furtherance of political or social objectives. The definition, on closer examination, is far more problematic than its apparently measured tones imply. Unlawful force also includes peaceful demonstrations where demonstrators unlawfully block highways in furtherance of political or social objectives, leading some to argue that they also fall under the definition of terrorist. For example, according to the BBC (Farley 2024), a UK government report proposed that protest groups such as Just Stop Oil and Palestine Action should be subject to the same kind of proscription, making support for or membership in them a criminal offence. In the UK, support for proscribed organisations is itself a criminal offence, irrespective of membership or affiliation to it (Terrorism Act 2000).

However, it is quite clear that an over-zealous application of these recommendations would represent a threat to free expression. For example, in 2024, five Just Stop Oil protesters were jailed for bringing a motorway in the UK to a standstill over four days. They received the longest sentences yet handed down to members of a protest group: Four members received four years and their perceived leader was sentenced to five years. These are sentences comparable to those handed out for supporting terrorist organisations. They are considered disproportionate to the offences charged, causing considerable protest from a range of people, not all readily associated with the protest group.

The definition of terrorism is not fixed, and the events at the time of writing demonstrate being reconsidered. On the 29th of July 2024, three children were murdered, and several others and two adults were seriously injured in a knife attack at a dance class in Stockport in the UK. Circulation of misinformation on social media about the person charged with the murders being an illegal immigrant rapidly resulted in violent gangs assembling at a mosque only a short distance away from the murder scene, intent on causing injury and damage. It escalated into similar riotous disorder in several cities in the UK involving attacks directed at asylum seekers and more particularly at police, even after it was disclosed that the individual arrested for the stabbing was not believed to be a terrorist. The rioters, whose appalling behaviour was clearly orchestrated, were described as terrorists by association. Neil Basu, the former head of counter-terrorism at the Metropolitan Police, stated in a BBC interview, later reported in *The Sun*: "I think we have seen serious acts of violence designed to cause terror to a section of our community" (Goodwin 2024). He suggested that the violence in the riots crossed the line into terrorism and that the legal definition of terrorism should be reconsidered:

> Not only does it fit the definition of terrorism, it is terrorism. It's nothing short of an attempt at a modern-day lynching and the people who did it should be facing life imprisonment, not a five-year sentence for violent disorder.
>
> *(Goodwin 2024)*

According to domestic legislation, Basu is correct. The United Kingdom's approach to defining terrorism followed the model encompassed by the FBI in 1987. The definition in the Terrorism Act 2000 identifies the actions (or threats of actions) that constitute terrorism as serious violence against a person, serious damage to property, endangering a person's life, creating a serious risk to the health or safety of the public or a section of the public and actions designed to seriously interfere with or seriously disrupt an electronic system. The underlying purpose (motive) that must be present: advancing a political, religious, racial or ideological cause.

Media cliches in terrorism stories

The media's interest in terrorism is self-explanatory: news is a product, violence is news and as a product it sells well. The psychology and sociology of this have also been subjected to endless scrutiny, which has led to a similar frustration in finding answers. To put it plainly, humans 'like' bad news. In the 1950s, American psychologist and psychotherapist Dr Albert Ellis, while developing rational emotive behaviour therapy, coined the expression 'catastrophic thinking' (Ellis 1955). Ellis described this as cognitive distortion, an irrational or exaggerated form of cognition, that he also described as magnification. Rational emotive behaviour therapy was the forerunner to our modern cognitive behavioural therapy. In his model, Ellis described catastrophic thinking as 'awfulizing', imagining the worst possible scenario even where there was a logical and simple explanation for an event that had just happened. It is easy to see that much of what we consume in our modern media contains clear evidence of such thinking. The consumer of news is not only keen to seek out the 'awful' but willing to accept the 'awfulizing' being packaged and presented to them.

Along with the exaggerating of awfulness, the myth of the new and unprecedented is the stock in trade of our news media. Indeed, unprecedented is a favourite word in the media lexicon often used in a flagrantly disingenuous way to describe an event or set of circumstances as if they had never been witnessed before. For the student of media history, it is very soon evident that virtually nothing in human experience is either new or unprecedented and for the investigator into the history of the study of conflict, the age-old clichés about history repeating itself become rapidly routine.

Another famous cliché regarding the media is delivered in the negative and tells us that "no news is good news". Many people are familiar with that expression, but few are aware of its origin or context. It originates in one of the earliest publications that we today can identify as a newspaper. In March 1611 the Catholic theologian and intelligencer Paolo Sarpi wrote to Groslot, the editor of *Protestanti*, saying,

> To have no newes is good newes. It is a symptom of a placid and quiet state of affaires. The subject of newes which is most enquired for is for the most part of wars, commotions and troubles or the composing of them.
>
> *(Sarpi 1931)*

It is the second part of Sarpi's observation that is omitted from our modern use of the cliché: "The subject of news which is most enquired of is for the most part of wars and commotions". Since the beginning of our modern media in the early 17th century, that is what our press has focused upon, and terrorism along with natural disasters is today the commotion we are conditioned to most fear. There is nothing new about terrorism, any more than there is anything new about the human desire for stories of catastrophe.

Analysing the use of words and phrases in reports helps us clarify some of the failings of the press to properly give a coherent narrative to terrorists' motives and methods. Applying syntactic to the word "terrorism" involves analysing how the word functions within the structure of sentences, focusing on its grammatical relationships with other words and phrases. It also relies on a contextual understanding of the words employed. The media can apply the syntax in a number of effective ways. We can start with terrorism as a noun. In the media, it can be used as a subject, object or complement in a sentence. The story might begin with the subject "terrorism is a threat to World peace", focussing our attention on the definition of the subject. The story may go on to tell us that "the security services are fighting terrorism", the object being to develop the story either negatively or positively. For instance, it might be complemented by assurances that the security services foiled more than 50 terror plots in the last 12 months or more, 'instinctively' catastrophising it.

Adjectives can be employed to create specific types or contexts. A favourite of the media in the last 20 years has been the concept of the Islamic terrorist which has, to a large extent, superseded political freedom fighters and made them obsolete. This type of terrorist is portrayed as by far the greatest threat of all. When referring to them, the hyperbole of the press can go into overdrive. For example, the use of the adjective 'unprecedented' is applied to the maximum. 'Unprecedented barbarity', 'unprecedented threat', not to mention the unprecedented use of the word 'unprecedented'. Adjectives are the media's favourite syntactical device. Not only do they modify the type and context of terrorism, but they also distort and hideously magnify both its causes and effects. Hyperbole and the lavish deployment of adjectives, articles and determiners undermine the efforts to develop a clear definition of terrorism which can be used to tackle the problem by the security services and law enforcement. The distorted media coverage and sensationalism around terrorism create a hyperreality (Baudrillard 1983) where the terror and fear seem more pervasive and immediate than they might be in an objective sense. It can lead to heightened states of anxiety and alter public and governmental responses to terrorism. In this respect, by amplifying and distorting the terrorists' actions, the media can correctly be argued to be making their points for them.

Tropes and the reporting of terrorism

The modern media is a mixture of story and tropes. The trope is both a product of the media and an affectation of it. They are excessive use of figurative or metaphorical language combined with recurrent themes. In many cases, they are the cause of both misinformation and bias rather than conspiracy theories. The constant over-analysis of the meaning of words often leads to a self-generating speculation as to what they really mean. In order to fully understand the effect of tropes on bias and political partiality, and by extension its effect on free expression, it is necessary to examine the use of tropes in media reporting.

The categorisation of terrorism by the use of certain words and phrases creates in the minds of the reader and listener an image. Since terrorism as a method of asymmetrical warfare needs the media platforms to produce the terror, it is often the terrorists who create the trope. In some respects, this is a declaration of the brand, and the media build a trope by describing terrorism in misapplied business or public relations terminology. Al Qaeda and Islamic State (IS) have on numerous occasions been described as 'franchises' in the way they are structured. This is because, unlike many other organisations, they appear to be autonomous operations with a common ideology. They are in fact very different organisations, but since they both fall neatly under the categorisation of 'Islamic Terrorism', it is their similarities that are emphasised rather than their differences.

How the excessive use of themes and tropes affects the understanding of the consumers of media can be better understood by looking at some of the most used examples: Sophistication, radicalisation, unprecedented and existential. These words are commonly found in reports of terrorist atrocities, and their use ranges from simple misapplication and the construction of a trope to the dangerous territory of glorifying terrorism or providing material useful to terrorists. The ad nauseum use of these tropes is misleading, and where this is taken to extremes, they can turn the news story into propaganda.

Sophisticated attacks

One word that too often occurs in the reporting of terrorism is 'sophisticated'. It runs the risk of playing to the terrorists' objective, which is that of frightening the target society. Describing a brutal attack as sophisticated suggests a complex enemy who is unbeatable. This both misrepresents the organisation and its message and is fundamentally untrue. The use of the term in common usage is a compliment that sends them a message that they are successful and are achieving their aims. In two thousand years of terrorism, virtually no organisation from the Sicarii to IS have been successful against their perceived enemy, yet news stories often convey the message they are 'winning'.

Terrorist attacks are rarely if ever sophisticated. Raw violence is a more potent terrorist weapon than sophistication. Even the apparently complex, expensive and deadly attacks require little in terms of intellectual planning. Yet, they are described as 'sophisticated' by media, politicians and national security services tasked with fighting terrorism. The circumstances of the attacks on the United States on 11 September 2001 by the Islamist group Al Qaeda are well known and need no reprise here. The complexity of the attack is well recognised, including the planning and execution by multiple individuals clearly under orders from some form of central planning. There is surprisingly little sophistication about deliberately crashing an aircraft into an undefended target. The attacks could not either be described as 'unprecedented'. Suicide attacks by groups of terrorists, not to mention regular armed forces, have been around since terrorism was first recognised over two thousand years ago. The attacks did not constitute any 'existential' threat, either; no terrorist organisation in history has ever constituted a threat to the actual existence of their perceived enemy and in most cases they do not even purport to. Al Qaeda was not a sophisticated, unprecedented, existential threat at all, except to individual victims of their barbarity. Yet, on 8 December 2001, just three months after the devastating attack in September, the Federal Bureau of Investigation, quoting a witness in a trial, described Al Qaeda as 'sophisticated' and having sophisticated training systems. The use of such hyperbole would of course have been picked up by the media and run with; we might well ask if the media can be blamed in such circumstances (Turner 2007).

Some commentators argue that government public relations (PR) influence the language used in the media. Nick Davies, an investigative reporter for the *Guardian*, stated in Flat Earth News (Davies 2008) that government PR, defined as 'strategic communications', has been orchestrated by the Pentagon "which has succeeded in engineering a significant expansion of its own ability to manipulate information as a weapon" (Davies 2008, 73). Rodgers (2012) also cites several other reporters, including himself as encountering this phenomenon. It does of course immediately raise the obvious questions. Firstly, there is no obligation on the press and media to run with this line, so the government and security services cannot be held fully liable when a complicit and often lazy media simply chooses to publish rehashed press releases. Secondly and relatedly, the press can do its own thinking and fact-checking. It seems odd that in reporting conflict the view of one of the combatants would be sufficient to satisfy a vigilant reporter.

Radicalisation

Another word used with mechanical regularity is 'radicalisation'. The word 'radicalise' according to the Cambridge Online Dictionary (2024) refers to making someone become more radical (= extreme) in their political or religious beliefs. This somewhat tautological definition does not assist in grasping what meaning it conveys. The press and politicians, within minutes of a terror suspect being identified, will begin asking the question about where the individual was radicalised. The word and concept are poorly defined and the repeated use of it in conjunction with other categories, such as 'British Muslims', is in part responsible for the wider dissemination of suspicion directed at the Muslim population. Interestingly, the word is rarely used in conjunction with terrorists from other ideological or religious backgrounds. The so-called 'right-wing' rioters have to date not been described as 'radicalised'. In fact, little analysis is currently being applied to why they attack mosques and hotels, except to keep repeating the 'right-wing thug' trope. For example, in their coverage of the riots in the UK in 2024, the media repeatedly referred to them as being orchestrated by 'right-wing thugs' but stopped short of calling them terrorists. In particular, on populist TV channels, such as GBTV and in the tabloid press, there is a disturbing trend to refer to them as people whose concerns are not listened to by the government. Ironically, the very same excuse is used by extremist environmental protesters, such as Just Stop Oil.

Unprecedented

There is never anything unprecedented about human violence in either scale or barbarity, but this too is a word much employed by the press in describing both motives and methods of attack. The history of terrorism will repeatedly demonstrate that little, if anything, in either style or method is new and therefore unprecedented. The terrible reality is that conventional symmetrical warfare involves just as much savage violence, often on an extremely disproportionate scale to that deployed by the terrorist. The current war in Gaza is a terrifying case in point. In retaliation to the murderous attacks carried out by Hamas terrorists on the 7th of October 2024, killing 1200 and kidnapping 252 civilians, the Israeli Defence Force, at the time of writing, killed over 41,000 Palestinians in Gaza, the majority of them non-combatants (OCHA 2024).

Existential threat

If any word is so misapplied and overused, it has to be that of 'existential' in combination with 'threat'. Quite simply, no terrorist organisation has ever been in reality any such thing and in many cases has never sought to be. The nationalist separatist insurrectionists are not intent on destroying the occupying power but simply removing them so that they may enjoy self-determination and sovereignty. The anarchist-ideological organisations, while particularly brutal in method, have never presented any coherent ideological objective but have a tendency to speak of objectives in vague or abstract terms. This has ironically led to them being held up as stereotypical cranks or simply criminals attempting to justify actions unworthy of any excuses whatsoever. Yet, media and politicians contribute to the overuse of this term. Rather than challenge the hyperbole, they adopt it for themselves to grab headlines. For example, when a gunman with links to Islamic State extremists killed 38 people in Tunisia, then-Prime Minister David Cameron described it as an 'existential threat', without elaborating on how this organisation was capable of actually extinguishing the British way of life and the media repeated his apocalyptic predictions with little to no criticism (see Wintour and Graham-Harrison 2015; BBC News 2015).

Writing for the Royal United Services Institute, Willasey-Wilsey (2022) argued that even in the UK, which has been a target for sustained terrorist attacks for over 50 years, terrorism was a small threat compared to crime and disease. According to his paper,

> Between 1970 and 2019, the UK lost a total of 3,416 lives to terrorism, but 84% of those were linked to Northern Ireland and 271 to the Lockerbie incident. Between 2005 and 2022, 93 people have died from terrorism, an average of under 6 per annum. This compares to 695 homicides in 2020, about 1,500 deaths each year from traffic accidents, and some 25,000 from influenza and pneumonia.
>
> *(Willasey-Wilsey 2022)*

Conclusion

A common feature of the news during the 1970s and 80s was that following a terrorist incident television news reporters would interview members of political parties affiliated with the paramilitaries, such as the Provisional Irish Republican Army. The format was repeated ad nauseam with the reporter asking the spokesperson for Sinn Fein to condemn the terrorist violence. The Sinn Fein spokesperson with clockwork regularity would state they condemned all political violence, including that perpetrated by the British Army. This infuriated then-UK Prime Minister Margaret Thatcher, leading to an almost farcical policy of banning the voices of these spokespersons so they were not heard. In a speech to the American Bar Association, she stated that 'we must try to find ways to starve the terrorist and the hijacker of the oxygen of publicity on which they depend' (Thatcher 1985). As a result, a spokesperson's statement would be overdubbed using the voice of an actor speaking, often in an unconvincing Northern Irish accent. The government had used powers under the Broadcasting Act 1981 to silence proscribed organisations. The partial gag on principally Irish Republican terrorists and their spokespersons had no demonstrable effect on terrorist activity but did deny information to the public. Mrs Thatcher justified the restrictions on the freedom of speech:

> We do sometimes have to sacrifice a little of the freedom we cherish in order to defend ourselves from those whose aim is to destroy that freedom altogether and that is a decision which we should not [be] afraid to take, because in the battle against terrorism we shall never give in.
>
> *(Thatcher 1988)*

If terrorism reporting is to inform the public and by doing so ensure the purposes of free expression, there needs to be an effort by both politicians and journalists alike. Commencing with politicians, there needs to be a review of anti-terror legislation. The exhaustive anti-terror legislation developed over the late 20th century and early 21st expanded the definition of encouragement and incitement by including more indirect forms of encouragement. They closed some loopholes but also impinged on the right to free expression in ways that go well beyond providing robust laws that protect life and property.

The legislation of the 21st century, in response to the 'new' threat of 'Islamist terrorists', made it impossible for a journalist to do interviews or even fully explain the motive of the asymmetrical insurgent. Both the Terrorism Acts of 2000 and 2006 place journalists in serious danger of facing prosecution by their own country's criminal justice system, adding to the rather obvious risk of approaching violent and sometimes desperate individuals and groups. In other words, the Terrorism Acts not only created a chilling effect by making talking to terrorists a crime but also put journalists at more risk of harm from terrorism themselves.

As well as governments adopting sensible anti-terror legislation that does not frustrate the media's role in explaining the phenomenon, the journalists themselves need to reform their practices. It is the role of serious journalists to report the news, not dramatise it. The use of incessant tropes designed around catastrophising the terrorist story distracts the public and denies them access to information. Keeping people in the dark may be frequently excused by politicians, but it should never be by journalists. Parroting terminology, some of which comes from official sources, is not doing the job. In 20 years of constantly reciting the word 'radicalised', we are still not quite sure what it means. The words existential, exponential, unprecedented and sophisticated now have parallel meanings in the media lexicon to the point of meaninglessness.

For a profession whose main tool is the use of words, this laziness is letting down those who need to be informed. It has of course always been a feature of sensationalist journalism which has expanded since the era of rolling news began. The desire to have the scoop has had the effect of creating a script for the story. The reporter on the scene must cobble the story together within minutes of the latest outrage. The handy lexicon of tropes helps to achieve that at the cost of a proper analysis and accurate telling of the story. Its impact has not been to increase the effectiveness of terrorism reporting.

Discussion questions

1. What do you think of the media style of reporting political conflicts? Do they intentionally or inadvertently encourage or glorify terrorism?

2. Can the media find a way to avoid the traps of categorisation by abandoning tropes and jargon?
3. What methods could reporters employ to make the coherent narrative simultaneously an explanatory narrative?

Further reading

Kearns, Erin M., and Amarnath Amarasingam. 2019. "How News Media Talk About Terrorism: What the Evidence Shows." *Just Security*, April 5. https://www.justsecurity.org/63499/how-news-media-talk-about-terrorism-what-the-evidence-shows/.

Marthoz, Jean-Paul. 2017. *Terrorism and the Media: A Handbook for Journalists*. UNESCO. https://unesdoc.unesco.org/ark:/48223/pf0000247074.

White, Jessica. 2020. "Terrorism and the Mass Media." *RUSI*, May 12. https://www.rusi.org/explore-our-research/publications/occasional-papers/terrorism-and-mass-media.

References

Baudrillard, Jean. 1983. *Simulations*. New York: Semiotext.

BBC News. 2015. "Tunisia Attack: Cameron Says IS Fight 'Struggle of Our Generation'." *The BBC News*, June 29. https://www.bbc.co.uk/news/uk-33307279.

Davies, Nick. 2008. *Flat Earth News: An Award-Winning Reporter Exposes Falsehood, Distortion and Propaganda in the Global Media*. London: Chatto & Windus.

Ellis, Albert. 1955. "New Approaches to Psychotherapy Techniques." *Journal of Clinical Psychology* 11 (3): 207–60.

Farley, Harry. 2024. "'Extreme' Protest Groups Face Ban Under Proposal." *The BBC*, May 12. https://www.bbc.co.uk/news/articles/c2qv7425gvwo.

Gearty, Conor A. 1991. *Terror*. London: Faber and Faber.

Goodwin, Harry. 2024. "Tough Punishment Riot Yobs Face Terror Charges, Britain's Top Prosecutor Says After Cops Hit With Petrol Bombs & Bricks in Carnage." *The Sun*, August 6. https://www.thesun.co.uk/news/29710529/violent-rioting-terrorism-met-terror/.

OCHA (The United Nations Office for the Coordination of Humanitarian Affairs). 2024. "Reported Impact Snapshot|Gaza Strip (18 September 2024)." *OCHA*, September 18. https://www.ochaopt.org/content/reported-impact-snapshot-gaza-strip-18-september-2024.

Pomerantz, Steven L. 1987. "The FBI and Terrorism." *FBI Law Enforcement Bulletin* 56 (11): 14–17.

Rodgers, James. 2012. *Reporting Conflict*. London: Chatto & Windus.

Sarpi, Paolo. 1931. "Letter to Groslot, March 29, 1611." In *Lettere ai Protestanti*, edited by Manlio Duilio Busnelli, Vol. 1. Bari: Laterza.

Silke, A. 2014. "Risk Assessment of Terrorist and Extremist Prisoners." In *Prisons, Terrorism and Extremism: Critical Issues in Management, Radicalisation and Reform*, edited by A. Silke, 108–21. London: Routledge.

Terrorism Act 2000, Part II. "S12. Support." https://www.legislation.gov.uk/ukpga/2000/11/section/12.

Terrorism Act 2006, Part 1. "Encouragement etc. of Terrorism." https://www.legislation.gov.uk/ukpga/2006/11/part/1.

Thatcher, Margaret. 1985. "Speech to American Bar Association." *Margaret Thatcher Foundation*, July 15. Accessed August 25, 2024. https://www.margaretthatcher.org/document/106096

Thatcher, Margaret. 1988. "Speech at Lord Mayor's Banquet." *Margaret Thatcher Foundation*, November 14. https://www.margaretthatcher.org/document/107380.

Turner, Barry. 2007. "Reporting Extremism: Why Do We Still Want to Shoot the Messenger?" *Ethical Space: The International Journal of Communication Ethics* 4 (3): 11–12.

Willasey-Wilsey, Tim. 2022. "Terrorism is Less of an Existential Threat Than Russia and China." *RUSI*, July 28. https://rusi.org/explore-our-research/publications/commentary/terrorism-less-existential-threat-russia-and-china.

Wintour, Patrick, and Emma Graham-Harrison. 2015. "Tunisia Attack: David Cameron Pledges 'Full Spectrum' Response to Massacre." *The Guardian*, June 29. https://www.theguardian.com/uk-news/2015/jun/29/tunisia-attack-david-cameron-pledges-full-spectrum-response-to-massacre.

11
JOURNALISM AND DISAPPEARANCES IN MÉXICO

Siria Gastelum and Darwin Franco

Introduction

The rise in disappearances in Mexico highlights a serious human rights crisis that underscores significant shortcomings in the rule of law and ongoing struggles to address widespread violence in the country. This crisis has been largely driven by several factors, including the growth of macrocriminal networks and the federal government's declaration of war on drug trafficking in 2006 (Reguillo 2021).

The problem gained international notoriety with the disappearance of 43 students from Ayotzinapa in the state of Guerrero on September 26, 2014, highlighting the involvement of both state and non-state criminal actors. It also became more visible due to the efforts of the "searching mothers" who, faced with the ineffectiveness of the Mexican state, took to the streets to protest and search for their missing loved ones.

In this regard, the media and journalists, especially freelancers, have played a crucial role in supporting the demands of the searching families and making visible the multiple human rights violations committed against the victims of disappearance and their families. A community of journalists has accompanied the more than 100 search groups for missing persons that have formed across the countries. Alongside the families, these journalists have dedicated themselves to using their profession to aid in the search and bring attention to this critical issue.

Disappearances are a social and public security problem intertwined with the activities of organized crime groups and the state's omission to address them. For those journalists who seek to understand why and how a person disappears, these events are not isolated incidents or personal or family issues but part of a network of structural violence that has turned this crime against humanity into a strategy of terror, allowing criminals to control and dominate crucial territories for the trafficking of illicit goods (Franco 2019).

The dynamics of violence and repression have also significantly impacted the media, rendering Mexico one of the most dangerous countries for journalists globally. This chapter examines how disappearances have influenced Mexican journalism and explores how journalists' work has become a crucial resource for victims of human rights violations, in particular for those searching for their disappeared loved ones.

Disappearing in Mexico, challenging narratives and the "official truth"

According to the International Convention for the Protection of All Persons from Enforced Disappearance, enforced disappearance is defined as:

> the arrest, detention, abduction, or any other form of deprivation of liberty by agents of the State or by persons or groups acting with the authorization, support, or acquiescence of the State, followed by a refusal to acknowledge the deprivation of liberty or by concealment of the fate or whereabouts of the disappeared person, which places such a person outside the protection of the law.
> *(UN 1993)*

Enforced disappearances are considered a crime against humanity under international law when committed as part of a widespread or systematic attack against a civilian population. They violate multiple human rights enshrined in various international instruments, including the Universal Declaration of Human Rights, the International Covenant on Civil and Political Rights, and the International Convention for the Protection of All Persons from Enforced Disappearance.

The Mexican State currently acknowledges the disappearance of 115,146 individuals, comprising 88,023 men, 26,576 women, and 546 individuals of unknown gender (Registro Nacional de Personas Desaparecidas y No Localizadas [RNPDNO] 2024).[1] Most of these individuals have gone missing since December 11, 2006, the date when former President of Mexico Felipe Calderon declared war against organized crime.

Despite these alarming statistics, during the administrations of Felipe Calderon (2006–2012) and Enrique Pena Nieto (2012–2018), the Mexican State systematically denied the existence of a human rights crisis. They repeatedly assured international bodies such as the Inter-American Court of Human Rights and the Office of the High Commissioner for Human Rights of the United Nations that there was no humanitarian crisis in the country due to violence (Vizcarra and Tzuc 2021).

Conversely, the government of Andres Manuel Lopez Obrador (2018–2024) acknowledged the human rights crisis in the country and the

State's responsibility for generating thousands of victims. However, there was no shift in the security strategy from his predecessors, and the number of disappearances continued to increase.

The historical context adds specific nuances to the phenomenon of disappearances in sociopolitical and sociocultural terms. The somewhat generic definition of disappearance and missing persons in international human rights treaties and legislation no longer encompasses all current forms of disappearance. These forms, which extend beyond the traditional designation of detainees-disappeared, reveal another type of disappearance orchestrated by crime and drug trafficking (Dulitzky 2016). Failing to consider the broad economic, political, and cultural panorama in which disappearances occur overlooks the growing instrumentalization of disappearances by organized crime and its negotiations with the state (Franco 2022). Consequently, this phenomenon tends to receive limited attention in public policy agendas, making it difficult to recognize victims and ensure their access to justice (Barooah et al. 2024).

Journalism plays a crucial explanatory and educational role in reporting disappearances, counteracting the official narrative that pretends to: 1) deny the existence of disappearances, 2) criminalize the victims of disappearance, and 3) minimize the search efforts carried out by families.

Journalists reporting on disappearances in Mexico devote considerable effort to dismantling "official truths" that obscure the state's role in the ongoing human rights crisis. Government narratives often criminalize victims and suggest that disappearances are the result of individuals' involvement with criminal organizations, reinforcing a binary narrative that separates the state from these groups.

Journalists challenge these narratives by collaborating with searching families and writing stories that portray the disappeared as individuals with dreams and aspirations, rather than mere judicial files or criminal statistics under different definitions, depending on the jurisdictions where this took place. To accurately portray the story of the disappeared, Mexican journalists bolster their reporting with academic research on disappearances in Latin America. They elucidate the symbols associated with the search for missing people, the psychosocial effects endured by searchers, and the empowerment of searching families who have evolved into human rights defenders over the years (Robledo 2017).

Navigating these complexities has been challenging for Mexican journalists. They have had to learn through personal pain and by assuming the same risks as the searching families. In this context, journalists themselves are criminalized, stigmatized, and attacked.

The victimization of journalists and their search for hope

According to Article 19, an international civil society organization, 164 journalists have been murdered, and 32 more have been missing in Mexico since

2000. In 2022, there was one attack against journalists or media houses every 13 hours, making Mexico one of the most dangerous countries for journalism worldwide (Articulo 19 2024).

The report "Voices Against Indifference" (Articulo 19 2022) indicates that 42% of attacks against journalists are committed by government officials, followed by criminal actors and private entities. The state itself poses the greatest threat to journalists' lives and dignity. These attacks often go unpunished, as authorities rarely investigate them and seldom link journalistic activity as a possible motive for the crime.

Márquez Ramírez (2023) emphasizes that in Mexico, symbolic violence against journalists and media, similar to direct violence, often originates from public officials. These officials use institutional communication mechanisms to discredit journalists who criticize or question government actions or decisions, frequently without substantiated evidence.

In the context of reporting on disappearances, this manifests when those in power downplay reports or investigations that reveal issues such as the statistical manipulation of the national registry of missing persons (Tzuc 2024). During his daily morning conferences, the president regularly denounces what he perceives as media attacks against his government. Government officials then refute journalistic investigations on live television and expose the personal information of reporters covering organized crime and corruption.

Covering disappearances in Mexico generally exposes journalists to direct violence. Perpetrators of this crime, including members of the Mexican state and organized crime, frequently threaten and harass journalists investigating the corruption and criminal networks behind these disappearances.

There is a significant gender component in violence against journalists in Mexico. According to the organization *Comunicación e Información de la Mujer* (The Women's Communication and Information) (CIMAC 2023), violence against women journalists has increased fivefold, with state officials being the main aggressors. This is particularly relevant in the context of covering disappearances, as women journalists are often the ones most closely accompanying the families of missing persons in their search and demand for justice.

Additionally, the limited resources available to cover disappearances may result in the publication of low-quality investigations. This situation also exposes journalists to lawsuits and other forms of harassment or attacks by authorities and criminals involved. Journalists focusing on disappearances often work under precarious conditions, facing low salaries, lack of benefits, job insecurity, and limited access to services such as housing and health (Del Palacio 2023, 17). What journalists experience mirrors some of the struggles of the families of the disappeared. Both groups face significant security risks and lack the economic resources to support their efforts, often relying on their own financial means and assuming all associated risks.

In response to this, a grassroots collective solution has emerged. Journalists who actively support the families of the disappeared have also committed to supporting, caring for, and training one another to ensure more ethical and safe coverage, with a focus on human rights.

Within this community, journalists have embraced their roles as human rights defenders. They recognize that their reporting on disappearances is highly socially relevant, not only for raising awareness of the issue but also for highlighting the structural violence that perpetuates these disappearances as an instrument of terror.

This solidarity stems from their shared experiences of accompanying families, acknowledging their own vulnerabilities, and striving for mutual physical and emotional well-being. Their goal is to use journalism as a tool for both search and hope.

The movements: families and journalists working together

Social organizations around the search for missing persons in Mexico date back to 1970, when the Committee of Family Members in Defense of Political Prisoners was formed in Guadalajara. According to journalist Guillén (2016), this was "one of the first organizations fighting against repression during the period known as the Dirty War."

The "Dirty War" in Mexico refers to a period from the late 1960s to the early 1980s characterized by state-sponsored violence and repression. Government authorities engaged in widespread human rights abuses, including forced disappearances, torture, and extrajudicial killings, targeting alleged political dissidents and social activists. Officially justified as a response to leftist guerrilla movements and national security threats, the victims often included innocent civilians such as students, intellectuals, and community organizers.

State-sponsored violence had a lasting impact on society, prompting civil society to seek justice and improve human rights protections. Since the "Dirty War," families of the disappeared, especially mothers, have organized with support from independent left-wing media. Notable media outlets include *Madera*, *El Martillo*, *Regeneración*, *Punto Crítico* (Mexico City), and *El Debate* (Guadalajara), which built trust with families by avoiding stigmatization. Disappearances persisted from 1980 to 2000 with minimal media coverage, until a resurgence of disappearances occurred after Felipe Calderón came to power in 2006.

In contemporary Mexico, three significant milestones are considered crucial for understanding the movement and struggle of the families of the disappeared: 1) Former President Felipe Calderón's declaration of war against organized crime, 2) The March for Peace led by poet Javier Sicilia on May 5, 2011, and 3) The forced disappearance of 43 students from the Ayotzinapa Rural Normal School in Guerrero on September 26, 2014.

The unilateral declaration of war against organized crime by Felipe Calderón on December 7, 2006, is viewed by various search collectives as the moment when disappearances began to be employed as a terror tactic (Fundenl 2016). Unlike disappearances during the "Dirty War," these were driven not by political-ideological motives but by territorial control and the establishment of large-scale criminal networks focused on drug trafficking and other illicit activities (Barooah et al. 2024).

A significant turning point in the "war on drugs" occurred on April 26, 2011, when Juan Francisco Sicilia, son of poet Javier Sicilia, was murdered by organized crime in Morelos. In response, the poet called for a national movement to end state violence in Mexico. This call led to the March for Peace on May 5, 2011, from Morelos to the Zócalo in Mexico City, uniting thousands of victims demanding justice for their murdered loved ones and the search for their missing relatives.

The monumental march led to the formation of the victims-led National Movement for Peace with Justice and Dignity. A key initiative was the Caravan for Peace, launched on September 9, 2011, which amplified victims' voices across various cities. Marcela Turati, a pioneering journalist in victim coverage in Mexico, reflects on the significance of this moment for the journalistic community:

> At that moment, we didn't grasp what the March and later the Caravan would mean for our work. We weren't prepared to cover the war, to understand the pain of so many people telling you the horror of the violence that, at that time, seemed distant to those of us practicing journalism in Mexico City. We truly didn't know what to do, so we listened, cried, and began to understand that we had to organize ourselves to report the pain, to support the victims through journalism.
> *(Turati, Personal communication, November 28, 2023)*

The movement prompted former President Felipe Calderón to engage in Peace Dialogues with victims, though he failed to fully acknowledge his administration's actions. Despite serious setbacks, such as the assassination of members, the movement persisted and inspired other collectives to be more active and vocal on the national stage. This culminated in the publication of the General Law for Victims in 2013, which recognized the state's responsibilities and victims' rights.

Concurrently, a network of journalists arose to support the search efforts of these collectives. One notable network was "Periodistas de A Pie" (On Foot Journalists) founded in 2007 by Marcela Turati with the aim of enhancing the quality of journalism in Mexico through training and the exchange of investigative techniques. Specifically, the organization sought to adopt a human rights perspective in journalistic coverage, an approach often lacking in mainstream reporting on victims of violence.

> Those of us in the Network, or even outside of it, began to notice that we had to educate ourselves on how to cover pain in better ways, to avoid revictimizing or criminalizing . . . I was concerned about that, but also about the safety and emotional stability of those covering . . . so I started calling them to discuss what we could do to continue supporting families.
> *(Turati, Personal communication, November 28, 2023)*

On September 26 and 27, 2014, Mexico witnessed one of the most harrowing episodes in its history of disappearances. Forty-three students from the Rural Normal School "Raúl Isidro Burgos" in Ayotzinapa, Guerrero, were forcibly taken by members of the municipal police of Iguala and Cocula, who subsequently handed them over to organized crime.

This event sparked a nationwide outcry, not only due to the sheer number of victims (later augmented by the deaths of three students) but also because of the apparent complicity of state actors. Thousands of people mobilized both within Mexico and abroad, demanding the safe return of all the abducted students.

The parents of the 43 students embarked on a cross-country journey in caravans, thrusting the issue of disappearances into the public spotlight like never before. In response, the Mexican government propagated an "official truth" narrative, asserting, without credible forensic evidence, that the students had been murdered and incinerated by members of organized crime.

This narrative was met with widespread skepticism and condemnation, as no substantive evidence was presented to substantiate these claims. Desperate for justice, the families of the students turned to international organizations for intervention, resulting in the establishment of the Inter-American Commission on Human Rights' Group of Independent Experts. After years of investigation, this group not only debunked the government's "official truth" but also classified the students' disappearance as a state crime, a case that remains unresolved to this day.

For journalism and the Mexican media landscape, the disappearance of the 43 students marked a significant turning point, thrusting disappearances into the forefront of news agendas. Families of thousands of disappeared victims seized upon this moment to demand that authorities devote similar resources and efforts to locate their missing loved ones.

In the ensuing years, two pivotal developments occurred in civil society. First, the *Movimiento Nacional por Nuestros Desaparecidos en México* (National Movement for Our Disappeared in Mexico) was established in 2015, comprising 35 search collectives dedicated to locating the disappeared and advocating for Mexico's first General Law on disappearances. Second, National Search Brigades were initiated, involving family members and volunteers conducting collaborative search efforts across the country.

These events facilitated the formation of a network of journalists covering the search brigades and their push for legislative reforms. These journalists worked closely with families, gathering testimonies and participating in field searches at clandestine gravesites and forensic facilities. Out of this collaboration emerged *A dónde van los desaparecidos* (Where do the disappeared go), the first specialized journalism project dedicated to disappearance coverage in Mexico.

From the collective learning and the need for specialized coverage of disappearances, *A dónde van los desaparecidos* emerged as more than a communication outlet. It became a haven for journalists dedicated to this cause, providing a platform to share their work and insights. This network evolved into a forum for collective reflection on sustaining investigative coverage and deepening understanding of these issues (A dónde van los desaparecidos 2019).

The group defines itself as

> a consortium of journalists hailing from diverse regions of Mexico, united in their commitment to reporting on disappearances through the lenses of memory and human rights, shedding light on the dynamics of disappearances in our nation and the arduous quests undertaken by families in search of their missing loved ones.
>
> *(A dónde van los desaparecidos 2019)*

Their mission, as articulated by the group, is twofold:

> A platform serving as a repository of memories and a real-time archive concerning the issue of disappearances in Mexico. Through this, our aim is to weave a shared understanding of the ongoing war, approaching it critically in contrast to the dominant narrative.

The role of 'A dónde van los desaparecidos' is profound, and as underscored by Barooah, Oliveira and Gastélum (2024, 13), "Journalism has played a key role in amplifying the voices of victims and communities, challenging official narratives and forcing authorities to address the issue."

Other journalistic endeavors, such as *ZonaDocs* in Jalisco, *Narrativas Dignas* in San Luis Potosí, and *Hasta Encontrarles* in Sinaloa, have proliferated. Similar to 'A dónde van los desaparecidos,' these platforms have been instrumental not only in reshaping the discourse around disappearances but also in challenging mainstream media to incorporate disappearance coverage into their news agendas. Through localized and nationwide investigations, they have questioned the official narrative, which either downplayed the severity of the issue or, worse yet, blamed the victims for their own disappearance.

However, these initiatives and collaborative networks have not been immune to challenges such as heightened risk, violence, and attacks. They also grapple with psychosocial impacts, including vicarious trauma, wherein journalists experience emotional distress as if the pain they cover is happening to them. As journalist Marcos Vizcarra, a member of *A donde van los desaparecidos*, attests:

> At some point, we had to acknowledge that we were not okay, that we had to talk about what we felt . . . acknowledge that we couldn't continue believing that nothing was happening to us; so we talked, listened to each other, and collectively sought help.
> *(Vizcarra, Personal communication, November 13, 2023)*

A symbiotic relationship has emerged between journalists collaborating to report on disappearances and the organized efforts of searching families. Journalists have gleaned insights into the complexities of searching for missing persons directly from those impacted, learning with them how to search for people and how to sensitively approach victims. Concurrently, families have acquired valuable information-gathering skills from journalists, fostering a mutually beneficial exchange of knowledge.

An illustrative example of this collaboration is the joint creation of independent databases documenting missing persons and clandestine graves. These regional records, compiled by both journalists and searching families, have facilitated the development of maps and virtual repositories containing comprehensive findings from families' search efforts.

Additionally, memory-focused projects have been initiated in locations where missing individuals have been tragically discovered, such as clandestine graves or abandoned extermination sites (locations where criminals carry out systematic killings or executions, usually of members of rival gangs). Journalists and searching families have collaborated to reframe and preserve the remains of those recovered.

For example, the organization *Técnicas Rudas* (Rough Techniques) trains local media to develop new narratives that combat the stigma surrounding victims of disappearance within a journalistic language.[2] Additionally, it facilitates the creation of technological platforms for information projects that humanize the victims, aiming to preserve their lives and memories. This approach aligns with UN recommendations on reporting and educating society about these crimes.

A case study: *Hasta Encontrarles* (until we find them)

The *Hasta Encontrarles* project originated in Culiacán, Mexico, in 2018, in response to the pressing need to transform the narratives surrounding disappearances. Leveraging memory as a tool, the project aimed to bolster the resilience of families of the disappeared while shedding light on the prevalence

FIGURE 11.1A AND B   Mural for missing people in Culiacán, Sinaloa

Source: Siria Gastelum

of disappearances in Sinaloa and the struggles faced by search collectives in the region.

This initiative was spearheaded by a group of journalists who had been covering disappearances in Sinaloa since 2016, in collaboration with mothers

FIGURE 11.1A AND B (Continued)

of the victims from collectives such as "Las Rastreadoras de El Fuerte (The Trackers of El Fuerte)" and "Sabuesos Guerreras de Culiacán (Culiacán Warrior Hounds)."

One of the founders, journalist Marcos Vizcarra, developed close personal relationships with the women from these groups by joining their field searches across the Sonora Desert and other rural and urban areas of northern Mexico. He accompanied them to autopsies, funerals, and court cases. Motivated by empathy and a shared frustration with the authorities' indifference, he proposed a series of personal narratives told by mothers of the disappeared to his newspaper, Noroeste (Vizcarra, Personal communication, November 13, 2023).

At the mothers' behest, Vizcarra secured permission from Noroeste to use a wall of their office building to paint the faces of their missing children. With the assistance of artist *El Dante*, the *Hasta Encontrarles* project was born, with the goal of empowering families of the disappeared with new tools to share their stories and dignify the memories of their loved ones.

Reflecting on the project's inception, Vizcarra noted the prevailing narrative surrounding disappearances, which often portrayed victims either as casualties of organized crime or as individuals who had voluntarily absconded to avoid financial or familial responsibilities.[3] The journalists behind *Hasta Encontrarles* sought to broaden this narrative, humanizing the disappeared and challenging the stigmatizing discourse perpetuated by the state (Vizcarra, Personal communication, November 13, 2023).

The Noroeste mural quickly became a monthly gathering place for mothers seeking solace and solidarity in their shared grief. In 2020, the collective of artists and journalists launched *HastaEncontrarles.com* (website), with support from the Resilience Fund and other international organizations. The site featured the first detailed map of clandestine graves in the state, with families actively involved in its creation and dissemination.

A fundamental aspect of the narrative shift facilitated by *Hasta Encontrarles* was the active involvement of searching families in crafting their stories for the media. The project served as a transformative model, providing families with tools and resources to advocate for their cause effectively while fostering unity among search collectives and overcoming communication barriers often imposed by authorities.

Hasta Encontrarles demonstrated that disappearance could be reported and understood through a human rights lens, to restore identity and dignity to the victims in their narratives. María Isabel Cruz Bernal, mother of Yosimar García Cruz and leader of the *Sabuesos Guerreras de Culiacán* (Culiacán Warrior Hounds), emphasized the crucial role journalists played in amplifying the voices of the families and bringing their plight to international attention.

> Journalists play a very important role because without them, we would have no voice. They have given us a voice; they have made us known internationally. Since I discovered that journalists were allies in what I was doing, I used them and have used them as much as I could . . . with *Hasta Encontrarles*, there was already total involvement . . . but they sought another way to document it, they documented it with sensitivity, with respect, with everything to avoid revictimizing the victims . . . for me, *Hasta Encontrarles* set a precedent in the search for the disappeared.
> *(Cruz Bernal, Personal communication, February 12, 2024)*

Similarly, journalists involved in *Hasta Encontrarles* underscored the invaluable lessons they learned from the families of the disappeared, As Vizcarra explained, journalists have learned from the families of the disappeared about the importance of collective actions. This way of working together has pushed journalists to collaborate and join forces to also denounce human rights violations against journalists (Vizcarra, Personal communication, November 13, 2023).

The solidarity has been reciprocal; in Culiacán when a journalist is attacked, the mothers of the disappeared stand behind the journalist's causes. They have joined journalists to protest the assassination of their colleagues, marching in the streets and supporting their quest for justice.

The future of a disappearing story

Reporting on disappearances has become increasingly challenging, reflecting the mounting risks to journalists. The stories about disappearances are vulnerable to disappearing from the news media agenda and from the government policies that aim to reduce services for victims under false claims of financial restraint. Speaking about disappearances is a contentious topic disliked by criminals and authorities alike.

For journalists in Mexico, silence is not an option. They are creating spaces for dialogue, innovating storytelling techniques, and developing new investigative tools to convey the painful stories many are weary of hearing. These journalists are organizing to protect themselves and share lessons with colleagues in Mexico and other countries beginning to cover disappearances.

Hasta Encontrarles stands as a testament to the power of collaborative journalism, challenging the status quo and demanding justice. It vividly reminds us that every story told, every mural painted, and every voice amplified contributes to a collective narrative calling the world to listen, act, and join the search until the missing are found.

The relevance of journalism amidst Mexico's severe crisis of disappearances is unquestionable. We are aware of the staggering scale of these crimes because journalists have risked their lives to report on them. The future of storytelling hinges on the protection of these journalists. The cost of being a journalist in Mexico is extraordinarily high, affecting their families and communities. Initiatives must also address the emotional toll on those covering these stories.

Innovative initiatives like *Hasta Encontrarles* and collaborative efforts like A dónde van los desaparecidos contribute to the understanding of the disappearance phenomenon, the location of missing people, as well as official and community-based resilience responses. They not only aid in comprehending the profound issue at hand, but also challenge the dominant (official) narratives that seek to downplay the involvement of state actors in crime and their persecution.

The future of journalism is the future of justice. Journalists in Mexico are documenting the magnitude of human-rights violations, corruption, and criminal violence. It is imperative to guarantee free speech and access to information, to keep authorities accountable and to prevent what can be prevented.

It is crucial to consider alternative ways of covering disappearances, devising new strategies, and crafting narratives that center around searching families and all the missing individuals. Initiatives must also address the emotional toll on those covering these stories. The successful pursuit of the search cause, locating the missing, can only be achieved through collaborative efforts.

The future of stories, as highlighted by projects like A dónde van los desaparecidos and *Hasta Encontrarles*, lies in the creation of journalistic endeavors that transform narratives and preserve the memory of this massive tragedy.

This type of collaborative journalism has offered us the real-data archives documenting the disappearance of individuals in Mexico, emphasizing the importance of remembering, understanding, and actively engaging with this profound human crisis.

Discussion questions

- What does it mean for journalists to cover the disappearance of people in one of the most dangerous countries for journalists?
- How would you describe the interaction between journalists and the families of the disappeared?
- How does this relationship affect journalists' practices when covering disappearances? How do you define their journalism?

Further Reading

"A dónde van los desaparecidos [Where Do the Disappeared Go]." https://adondevanlosdesaparecidos.org.

Gisbert, Manuel Bayo. 2024. "Looking for the Missing People of Mexico." *International New York Times*, May 28.

"Observatorio sobre Desaparición e Impunidad en México [Observatory on Disappearance and Impunity in Mexico]." https://odim.juridicas.unam.mx.

"Volver a desaparecer [Disappear Again]." https://volveradesaparecer.datacivica.org.

Notes

1. Statistics as of June 17, 2024.
2. Here are two examples of the work of this organization: *Narrativas y Memoria* (Narratives and Memory of the disappearance in Mexico): https://www.narrativasymemorias.org and *Desaparecer en pandemia* (Disappear in pandemic): https://desaparecerenpandemia.org.
3. Mothers searching for their missing children often recount similar experiences when reporting disappearances to authorities. They are frequently told their sons must be involved in criminal activity and are blamed for their responsibility. When women go missing, authorities often assure mothers that they must have "run away" with their partners. In cases of young missing children, authorities tend to minimize the situation, attributing it to disputes between fighting parents.

References

A dónde van los desaparecidos. [Where the Disappeared Go]. 2019. "Acerca de." https://adondevanlosdesaparecidos.org/nosotros/.

Artículo 19. 2022. *Voces contra la indiferencia.* [Voices Against Indifference]. Informe Anual 2022. México: Artículo 19. https://articulo19.org/wp-content/uploads/2023/03/Voces-contra-la-Indiferencia-INF-A19-22-PDF-Prel-vf.pdf.

Artículo 19. 2024. *Periodistas asesinados y desaparecidos en México* [Journalists Assassinated and Disappeared in Mexico]. https://articulo19.org/periodistasasesinados/.
Barooah, R., A. Oliveira, and S. Gastélum. 2024. *We Just Want to Find Our Children 'Understanding Disappearances as a Tool of Organized Crime'*. Switzerland: Global Initiative Against Transnational Organized Crime.
CIMAC. 2023. *Palabras impunes: Estigmatización y violencia contra mujeres periodistas en México* [Unpunished Words: Stigmatisation and Violence Against Female Journalists in Mexico]. 2019–2022. México: CIMAC.
Comisión Nacional de Búsqueda de Personas (CNB). 2022. "Personas desaparecidas y no localizadas por año [Disappeared and Untraced Persons by Year]." https://versionpublicarnpdno.segob.gob.mx/Dashboard/Sociodemografico.
Cruz Bernal, M. 2024. Personal communication, February 12, 2024.
Del Palacio, C. 2023. *El estado de la libertad de expresión y violencia contra periodistas en Jalisco*, [The State of Free Speech and Violence Against Journalists in Jalisco]. En *El estado de la libertad de expresión en Jalisco [The State of Free Speech in Jalisco]*, Coord. C. Del Palacio, 12–32. México: Universidad de Guadalajara.
Dulitzky, A. 2016. *Derechos humanos en Latinoamérica y el Sistema Interamericano Modelos para (des)armar [Human Rights in Latin America and the Inter-American System Models for (Dis)arming]*. México: Instituto de Estudios Constitucionales de Querétaro.
Familias Unidas por Nuestros Desaparcidos Nuevo León (Fundenl). 2016. *La presencia de la ausencia. Historias de personas desaparecidas y reflexiones en torno a la desaparición en México [The Presence of the Absence. Stories of Missing People and Reflections on Disappearances in Mexico]*. México: Universidad Autónoma de Nuevo León (UANL).
Franco, D. 2019. "The Quadruple Disappearance: Analytical Proposal to Reflect the Social and Media Representation of the Victims of Disappearance in Jalisco, Mexico." *Revista Políticas, Globalidad y Ciudadanía* 5 (9): 80–97. http://revpoliticas.uanl.mx/index.php/RPGyC/article/view/113.
Franco, D. 2022. *Tecnologías de la Esperanza. Apropiaciones Tecnológicas para la búsqueda de las personas desaparecidas en México [Technologies of Hope: Technological Appropriations for the Search for the Disappeared in Mexico]*. México: Tintable.
Guillén, A. 2016. "Jalisco, tierra de desaparición y colectivos de búsqueda [Jalisco, Land of Disappearances and Search and Rescue Collectives for Missing Persons]." https://christus.jesuitasmexico.org/jalisco-tierra-de-desaparicion-y-colectivos-de-busqueda/.
Márquez-Ramírez, M. 2023. "Mapping Anti-Press Violence in Latin America: Challenges for Journalists 'Safety'." In *The Routledge Companion to News and Journalism*, edited by S. Allan, 2a edición. Routledge.
Registro Nacional de Personas Desaparecidas y No Localizadas (RNPDNO). 2024. *Informe estadístico [Statistical Report]*. Ciudad de México: Secretaría de Gobernación. https://rnped.segob.gob.mx/
Reguillo, R. 2021. *Necromáquina: cuando morirse no es suficiente [Necromachine: When Dying Is Not Enough]*. Madrid: Ned Editores.
Robledo, C. 2017. *Drama social y política del duelo. Las desapariciones de la guerra contra las drogas en Tijuana [Social Drama and the Politics of Grief: The Disappearances From the Drug War in Tijuana]*. Ciudad de México: El Colegio de México.
Turati, M. 2023. Personal Communication, November 28, 2023.
Tzuc, E. 2024. "Decenas de personas 'localizadas' por el Gobierno siguen desaparecidas" [Dozens of People 'Found' by the Government Are Still Absent]. https://adondevanlosdesaparecidos.org/2024/03/06/decenas-de-personas-localizadas-por-el-gobierno-siguen-desaparecidas/.
UN. 1993. Resolución 47/133. "Declaración sobre la protección de todas las personas contra las desapariciones forzadas [1993 Resolution 47/133. Declaration on the Protection of All Persons From Enforced Disappearance]." http://www.un.org/es/comun/docs/?symbol=A/RES/47/133&Lang=S.

Vizcarra, M. 2023. Personal communication, November 13.
Vizcarra, M., and E. Tzuc. 2021. "En México, las desapariciones continúan, son generalizadas y siguen en la impunidad: Comité de la ONU" [In Mexico, Disappearances Continue, Are Widespread and Remain Unpunished: UN Committee]. https://adondevanlosdesaparecidos.org/2021/11/26/en-mexico-las-desapariciones-continuan-son-generalizadas-y-siguen-en-la-impunidad-comite-de-la-onu/.

12
REPORTING ON CLIMATE CHANGE THROUGH THE LENS OF HUMAN RIGHTS

Jhesset Thrina Enano

Introduction

When Super Typhoon Haiyan slammed into Eastern Visayas in central Philippines in November 2013, newspaper journalist DJ Yap recalled it was akin to meeting a monster. A longtime reporter of the English broadsheet *Philippine Daily Inquirer*, Yap was no stranger to covering typhoons – a perennial hazard for the archipelago sitting on the western Pacific Ocean. But Haiyan, locally known in the Philippines as "Yolanda," was no ordinary typhoon. Yap arrived in Tacloban City in Leyte province a day before the storm's expected landfall. In the early morning of November 8, 2013, he and photojournalist Niño Jesus Orbeta woke up to howling winds and booming sounds as Haiyan began to unleash its fury on the city. In an essay published 10 days after their ordeal, Yap recalled: "In the darkness we listened in silence to Yolanda's roar."

After the typhoon passed, the two journalists documented the harrowing destruction that the typhoon left in its wake: dead and decaying bodies on the streets, collapsed buildings, and little to no food and water for thousands of people reeling in shock and grief.

Yap, now an editor for the newspaper, recalled in his essay:

> I arrived in Tacloban a veteran reporter of disasters, mistakenly believing I had seen it all. I left the broken city humbled and grateful, sure only of the knowledge that I knew nothing at all. I won't ever forget what happened there. May it never happen again.

Haiyan struck the Philippines more than a decade ago, leaving more than 6,000 dead. It is one of the most powerful tropical cyclones ever recorded, and

DOI: 10.4324/9781032662589-15

among the deadliest that hit the Philippines. Since then, many more destructive typhoons devastated towns and cities across the country, threatening the lives, livelihood, and safety of millions of Filipinos.

With anthropogenic climate change, these hazards are further magnified. While not every extreme weather event can be immediately attributed to climate change, scientists have said that climate change has "increased the occurrence of the most intense and destructive storms" (Clarke and Otto 2022). Other physical impacts of climate change, such as heatwaves, sea level rise, and ocean warming and acidification, are acutely felt across the world. In this landscape, journalists are at the frontlines of witnessing, documenting, and reporting climate change and how it threatens human rights, including the rights to life, health, food and water, shelter, development, and self-determination.

This chapter explores the experiences of journalists from different countries who are reporting on the nexus of climate change and human rights. It discusses the findings based on the analysis of interviews with reporters about their on-the-ground experiences in their respective home countries or countries of assignment. This chapter also provides an overview of how they approach and frame their reporting, and the challenges that they face in their line of work. Finally, it considers the journalists' observations on the impact of their stories, as well as the effect of their reporting work on themselves as they witness disasters and violations of human rights exacerbated by climate change.

The purpose of this chapter is to present the experiences of climate, environment and human rights journalists, predominantly from the Global South, and to provide motivation, inspiration, and guidance to journalists seeking to report on the same intersections.

The link between climate change and human rights

In 2022, the United Nations (UN) General Assembly passed a resolution that recognized the right to a clean, healthy, and sustainable environment as a human right. While not legally binding, the document recognized environmental degradation and climate change as some of the "most pressing and serious threats to the ability of present and future generations to effectively enjoy all human rights" (UN General Assembly 2022).

In its Sixth Assessment Report, the Intergovernmental Panel on Climate Change (IPCC), a UN body that assesses the latest scientific knowledge on man-made climate change, said human activities have "unequivocally" caused global warming. This was primarily through the emissions of greenhouse gases from unsustainable energy use, land use, and lifestyles and patterns of consumption and production. Scientists reported that climate change is projected to increase the severity of impacts across natural and human systems. Some examples include heat-humidity risks to human health; increases in flooding in coastal and low-lying cities and regions; an uptick in food-, water-, and vector-borne diseases and mental health challenges, and decreases in food production. Different parts of the world will experience these threats to varying degrees (IPCC 2023).

Given these impacts, it is clear that climate change undermines a wide array of human rights. In its "Climate Change and Human Rights" report, the UN Environment Programme (UNEP) said climate change is "not merely an abstract, future possibility" (UNEP 2015, VIII) but an already occurring threat. The report highlighted several challenges; for instance, as climate change increases the frequency of droughts and heat waves, the peoples' rights to water, sanitation, and health are affected. Sea level rise and storm surges can impact the rights to housing and adequate standards of living of people residing in low-lying and coastal areas. Amid the scarcity of natural resources, climate change can also threaten human security, resulting in displacement, migration, and even conflict. It could also compromise culture, identity, and history (UNEP 2015).

At the same time, some responses to climate change can also have an impact on the enjoyment of human rights. For example, massive renewable energy projects, without proper consultation and participatory measures, can displace local and Indigenous peoples and destroy natural ecosystems.

With the links between climate change and human rights becoming apparent, any effort to mitigate and adapt to these challenges should also abide by human rights norms and principles, such as the rights to non-discrimination, participation, information, and transparency. According to a policy document of the UN Office of the High Commissioner on Human Rights (OHCHR), climate change is "a human rights problem and the human rights framework must be part of the solution" (UN OHCHR 2015, 6).

It is also important to note that the impacts of climate change are disproportionately felt by certain groups. Women and girls, people living in poverty, and Indigenous peoples bear the brunt of the climate crisis differently. Often, those who experience the worst of the climate impacts already live in disadvantaged areas where they no longer fully enjoy their inherent human rights. They are also often the least contributor to the climate crisis, with minimal greenhouse gas emissions, yet they suffer the most under these new realities. This recognition forms the core idea of climate justice, where those who are most responsible for the climate crisis are held accountable for the harms that they cause.

Communities and individuals have recognized these harms. Many are taking action, not just in the streets, but in the legal system as well. In 2015, two years after Haiyan devastated cities and towns in the Philippines, a petition was filed before the Philippine Commission on Human Rights (CHR) by campaigning network Greenpeace Southeast Asia and individual survivors of different typhoons. They asked the commission to examine the impacts of climate change on Filipinos and the role of "carbon majors," or companies engaged in coal, oil, gas and other fossil fuels, in the climate crisis. It was the first petition of such kind before a national human rights body that specifically looked into corporate responsibility. Seven years later, the CHR ruled that the fossil fuel companies had early knowledge of the adverse impacts of fossil fuels and that they have the responsibility to undertake human rights due diligence and provide remediation (CHR 2022).

Also in 2015, the Lahore High Court in Pakistan made history after it ruled that the national government's "delay and lethargy" in implementing its National Climate Change Policy and Framework for Implementation of Climate Change Policy violated the fundamental rights of its citizens.

As of December 2022, there have been 2,180 climate-related cases filed in different jurisdictions, including international courts, tribunals, and quasi-judicial bodies (UNEP 2023). This marked a steady increase in recent years, with children, women, and Indigenous peoples taking prominent roles in bringing these cases to the courts.

Conversations with journalists reporting on climate change and human rights

The discussions in this chapter are based on the analysis of semi-structured in-depth interviews with nine journalists, predominantly from the Global South. This sampling was intentional because while the impacts of climate change are experienced across the world, these are more pronouncedly and disproportionately felt in developing countries.

Eleven journalists covering climate change and its impacts on human rights were initially contacted for this chapter. From this effort, nine journalists agreed and were interviewed via video conference and e-mail correspondences between January and March 2024. They consented to have the conversation recorded, and agreed to speak on the record and be quoted for the succeeding discussion.

While the journalists interviewed represent only a small sample of media professionals reporting on climate change and human rights, they come from diverse backgrounds and years of reporting work. This allowed for a variety of experiences, stories, and challenges faced by reporters on the field. The quotes in this chapter are directly lifted from the interviews to allow the journalists to share their insights in their own words. These have been lightly edited for clarity.

Of the interviewees, five were biologically female and four men. Two were visual journalists, while the rest were text and/or multimedia reporters. The majority were freelancers or independent journalists who work for different local and foreign publications and media organizations.

Despite best efforts and with the limitations in time and resources, the chapter author was not able to interview journalists from other key continents, such as Oceania and Africa. It is critical to note that the experiences of climate

Reporting on climate change through the lens of human rights 171

TABLE 12.1 Journalists interviewed for the chapter

Name	Position & Affiliation	Place of Assignment
Adi Renaldi	Freelance multimedia journalist	Indonesia
Aryn Baker	Senior international climate and environment correspondent, TIME	Global (based in Rome)
Elisângela Mendonça	Senior forests investigator, Global Witness	Brazil (based in London)
Meral Jamal	Independent journalist	Canada (Nunavut in the Canadian Arctic)
Rafael Vilela	Independent photographer	Brazil
Rafiqul Montu	Freelance journalist	Bangladesh
Ritwika Mitra	Independent journalist	India
Zakir Hossain Chowdhury	Visual journalist	Bangladesh
Zuha Siddiqui	Labor & Tech fellow, Rest of World	Pakistan

change and human rights journalists reporting from and about these regions are just as important. This limitation can be the jump-off point for a more expansive study on the topic.

Climate change and human rights: the inevitable story

When Indian journalist Ritwika Mitra first started reporting from the Sundarbans, one of the world's largest mangrove forests that lies on the delta in the Bay of Bengal, she initially pitched a story to look into the situation of girls and children being trafficked from the area. Mitra said: "That was the lens I started covering it from: from a very core human-slash-feminist point of view. I wanted to look at it from a child rights issue" (Mitra, Personal Interview, 2024).

When she began to report extensively from the ground, she eventually realized that the story was not just of human rights violations alone. She saw it in the context of how these violations were taking place "as a kind of ripple effect" of the climate crisis (Covering Climate Now 2023).

Dubbed the "cyclone capital of India," the Sundarbans face not only intense cyclones, but also flooding and sea level rise due to subsidence and climate change. In her report for *The Fuller Project*, Mitra wrote that these disasters and environmental changes have resulted in its population being more vulnerable to participate in or become victims of human trafficking. Recalling her first stories from the Sundarbans, Mitra said:

> It was like a moment of epiphany . . . I think that totally kind of changed the lens for me, not only in terms of trafficking, hunger, poverty. . . . For

every story, there was a climate story. Suddenly, I felt like it was so evident to me that there is this need to mount this lens.

(Mitra, Personal Interview, 2024)

In the interviews with journalists for this chapter, a clear consensus emerged: Climate change and its impacts on and intersections with human rights can no longer be ignored, especially by journalists who cover these topics. Across different regions, the climate crisis is now the context by which every story exists. Turning a blind eye to the human rights challenges in a rapidly warming world would be to leave out narratives and voices of populations and sectors that are often already disadvantaged even before climate change enters the picture.

London-based Brazilian journalist Elisângela Mendonça, who reports on deforestation in the Amazon Rainforest, said: "The climate crisis is impacting everything. So I feel that we can't dissociate. . . . We cannot look into that as two different things. . . . It's one aspect of the same problem" (Mendonça, Personal Interview, 2024).

The journalists started out reporting on the nexus of human rights and climate change in different ways. Most of them started as reporters already covering human rights concerns in their home countries or countries of assignment. They were producing reports that investigated the conditions of women, children, and Indigenous peoples; the rights to decent shelter and dignified work, and access to proper healthcare, among others.

Eventually, they saw how the impacts of climate change, such as more severe cyclones and fast-rising seas, deepened the inequalities in the communities they cover. In some scenarios, the climate crisis may not be the historical reason for suffering or injustice. However, repeated bouts of extreme precipitation or intense heat and the increase in salinization of agricultural lands have forced migration and displacement, unjustly affected women, children, and the elderly, and pushed people deeper into poverty and hunger.

In 2012, Aryn Baker, an American foreign correspondent for more than two decades, began looking more closely at how climate change intertwined with human rights and foreign coverage. She recalls in particular her reporting of the Arab Spring, a series of protests and uprisings in the Middle East and North Africa in the early 2010s amid corruption and economic instability. She said:

> When I was interviewing a Middle East agricultural specialist about the roots of the conflict, he was the first person that brought up the issue of the drought in the 1990s. For me, it was like the penny dropped. I realised it was much more complicated than just an uprising – there are antecedents in climate.
>
> *(Baker, Personal Interview, 2024)*

Bangladeshi visual journalist Zakir Hossain Chowdhury echoes a similar sentiment. According to him, the recognition of how human rights weave into environmental changes could be a "revelation" for some journalists. He said: "Connecting this understanding to the plight of vulnerable communities broadens the narrative, revealing the urgent and complex human dimensions of the climate crisis" (Chowdhury, E-mail Correspondence, 2024).

The growing awareness and knowledge on climate change among the public also influenced their reporting on this topic, according to some of the journalists. In 2018, climate change began making more headlines as young people around the world organized global strikes. These movements followed the actions of then-15-year-old Greta Thunberg, who protested in front of the Swedish Parliament in August that year.

Some newsrooms began to reflect this heightened consciousness, journalists said. For the freelancers working in climate-vulnerable countries, they noted that editors from foreign news agencies would specifically look for or assign stories on how climate change is affecting their respective countries.

While most of the journalists interviewed for this chapter focused first on human rights issues before incorporating the climate lens, others approached it first from the environment and climate perspective. This depends on their reporting assignment or on the places from which they report.

Meral Jamal, who is among the very few journalists reporting from the Canadian Arctic, said she actively looks for the climate stories first, since that is her own strength as a reporter. Then she digs deep into the human rights angle, particularly how the Indigenous communities in the Nunavut territory are affected by climate change impacts or the extraction and development of resources from their lands.

Jamal said reporting on climate change through and with the human rights aspect shows that the crisis is not just about its physical impacts, but about how people are affected on personal and political levels. She said:

> When you bring in that human rights report, it's a way to find that accountability aspect. . . . Reporting on human rights within climate change is that opportunity to bring Indigenous resistance, Indigenous voices, Indigenous acts and actions, and Indigenous resilience into your reporting.
>
> (Jamal, Personal Interview, 2024)

Approaches and story framing

For *National Geographic*, freelance multimedia journalist Adi Renaldi explored how climate change and land subsidence threaten parts of Indonesia, including its capital, Jakarta, where he is based.

Reporting from the north coast of Java in 2021, he reported how rising seas and sinking lands were pushing a graveyard in the village of Timbulsloko underwater. It was one of the last few places, he wrote, that connected its villagers with their history. Recalling a scene where he watched a mother and her son pray in a flooded cemetery at sunset, he said:

> [I thought about how] all your memories are going to be wiped out by the sea level rise. That freaks me out in such a way that the threat is so real. You can lose everything; you can lose not just your home, but all your memories also.
> *(Renaldi, Personal Interview, 2024)*

Similar to Renaldi, the journalists reporting on the intersections of climate change and human rights already feel the impacts of climate change on their doorstep – literally and figuratively.

In terms of framing their reports, journalists shared varied ways of approaching their work. The general sentiment is that their angles depend on the particular topic, project, or assignment they are pursuing. Still, all of them emphasized that their stories put people and their experiences in the center, and that their reporting is grounded in science.

Renaldi, for instance, said he often looks at the human impacts of environmental challenges and degradation first, before doing more research on how climate change affects or exacerbates these situations. He underscored how climate change can be reported from different angles:

> I think climate stories are very complex because they involve multidimensional angles. . . . You'll never end up writing just one angle. . . . It won't do justice (to) the bigger portrait and the bigger picture.
> *(Renaldi, Personal Interview, 2024)*

Mendonça, who was previously an environment reporter for *The Bureau of Investigative Journalism* in London, said she usually looks first at the environmental impacts of certain activities, then investigates the impact on the people. This reporting approach, however, can reflect differently in her writing: "When you're writing it, you have the option of putting people first" (Mendonça, Personal Interview, 2024).

In one of her reports produced with the support of the Pulitzer Center's Rainforest Investigations Network, she and her fellow reporters scrutinized the supply chain of collagen, a sought-after ingredient in the wellness industry. Their investigation was the first to draw the connection between collagen sourced from cattle with forest loss in the Brazilian Amazon and violence against Indigenous peoples.

The journalists interviewed for this chapter also underscored that it is critical to capture the historical nuances and contexts of the communities that they cover.

Rafiqul Montu, who reports on the plight of coastal communities in Bangladesh, said many of the people who are living in places that are at the highest risk for climate disasters are already deprived of many basic rights to begin with. As the climate crisis ravages their communities and puts their livelihood and identities under threat, they are further forced to "give up" many of their rights, he said (Montu, Email Correspondence, 2024).

Mitra, who explores stories on gender-based violence, caste, and climate change across India, emphasized that it is also important that the climate change lens is not forced on the narratives of the people that journalists write about. She is highly conscious about the way that climate change is perceived in the communities and its actual role in their current plight, if any. While many stories of injustices can be linked to and are intertwined with climate change, she stressed that it is necessary to capture the complexities of peoples' experiences and contexts to get an accurate story.

Mitra takes a step back and listens closely to the stories of the communities themselves. She also speaks with other stakeholders who have worked on these intersecting topics more extensively than she has. She said:

> We are often going with our own assumptions. . . . I think we need to undo a lot of those binaries when we are going to the field. . . . I think this is where more and more the intersectional lens will be useful, because we really cannot report in isolation.
>
> *(Mitra, Personal Interview, 2024)*

Challenges in reporting

Despite the headways in climate change journalism and human rights reporting, different challenges still hound journalists reporting on these two difficult topics and their intersections.

A common concern raised by the reporters was the current structure of newsrooms. Investigations on climate change and human rights violations take a lot of time and resources to pursue. Many publications and media organizations around the world do not have dedicated climate and/or human rights reporters, leaving a huge gap in the reporting.

Zuha Siddiqui, who covers climate, technology, and labor stories, described the situation in her home country, Pakistan: "There is very little climate reporting to begin with, let alone climate and human rights . . . primarily because local newsrooms don't really see climate as a beat that is pressing or urgent" (Siddiqui, Personal Interview, 2024). At the time of writing this chapter, she was a Labor and Tech fellow for *Rest of World*, a global nonprofit publication that covers the impact of technology around the world. Before venturing into these intersections, Siddiqui was a freelancer reporting primarily on human rights, which she felt was the topic of interest of international editors seeking stories from Pakistan. She shared that climate change and human rights both receive very little coverage locally:

> It was really bizarre in the sense that they didn't sort of illustrate what was happening on the ground, not just in terms of the dire impact, but also in terms of what local groups are doing. . . . There is actually a local climate action movement that's been rallying for a very long time . . . [but] I really didn't see those voices represented.
> *(Siddiqui, Personal Interview, 2024)*

Another challenge identified by journalists was the need to grasp technical knowledge and information on climate change, given the fact that many of them do not come from scientific backgrounds. One journalist shared that they still face a learning curve in understanding the latest climate science and incorporating this in their reporting. Another reporter raised the difficulty in accessing data and information for their stories. In their reporting, either their governments do not have enough data or are unwilling to release them to reporters.

In the end, one of the biggest predicaments for journalists reporting on climate and human rights is getting people to read their stories and care for those who are heavily affected by these twin crises.

Baker, who specifically reports on the human impacts of climate change for *TIME*, said getting people to care about human rights reportage is already difficult, and climate change journalism poses a similar task. Put together, they present a daunting ordeal for the public. The major obstacle, according to Baker, is battling despair and indifference from the readers:

> There's so much despair involved. I think there's a tendency of readers to want to look away because I think there's a tendency of these stories to be very much doom-and-gloom. . . . It really invokes a sense of passivity in the readers. It's a challenge to battle that: to always make the point that it is not set in stone. We can stop the worst from happening.
> *(Baker, Personal Interview, 2024)*

Measuring impact

When asked about the impact of their reporting on policy and public perception, the journalists echoed a common view that measuring the impact of their individual stories or even a body of journalism work is a difficult task. Not all stories immediately lead to significant changes, with one journalist calling the work a "long-term game." Still, they observed positive reception and developments that stemmed from their reporting.

The majority of the reporters took note of the increased awareness about climate change on the communities and sectors that they cover. One journalist saw how local media had begun covering similar issues that they had been reporting on in their country. Another reporter shared that some of their readers have reached out to help the disadvantaged communities that were featured in their stories.

For others, their reports have pointed toward or contributed to significant systemic changes. Baker said her reporting on the sweltering conditions faced by migrant workers in the Arab Gulf for *TIME* helped amplify the issues of the laborers, considering the extensive reach of the high-profile magazine. She said: "I think there's no direct [way that] I can say like my story did this or that. But I think it furthers the conversation" (Baker, Personal Interview, 2024).

Sometimes, concrete changes can happen more swiftly as a result of good journalism. Global brand Nestlé dropped a major supplier linked to the purchase of bovine from seized Indigenous lands in the Amazon, following the stories published by Mendonça and her team that showed the intricate links between food, rainforests, climate, and Indigenous rights in the vast rainforests of Brazil.

Journalists as witnesses: covering an existential crisis

As the climate crisis continues to undermine fundamental human rights across the world, journalists find themselves in an increasingly difficult position as witnesses and producers of the first drafts of history.

When asked about the impact of their reporting work on themselves, all the interviewed journalists expressed feelings of fatigue and depression. They shared frustration over the lack of urgency from governments and institutions to protect the most vulnerable populations whose stories they witness and gather.

They also expressed heightened consciousness about their lifestyles. Renaldi from Indonesia said his own reporting has influenced his individual choices. He has worked on lessening his air travels, given the massive emissions that come from flying. He has also decided not to buy an electric vehicle, in consideration of the human rights abuses linked to the extraction of critical minerals used to manufacture them. Reflecting on the impact of his work on his personal life, he said:

> It depresses me in some certain way. . . . It makes me think about what my kids will be [experiencing] in the next 10 years. . . . So I think I should do better, but I don't know. How can I do better? Maybe I can contribute, but maybe not. But at least, I try to do better in journalism.
>
> *(Renaldi, Personal Interview, 2024)*

The majority of the journalists talked about the need to take the time off to decompress and process their experiences after covering highly sensitive issues linked to human rights and climate. They also underscored, however, the difficulty of dissociating and detaching from their reporting work. Talking about the limitations of journalism in enacting change, Mendonça said:

> Usually, you can just inform or shed light on a problem. But ultimately, you don't have the power to change things. And the feeling of powerlessness, for me, is what strikes me the most. It's like a moral injury of being there, seeing what's going on, reporting about it, and ultimately, not seeing anything changing.
> *(Mendonça, Personal Interview, 2024)*

Photographer Rafael Vilela, who reports on social injustice and the environmental crisis in Brazil, shared that he finds ways to help beyond his journalism work. His ongoing project titled "Forest Ruins" explores the role of cities in the climate crisis from the perspective of the Indigenous Guarani Mbyá in the city of São Paulo. Outside of his work as a photographer, he remains active in extending help to communities in his area. When asked about his ethical considerations, Vilela said that for him, the debate on the supposed neutrality of journalists is "over":

> You can always be balanced. You can listen to both sides. But for me, it's impossible to not take a side. Our planet is literally in a huge crisis. . . . So it's hard for me to think [that] neutrality is something good right now. I think we cannot be neutral. We need to be active in reaching people's minds and try to change the context we have right now.
> *(Vilela, Personal Interview, 2024)*

Journalists living and working in countries that are at high risk from climate change also shared how they are cautious that they are not the center of their stories, even if they are feeling the impacts themselves.

Siddiqui, who lives in a low-lying reclaimed land also under threat of climate change, said:

> Your primary objective at this point is to report their story and not your own. . . . It's scary to think about the consequences of what might happen as a result of climate change, but at the moment, the stories that I am reporting are not my stories.
> *(Siddiqui, Personal Interview, 2024)*

Conclusion

Climate change is already undermining fundamental human rights that are inherent to every human being, regardless of nationality, race, sex, religion, or other status. Journalists reporting on climate change through the lens of human rights play a critical role in showing and exposing these ongoing realities. As climate change continues to pose a threat to every region in the world, journalists must be equipped with an intersectional lens to better report on this crisis.

The experiences of journalists featured in this chapter showed that reporters see themselves bearing a huge responsibility in reporting on climate change and its impacts in a holistic manner. Issues affecting vulnerable populations can no longer be reported in silos; instead, climate change has become the necessary context for many of these injustices, both historical and new. For many journalists, navigating this nexus is also a learning opportunity: a chance to shed assumptions and challenge existing beliefs.

While the approach of each journalist varies, it is apparent that climate change and human rights stories are people-driven. They feature powerful human narratives that underscore universal experiences and universal rights. Uncovering injustice and reporting on climate justice is also about accountability reporting, or holding institutions and individuals in power responsible for the crises that we face. In this sense, journalists practice their watchdog function.

While reporting on this intersection, journalists must also strive to report the nuances and historical contexts of the communities they cover. While climate change virtually affects everything in existence, reporters must take care not to always force this lens. Instead, the actual experiences of communities and populations must be heard and reflected in the story.

The challenges that already plague the journalism industry, such as rigid newsroom structures and dwindling resources, are also encountered by reporters covering climate change and human rights. To tackle these obstacles, systemic changes are necessary to ensure that more journalists consistently cover these difficult topics, while making certain that they are not placed in precarious situations without adequate newsroom and community support. Journalists and newsrooms must also find ways to closely engage with the public to counter climate fatigue and news avoidance. These could include an increased emphasis on climate solutions and grassroots adaptive responses, while still reporting on the terrifying realities in a warming world.

While the impacts of climate change and human rights journalism are quite tricky to measure, journalists see their work as important and necessary for the populations they cover. However, as they continue to witness, document, and report, they too find themselves in difficult positions. They experience moral injury, depression, frustration, and fear over the existential question that they probe and investigate. As such, journalists reporting on the nexus of climate change and human rights also need support and resources to ensure the sustainability of their important work and of the journalism profession.

In the end, journalists will persist in holding up a mirror to society, letting us confront the devastation that we humans have brought to our planet while reminding us of the hope and action needed for change. In the face of our uncertain and terrifying realities, the world needs responsible, courageous, and ethical journalists to tell the most important story of our time.

Advice for journalists covering climate change and human rights

For journalists seeking to pursue stories on the nexus of climate change and human rights, here is some advice from the journalists featured in this chapter, as well as from the chapter author:

1. **Start reporting on climate change now.** You don't need to wait 10 years to start reporting on how climate change is affecting your community or your region. The crisis is urgent, it is real, and it is already affecting the rights of many people. Start where you are, now.
2. **Turn to science and data, and seek different sources of knowledge.** Climate change stories must be grounded in science. Seek out experts and scientists and ask questions. Acknowledge also that there are different bearers of knowledge; Indigenous and traditional knowledge is just as valuable as Western knowledge.
3. **Learn from and listen to communities.** The best way to understand the human impacts of climate change is to report from the field and learn from the communities and their lived experiences. Our reports must reflect their richness of their lives, while not downplaying the problems that they face.
4. **Amplify human narratives.** Find a compelling character with a universal and relatable story. Present a human face in your climate story. Some questions to ask: Who benefits? Who loses?
5. **Make stories complex and be ready to challenge your own assumptions.** Ensure that your reporting captures the necessary contexts and nuances in the story that you are covering. Do not force the climate change lens when it isn't present. You can instead explain how the climate crisis or the inaction toward its impacts can further exacerbate the challenges that the communities deal with.
6. **Visualize your climate stories.** Visual narratives can help communicate complex scientific topics and present the social dimension of climate change. Always practice sensitivity and journalistic ethics when creating visuals and images. Seek consent before capturing an image or video, and practice respect and professionalism.
7. **Challenge newsroom structures.** If there is no dedicated climate reporter in your newsroom, have the initiative to incorporate the climate and human rights angles in your reports, regardless of what beat you are covering. Emphasize the intersectionality of these issues to make them a newsroom priority.
8. **Collaborate with other journalists and even across disciplines.** The climate change story is profound and all-encompassing. Collaborate and work with other journalists, editors, and even newsrooms to produce more

compelling reports. Consider engaging people from other disciplines as well, such as educators and artists, to find innovative and impactful ways to tell the climate story.

Discussion questions

1. How does climate change disproportionately affect certain sectors of society?
2. How can journalists and newsrooms better report on the impact of climate change on human rights?
3. What kinds of support can be extended to journalists reporting on climate change through the lens of human rights?

Further reading

Baker, Aryn, and Ed Kashi. 2022. "Thousands of Migrant Workers Died in Qatar's Extreme Heat. The World Cup Forced a Reckoning." *Time*, November 3. https://time.com/6227277/qatar-extreme-heat-world-cup-2022/.

Mendonça, Elisângela, Andrew Wasley, and Fábio Zuker. 2023. "Collagen Craze Drives Deforestation and Rights Abuses." *The Bureau of Investigative Journalism*, March 6. https://www.thebureauinvestigates.com/stories/2023-03-06/collagen-wellness-industrys-star-product-drives-deforestation-and-rights-abuses/.

Mitra, Ritwika. 2022. "In the Sundarban, Climate Change Has an Unlikely Effect: On Child Sex Trafficking." *The Fuller Project (Co-Published With the Wire)*, January 20, 2022. https://fullerproject.org/story/sundarban-climate-change-child-sex-trafficking/.

Renaldi, Adi. 2022. "Their Homes Are Sinking Fast: Can Their Community Survive?" *National Geographic*. https://www.nationalgeographic.com/magazine/article/their-homes-are-sinking-fast-can-their-community-survive-feature.

Siddiqui, Zuha. 2022. "Pakistan Floods Pose Urgent Questions Over Preparedness and Climate Reparations." *The New Humanitarian*, September 5. https://www.thenewhumanitarian.org/news-feature/2022/09/05/Pakistan-floods-urgent-questions-climate-crisis.

References

Baker, Aryn. Personal Interview with Author, February 14, 2024.
Chowdhury, Zakir Hossain. Email Correspondence with Author, February 21, 2024.
Clarke, Ben, and Friederike Otto. 2022. *Reporting Extreme Weather and Climate Change: A Guide for Journalists*. World Weather Attribution. https://www.worldweatherattribution.org/wp-content/uploads/ENG_WWA-Reporting-extreme-weather-and-climate-change.pdf.

Commission on Human Rights of the Phillipines. 2022. *National Inquiry on Climate Change Report*. December 2022. https://chr2bucket.storage.googleapis.com/wp-content/uploads/2022/12/08152514/CHRP_National-Inquiry-on-Climate-Change-Report.pdf.

Covering Climate Now. 2023. "Q&A: Ritwika Mitra's Reporting on Gender Shows Climate Change's Fingerprints." *Covering Climate Now*, October 26. https://www.cjr.org/covering_climate_now/qa-ritwika-mitras-gender-climate-change-sundarbans-india-bangladesh.php.

Intergovernmental Panel on Climate Change. 2023. "Summary for Policymakers." In *Climate Change 2023: Synthesis Report. Contribution of Working Groups I, II and III to the Sixth Assessment Report of the Intergovernmental Panel on Climate Change*, edited by Core Writing Team, H. Lee, and J. Romero, 1–34. Geneva, Switzerland: IPCC. https://doi.org/10.59327/IPCC/AR6-9789291691647.001.

Jamal, Meral. Personal Interview with Author, January 29, 2024.

Mendonça, Elisângela. Personal Interview with Author, February 20, 2024.

Mitra, Ritwika. Personal Interview with Author, January 17, 2024.

Montu, Rafiqul. Email Correspondence with Author, February 20, 2024.

Renaldi, Adi. Personal Interview with Author, February 6, 2024.

Siddiqui, Zuha. Personal Interview with Author, January 16, 2024.

UN Office of the High Commissioner on Human Rights (OHCHR). 2022. "I Lost Friends, Relatives, Our House." *OHCHR*, July 26. https://www.ohchr.org/en/stories/2022/07/i-lost-friends-relatives-our-house.

United Nations Environment Programme. 2015. "Climate Change and Human Rights." https://wedocs.unep.org/bitstream/handle/20.500.11822/9530/-Climate_Change_and_Human_Rightshuman-rights-climate-change.pdf.pdf?sequence=2&amp%3BisAllowed=.

United Nations Environment Programme. 2023. *Global Climate Litigation Report: 2023 Status Review*. Nairobi.

United Nations General Assembly. 2022. "The Human Right to a Clean, Healthy and Sustainable Environment: Draft Resolution." Seventy-sixth session. A/76/L.75, July 26. https://digitallibrary.un.org/record/3982508?ln=en&v=pdf.

United Nations Office of the High Commissioner for Human Rights. 2015. "Understanding Human Rights and Climate Change." https://www.ohchr.org/sites/default/files/Documents/Issues/ClimateChange/COP21.pdf.

Vilela, Rafael. Personal Interview with Author, March 6, 2024.

Yap, D. J. 2013. "Meeting a Monster: First Person Account." *Philippine Daily Inquirer*, November 17. https://newsinfo.inquirer.net/528483/meeting-a-monster-first-person-account.

13
MIGRATION AND FORCED DISPLACEMENT

Transnational phenomena challenging journalism research and education

Susanne Fengler and Monika Lengauer

Introduction

Journalism representing perhaps "our only hope to secure human rights" (OHCHR 2023) seems too much for the profession to shoulder especially vis-à-vis the growing challenges journalists face in covering migration and forced displacement: By the second anniversary of the full-scale Russian invasion on Ukraine in February 2024, around six million European refugees had been added to six and a half million refugees from Syria, and six million people with protection needs in the Americas (UNHCR 2023), while Sudan may be "today's worst war in sheer numbers of people killed and displaced" (Crisis Group 2024). Persecution that equals genocide forces Rohingya to flee from Myanmar (Becker 2020). As small island nations in the South Pacific are becoming uninhabitable, islanders are at risk of becoming stateless (Gaynor 2020; Speelman, Nicholls and Safra de Campos 2021). These are only paradigmatic African, American, Arab, Asian, European and Oceanian protection cases under the mandate of the United Nations High Commissioner for Refugees (UNHCR). Under its specific mandate, the United Nations Relief and Works Agency for Palestine Refugees in the Near East (UNRWA) has provided assistance and protection to around six million Palestine refugees for over 70 years (Lengauer 2021a). Protection needs increased massively (UNRWA 2024) after the Palestinian group Hamas led "the worst massacre [against Israeli civilians] since the Holocaust" (Los Angeles Times 2023). Hamas's attack on 7 October 2023 and the ensuing war caused multiple human rights abuses, including sexual violence (United Nations 2024). The war, during which Hamas kept Israeli hostages on end, was also discussed as genocide (Journal of Genocide Research 2024).

DOI: 10.4324/9781032662589-16

Besides these forcibly displaced persons under the mandates of the UNHCR and the UNRWA, the International Labor Organisation (ILO) is concerned with around 170 million international migrant workers (ILO 2022), including around 58 million irregular migrant workers. The key function of the International Organization for Migration (IOM) is to facilitate orderly migration flows by providing services (Bradley 2023). With the growth of people on the move (voluntary or obliged mobility) and on the run (forced displacement), the eyes of the world have increasingly been set on managing flows of human mobility, and thus on the four international organizations (IOs) UNHCR, UNRWA, ILO and IOM, whose human rights compliance is also a matter of discussion (Geiger and Pécoud 2020; Bradley and Erdilmen 2022; Bradley, Costello and Sherwood 2023). All beneficiaries – almost 280 million people worldwide by mid-2020 (Migration Data Portal 2024) – of these IOs enjoy rights including human rights, but not all rights equally apply to all groups of migrants, labour migrants, irregular migrants, refugees, asylum seekers, stateless people, Palestine refugees and others. Migrants – a term that remains fuzzy – enjoy human rights that are mostly non-binding. Conversely, the term refugee is clearly defined in the 1951 Refugee Convention and the 1967 Refugee Protocol, and it is individualized, which opens the way to political asylum, residence, citizenship and other rights (Akram 2002; Crock 2015; Hathaway 2021; United Nations 2018a).

A complex field for journalistic coverage

Mass communication scholarship impacts the field increasingly in cross-cultural comparative research that not only informs journalism educators but also helps practicing journalists to navigate the complex field. Journalism educators in academic and training settings across the globe are challenged to prepare practitioners for covering human mobility. Journalists are expected to publish rounded stories that represent all actors' voices, adding the hitherto largely missing narratives of migrants and refugees. Based on comprehensive education, the reporting on migration and forced displacement is supposed to be knowledge- and know-how-based as in research and skills. Thus prepared, practitioners can be conscious of human rights in mobility, cross-culturally oriented, aware of terminologies and reliable sources, reflective, unbiased, mastering various storytelling techniques and strictly observing the profession's ethics and objective to inform responsibly and competently (Lengauer, 2024). As transnational fields of inquiry, migration and refugee studies involve more than political, economic, social, anthropological, psychological, developmental, mass communication, humanitarian and human rights perspectives (Black 2001; Bloch 2020; Castles and Miller 1993; Levitt and Jaworsky 2007; Rodrigo and Priorelli 2023), a profundity that journalists need to reflect, and deconstruct into knowledge-based, accurate, relevant and relatable stories for diverse transnational audiences, revealing individual human experiences (Stein and Tomasi 1981). Current scholarship on migration has largely abandoned the "simplistic pull-push models" (de Haas 2021, 1) that date back to the beginning of theorizing with a focus on economic drivers, mainly by Ravenstein (e.g., 1885) and Lee (1966). Ravenstein established distance as a factor in migration flows whereby migrants intend to improve their living conditions. Lee suggested that factors pull people from their origin country and/or push them into destination countries; he also addressed "intervening obstacles" such as immigration laws and migrants' perceptions, notions that reverberate in discussing these matters until today.

Migration theories of the early 20th century discussed the integration of immigrants, often outlining them as "strangers", into the distinctively different cultures of host societies (e.g., Park 1928). While the immigrant was described as asking for acceptance, host societies were profiled as seeking loyalty from the immigrant. The process of immigration was modelled as a set of stages migrants were passing through, which also included phases of competition between migrants and host societies and conflict. Early scholars emphasized the objective of the migrants' full assimilation into the destination society, while ensuing studies also take into account the impact of the migrants' culture on the culture of receiving societies, stressing pluralism and transnationalism. Different ethnic groups were found to have different modes and capabilities of coping with assimilation (e.g., Eisenstadt 1953), whereby the assimilation debate is now largely seen as noncompliant with the human rights of migrants (e.g., Hieronymi 2005).

The academic shift in migration studies is relevant to journalistic practice in several ways. One aspect of great importance is the education that future practitioners across the globe increasingly obtain in academic programmes (Josephi et al. 2019). These curricula, based on the interdisciplinary research field of mass communication, aim at professionalization through a balance of research-based knowledge and the profession's know-how (Lengauer 2021b). Combined with the interdisciplinary research fields of refugee studies on the one hand and of migration studies on the other hand, educating journalists on the coverage of migration and forced displacement addresses the complexity of the reporting realities. Another relevant academic shift relates to the new research attention on the individual, acknowledging each person's human agency and the "fact that the vast majority of migrants move of their own free will" (de Haas 2021, 15). The attention on the individual has been largely missing in the past, as global comparative studies by Fengler et al. (2022) and Fengler and Kreutler (2020) have revealed.

Refugee studies as an academic discipline has developed progressively since its inception but it is still short of "a central body of theories that summarises, generalises and systematises the accumulated insights of a vast amount of empirical research" (de Haas 2021, 2). Nonetheless, it has been established as a burgeoning interdisciplinary and international research field with university-based refugee studies centres, for instance the Refugee Studies Centre at the University of Oxford; with topical journals such as the Journal of Refugee Studies; with topical manuals from peers for peers on journalistic coverage of refugees and asylum seekers (e.g., the International Journalists' Network 2021). Research and policy formulation were linked from the onset for both migration studies and refugee studies (Bakewell 2008; Black 2001; Bloch 2020; Freedman and de Andrade 2024; Levitt and Jaworsky 2007; Rodrigo and Priorelli 2023), prompting Stein and Tomasi (1981, 6) to lament the "scholarly inattention" of forced displacement. The research-policy nexus has recently been projected in the UN General Assembly's 2016 Declaration for Refugees and Migrants via the Global Compact for Migration and the Global Compact on Refugees (Kraly and Hovy 2020). Both compacts are generally aligned with the definitional distinction of refugees and migrants. They are profoundly grounded in human rights, yet the Refugee Compact was able to further the longstanding body of international law while the Migration Compact represents a starting point for the global regulation of migration (McAdam 2018). Regarding press freedom as a human right, the two compacts differ greatly: The Refugee Compact looks at the media alongside many other actors – within and outside the UN system, including the humanitarian sector, local governments, international and regional institutions, civil society organizations (CSOs), academia and refugees themselves – as stakeholders in "sharing of the burden and responsibility for hosting and supporting" refugees. The compact remains vague about the media's role but highlights the "power and positive impact" of the media and others (United Nations 2018b, 2, 33). The Migration Compact is more detailed in outlining the media's role. Aimed to "promote evidence-based public discourse", it intends to build on "independent, objective and quality reporting . . . in full respect for the freedom of the media" and the "education of media professionals" (United Nations 2018a, 24). This document regards press freedom and academic freedom as human rights (Scholars at Risk 2023).

The research-policy nexus is also part of mass communication scholarship on migration and forced displacement. The diverse field comprises research in the global context, emphases on ethnic and cultural pluralism of immigration (Glazer and Moynihan 1963), on tensions related to imbalances between nations (which may foster the desire to migrate among members of societies perceived as less powerful and prestigious (Hoffmann-Nowotny 1970), to mention just a few fields. In a global society, international migration has been described as mutually beneficial for crowded labour markets in countries of origin on the one side, and for destination countries in need of labour on the other side. Migration also represents a vehicle for upward social mobility for individual migrants and their families or communities (Sassen 2007). As brain drain may initially weaken sending societies and brain gain potentially benefits receiving societies, circular migration may favour both (Dao et al. 2018). This is especially true under conducive conditions as for instance outlined in the World Bank's (2023) "Match and Motive Matrix" that assumes a match when "the degree to which a migrant's skills and related attributes meet the demand in the destination country" (p. 21). Origin countries and destination countries are often connected by historical patterns, cultural and ethnic ties, traditional trade relationships, language, religion etc.; together, they form a system of migration, interconnected by financial transactions (remittances) and communication. Exchange between those community members who stayed at home with those who settled in the diaspora may lead to more migration, a "pull factor" furthered by shrinking distances due to technological achievements (Douglas et al. 1994). The internet and social media enable international migrants to remain closely connected to their networks in their countries of origin, resulting in their hybrid identities (Dekker and Engbersen 2014).

Communication scholarship on the coverage of migration and forced displacement is on the rise but it still largely assumes the vantage points of migrants' and refugees' destination countries (Fengler 2021). This applies to the coverage of mobility within Europe (Bulgaria to the UK; Balabanova and Balch 2010) as well as of mobility from Africa to Europe (Fengler et al. 2022; Horsti 2008) respectively to the Global North (Fengler and Kreutler 2020). Comparative research of migration and forced displacement oftentimes yielded more differences than similarities; for instance, Swedish publications at the time of the refugee crisis 2015–2016 were more positive than those in the UK (EJO 2015; Berry et al. 2015). Regularly, migrants and refugees were not quoted in journalistic work, and the contexts of their lives and migration decisions remained vague for reasons also embedded in journalists' lack of knowledge (Fotopoulos and Kaimaklioti 2016; Georgiou and Zaborowski 2017); they were not shown as sovereign actors but as helpless victims, lacking agency (de Haas 2021).

Future research directions are multifarious from all vantage points in migration and refugee studies, including human rights inquiry and mass communication (Lecheler, Matthes and Boomgaarden 2019; Smets et al. 2020). One may point out durable solutions and borders with bordering practices as the most discernible research agendas, all with strong human rights and mass communication implications. Both topics are most prevalent in the increasingly global public debate with human mobility often playing a central role. Cross-cultural research agendas and journalism education curricula reflect the complexity of the field. The wealth of literature on durable solutions and borders with bordering practices cannot be discussed here; regarding borders, for instance, Australia's, the EU's and UK's pushback policies are main fields of inquiry under the human rights and mass communication perspectives (e.g., Andro 2022; Dastyari, Nethery and Hirsch 2023; Freier, Karageorgiou and Ogg 2021; Trimikliniotis 2020); regarding durable solutions, enquiry has included main destination countries such as South Africa, Pakistan or Turkey (Ferris 2023; Handmaker, La Hunt and Klaasen 2008; Siddikoglu and Sagiroglu 2023). Erdilman (2019) has pointed to the lack of studies covering destination countries of the Global South where the majority of displaced people stay. The picture is, however, very varied and changing over time. While international migrants in search of the greatest opportunities predominantly settle in the high-income countries like the USA, Germany and Saudi Arabia, new asylum claims are routinely registered in the Global North, mainly the USA and Germany (IOM 2021; UNHCR 2023). To reach these destinations (in irregular ways) often requires to overcome great distances, "intervening obstacles" such as immigration laws and life-threatening hazards (Lee 1966; Ravenstein 1885) as the Darien Gap, Sahara Desert or Mediterranean Sea etc. The majority of refugees, however, seek refuge in low- and middle-income – often neighbouring – countries. For instance, large numbers of international migrants live in another African country (IOM 2021). This significant human mobility is not reflected in African news media. They often replicate stereotypes of Africa from foreign media, according to the former head of the African Media Initiative (AMI), Eric Chinje. He deems the adequate coverage of migration and forced displacement within and from Africa to be a precondition for the development of a critical constituency in Africa, for citizens who are empowered to fight for policies that effectively address the root causes of (irregular) migration (cited in Fengler 2021); this view reverberates elsewhere, for instance the Arab world (Hamad 2023; Maharat Foundation 2016). A study by the United Nations Development Programme (UNDP 2019) has shown that the vast majority of migrants would redo the treacherous journey if they were (voluntarily) returned to their country of origin. Against this backdrop, it is important, as Eric Chinje has hinted, for journalists to balance the – much needed – critical coverage with positive examples. Young migrants may then decide to avoid the "intervening obstacles" (Lee 1966) of irregular migration. This is also part of the media's social responsibility (Fengler 2021), facilitating a public debate that is unbiased, fair, inclusive of diverse voices from across stakeholders in countries of origin, transit and destination, applying research-based knowledge and know-how that ably contextualizes the reasons behind mobility.

The discourse in origin and destination countries analysed in mass communication scholarship

The analysis of migration and forced displacement in mass communication suggests future research (Lecheler, Matthes and Boomgaarden 2019; Smets et al. 2020) should encompass comparative research, geographical balance, methodological and theory development as well as particular aspects of teaching. Addressing the research gap of comparative studies, we have devised two cases that will be discussed in some detail. Both cases analyze journalistic work published during the 2015 to 2016 period of significant mobility of migrants and refugees into Europe.

The *first case* (Fengler et al. 2022) represents a comparative study of migration and forced displacement coverage in origin and destination countries alike. It aims to identify the similarities and differences in the coverage in selected African and European media outlets. Analysing a sample of 22 news outlets across Africa (10) and Europe (12), the study shows that migration is greatly underreported in the African news outlets (Connor 2018; Lengauer 2021c; Okunna 2021) and that individual migrants and refugees are barely quoted in their own words. In these respects, African and European results differed. Based on 1,512 news articles published between 1 June 2015 and 31 May 2016, over 88 percent of the articles (1,337) originated in European media, and only 11 percent (175) in African media. In this study, the category 'main actors' comprised different groups of people quoted in the articles of the sample; these groups included individuals from the countries in the sample such as citizens, politicians in government and opposition, people working in that country such as representatives of IOs and of CSOs, as well as migrants and refugees currently present in that country. The representation of migrants and refugees varied considerably between the African and the European sample: Migrants were represented as main actors in almost six percent of the African articles versus in over ten percent of European articles, and refugees were main actors in around five percent of the African articles versus almost 14 percent of the European ones. Politicians were dominant as main actors in both samples. IOs played a prominent role as main actors in the African media (15 percent), coming in second after politicians. This result confirms earlier studies that, too, point to higher salience of the topic in destination countries (Assopgoum 2011; Eberl et al. 2018).

The content of the African and European coverage also differed. European news media focused on domestic issues like border security and migration policy. African media outlets in this study were primarily concerned with disasters involving African migrants, while they otherwise often mirrored European news agendas. They disproportionately referenced aspects of migration in European over African countries. For instance, they discussed integration of African migrants in Europe (almost six percent of the sample) while snubbing the integration of migrants in African countries – despite the fact that most African migration takes place within the African continent. Exploring the reasons for these findings, the study suggests limited press freedom, anaemic reporting resources, poor editing and negative assumptions about the public's interest in political affairs, among other adverse conditions.

The *second case* (Fengler and Kreutler 2020) analyses actors, topics and tone of mass media coverage of migrants and refugees in 17 countries of the Global North. It is built on a dataset of 2,417 news articles published in six exemplary weeks (August 2015 to January 2016 and October 2017 to March 2018). The data involved two agenda-setting print or online media outlets per country.

Individual migrants and refugees, this study discerns, are also under-represented in the coverage (six percent of all articles that were part of the study), with zero reference in a Ukrainian news portal, and the highest visibility in the US media. Reporting is often assumed under a domestic policy viewpoint rather than foreign coverage. Politicians again outnumber other groups as the main actors (over 50 percent of all articles in this study), and only one percent of the articles focused on individual motives for people to migrate or to flee. Even as groups, people on the move and on the run remain fuzzy, with the majority of articles unclear about the definitions of migrants and refugees. Identifying key topics in the media coverage, the study points to political debates as the main theme in close to 50 percent of the articles compared to only four percent of the articles dedicated to individual stories of migrants and refugees. Equally deficient (four percent as well) was the inclusion of statistical and background information on migration and forced displacement in the coverage.

In an important result for journalism education, the study reinforced the training needs of European journalists for research-based coverage, particularly given the fact that the Russian war on Ukraine brought matters of migration and forced displacement back to the heart of Europe.

Research-based and collaborative: two projects in media and migration

Covering migration and forced displacement as a transnational topic in appreciation of the interdisciplinarity of the three related research fields – migration, refugee studies, mass communication – and with a focus on human rights is a complex assignment that requires professional education. As a contribution to advance this objective, and with the collaboration of educators from East and West Africa, our UNESCO Handbook for Journalism Educators "Reporting on Migrants and Refugees" (Fengler, Lengauer and Zappe 2021) addresses journalism educators in the Global South and in the Global North. It is available in Arabic, English, French, Kiswahili, Russian and Spanish. Concerned with the media coverage of migrants, refugees, internally displaced persons, stateless people and their host communities alike, the handbook's interdisciplinary approach comprises all aspects needed to educate and train journalistic analysis, research, presentation, editorial marketing and ethics of migration coverage. Specific modules prepare journalists on how to generate needs-assessed story ideas, pitch a story to editors, and use social media to address larger audiences for migration-related journalistic stories.

Supporting journalism education to advance quality reporting on migration and forced displacement in Africa is the main target of the Erasmus+

CoMMPASS (2024). The project develops a distance learning platform on reporting on migration and forced displacement that will be available in English, French, Portuguese and Kiswahili. Based on a series of workshops with leading African journalism educators, the CoMMPASS project team has jointly identified specific challenges that need to be addressed in higher journalism education and newsrooms in African countries when it comes to covering migration. The online course intends to bridge the academia-practice divide by offering content to classrooms and newsrooms. By offering digital content based on the latest knowledge and know-how, it responds to the growing number of African students who aspire to a university education. Much has been said about the African youth bulge. This project contributes efficiently and sustainably to turning the youth bulge into a dividend by offering learning opportunities. The relevance of educating youth in three research fields that are most relevant for their societies – journalism as a pillar for democratic transition and migration and refugee studies that help youth to make informed decisions.

Conclusion

Through mass communication research and journalism education, the call to tell the global and human rights-based story of migration and forced displacement is advancing. By reflecting the human rights of migrants, refugees and members of host communities, journalists innovate the storytelling in many ways: They add depth by asking individuals at all junctions of human mobility to speak for themselves. This is a sea change in many journalism cultures from a dominance of officials towards a new diversity of voices that include directly affected individuals – in systems of limited freedoms this may be perceived as a step towards democratic transition. Appreciating the individual in reporting on migration and forced displacement is long overdue, considering the year 1951 when the significant change to an individualized definition of a refugee was enshrined in the Refugee Convention. Journalists are moving from reporting *on* migrants towards reporting *with* migrants, granting their interviewees space with full agency. Innovative storytelling in the global policy field also departs from a domestic viewpoint to the multiplicity of transnationalism that characterizes migration and forced displacement. Against this backdrop, the education of aspiring journalists and the training of practitioners is imperative. In response, journalism educators pursue a balanced curriculum of research-based knowledge and the profession's know-how. This chapter has shown two current examples in the UNESCO Handbook for Journalism Educators (Fengler, Lengauer and Zappe 2021) and the e-learning platform developed by the CoMMPASS (2024) project. They offer solutions to needs that were identified in comparative research. It has been shown that migration and forced displacement are underreported in many journalism cultures, and that, if covered, articles often lack definitional clarity of key terms, statistical and background information. They are also one-sided – European media focus on border security and migration policy; African media cover the integration of African migrants in Europe but snub reporting on the integration of African migrants in African countries where the majority of African migrants settle. Through collaborative work with scholars and practitioners from various world regions, these resources aspire to empower practising journalists so they convey transnational stories based on knowledge and know-how, in full acknowledgement of cross-cultural diversity and human rights. These are building blocks to create the conditions for original research and reporting practice. Human rights are crosscutting the inquiry in all facets of migration and forced displacement including questions of border security and externalization of border control. For communication research, and for journalists reporting on the matter, press freedom and academic freedom are indispensable human rights. Journalism representing perhaps "our only hope to secure human rights" (OHCHR 2023), indeed, seems a lot for the profession to shoulder, but journalism educators accept the challenge.

Discussion questions

1. Which innovative approaches are expected from journalism education to further build the knowledge and know-how of aspiring journalists across journalism and educational cultures in reporting migration and forced displacement as a transnational matter?
2. How are the disciplines of mass communication, migration and refugee studies envisioning collaborating in order to advance the joint research field, and how does the cross-cultural perspectives inform the perspectives?
3. What research questions need to be developed in order to meet the complexities of 360-degree reporting of the "African" and other spatially-related stories?

Further reading

Chernov, M. 2023. *20 Days in Mariupol.* PBS Frontline and AP.
Rothenberger, L., M. Löffelholz, and D. H. Weaver. 2023. *The Palgrave Handbook of Cross-Border Journalism.* Springer International Publishing.
White, A. 2015. *Moving Stories.* London: Ethical Journalism Network.

References

Akram, S. 2002. "Palestinian Refugees and Their Legal Stauts: Rights, Politics and Implications for a Just Solution." *Journal of Palestine Studies* 31 (3): 36–51.
Androff, D. K. 2022. *Refugee Solutions in the Age of Global Crisis: Human Rights, Integration, and Sustainable Development.* Oxford University Press.

Assopgoum, F. T. 2011. *Migration aus Afrika in die EU: Eine Analyse der Berichterstattung in deutschen und senegalesischen Zeitungen*. Wiesbaden: VS Verlag für Sozialwissenschaften.

Bakewell, O. 2008. "Research Beyond the Categories: The Importance of Policy Irrelevant Reseach into Forced Migration." *Journal of Refugee Studies* 21 (4): 432–543.

Balabanova, E., and A. Balch. 2010. "Sending and Receiving: The Ethical Framing of Intra-EU Migration in the European Press." *European Journal of Communication* 25 (4): 382–97.

Becker, M. A. 2020. "The Plight of the Rohingya: Genocide Allegations and Provisional Measures in the Gambia v Myanmar at the International Court of Justice." *Melbourne Journal of International Law* 21 (2): 428–49. https://search.informit.org/doi/10.3316/agispt.2021101105485956.

Berry, M., I. Garcia-Blanco, and K. Moore. 2015. "A Press Coverage of the Refugee and Migrant Crisis in the EU: A Content Analysis of Five European Countries." https://www.unhcr.org/protection/operations/56bb369c9/press-coverage-refugee-migrant-crisis-eu-content-analysis-five-european.html.

Black, R. 2001. "Fifty Years of Refugee Studies: From Theory to Policy." *The International Migration Review* 35 (1): 57–78.

Bloch, A. 2020. "Reflections and Directions for Research in Refugee Studies." *Ethnic and Racial Studies* 43 (3): 436–59.

Bradley, M. 2023. "Who and What is IOM For? The Evolution of IOM's Mandate, Policies, and Obligations." In *IOM Unbound? Obligations and Accountability of the International Organization for Migration in an Era of Expansion*, edited by M. Bradley, C. Costello, and A. Sherwood, 43–184. Cambridge University Press.

Bradley, M., C. Costello, and A. Sherwood, eds. 2023. *IOM Unbound? Obligations and Accountability of the International Organization for Migration in an Era of Expansion*. Cambridge University Press. https://doi.org/10.1017/9781009184175.003.

Bradley, M., and M. Erdilmen. 2022. "Is the International Organization for Migration Legitimate? Rights-Talk, Protection Commitments and the Legitimation of IOM." *Journal of Ethnic and Migration Studies* 49 (9): 2332–54.

Castles, S., and M. J. Miller [J. Mark]. 1993. *The Age of Migration: Population Movements in the Modern World*, 1st ed. Longmans, Green.

Connor, P. 2018. *International Migration From Sub-Saharan Africa Has Grown Dramatically Since 2010*. Pew Research Center. https://www.pewresearch.org/fact-tank/2018/02/28/international-migration-from-sub-saharan-africa-has-grown-dramatically-since-2010.

Crisis Group. 2024. "10 Conflicts to Watch 2024: More Leaders Are Pursuing Their Ends Militarily. More Believe They Can Get Away With It." https://www.crisisgroup.org/global/10-conflicts-watch-2024

Crock, M., ed. 2015. *Migrants and Rights*, 1st ed. London: Routledge. https://doi.org/10.4324/9781315248967.

Dao, T., F. Docquier, M. Maurel, and P. Schaus. 2018. "Global Migration in the 20th and 21st Centuries: The Unstoppable Force of Demography." Fondation pour les études et recherches sur le développement international. Working Paper No. P223. https://ferdi.fr/publications/global-migration-in-the-20th-and-21st-centuries-the-unstoppable-force-of-demography.

Dastyari, A., A. Nethery, and A. Hirsch, eds. 2023. *Refugee Externalisation Policies: Responsibility, Legitimacy and Accountability*. Milton Park, New York: Routledge.

de Haas, H. 2021. "A Theory of Migration: The Aspirations-Capabilities Framework." *Comparative Migration Studies* 9. https://doi.org/10.1186/s40878-020-00210.

Dekker, R., and G. Engbersen. 2014. "How Social Media Transform Migrant Networks and Facilitate Migration." *Global Networks* 14 (4). https://onlinelibrary.wiley.com/doi/epdf/10.1111/glob.12040.

Douglas, S. M., J. Arango, H. Graeme, A. Kouaouci, A. Pellegrino, and J. E. Taylor. 1994. "An Evaluation of International Migration Theory: The North American Case." *Population and Development Review* 20 (4). https://doi.org/10.2307/2137660.

Eberl, J. M., C. Meltzer, T. Heidenreich, B. Herrero-Jiminez, N. Theorin, F. Lind, R. Berganza, H. G. Boomgaarden, C. Schemer, and J. Strömbäck. 2018. "The European Media Discourse on Immigration and Its Effects: A Literature Review." *Annals of the International Communication Association* 42 (3): 207–23.

Eisenstadt, S. N. 1953. "Analysis of Patterns of Immigration and Absorption of Immigrants." *Population Studies* 7 (2). https://doi.org/10.2307/2172030.

EJO. 2015. "Wie Zeitungen aus West- und Osteuropa über die Flüchtlingskrise berichteten." https://de.ejo-online.eu/forschung/wie-zeitungen-in-europa-über-die-flüchtlingksrise-berichteten.

Erasmus + CoMMPASS Project. 2024. "Erasmus+ Communicating Migration and Mobility: E-Learning Programs and Newsroom Applications for Sub-Saharan Africa (CoMMPASS)." https://commpass.org/partner-institutions/.

Erdilman, M. 2019. *Durable Solutions and the Humanitarian-Development-Nexus: A Literature Review*. Ottawa: The Local Engagement Refugee Research Network, Carlton University. https://carleton.ca/lerrn/?p=708.

Fengler, S. 2021. "The Media and the Migration Story: An Analysis Across Countries." In *UNESCO Series on Journalism Education: Reporting on Migrants and Refugees: Handbook for Journalism Educators*, edited by S. Fengler, M. Lengauer, and A.-C. Zappe, 97–112. Paris: UNESCO.

Fengler, S., M. Bastian, J. Brinkmann, A.-C. Zappe, V. Tatah, M. Andindilile, E. Assefa, M. Chibita, A. Mbaine, L. Obonyo, T. Quashigah, and M. Lengauer. 2022. "Covering Migration: In Africa and Europe: Results From a Comparative Analysis of 11 Countries." *Journalism Practice* 16 (1): 140–60.

Fengler, S., and M. Kreutler. 2020. *Migration Coverage in Europe's Media: A Comparative Analysis of Coverage in 17 Countries* (OBS Working Paper No. 39). Frankfurt am Main. Otto Brenner Stiftung. https://www.otto-brenner-stiftung.de/fileadmin/user_data/stiftung/02_Wissenschaftsportal/03_Publikationen/AP39_Migration_EN.pdf.

Fengler, S., M. Lengauer, and A. C. Zappe, eds. 2021. *UNESCO Series on Journalism Education: Reporting on Migrants and Refugees: Handbook for Journalism Educators*. Paris: UNESCO. https://unesdoc.unesco.org/ark:/48223/pf0000377890.

Ferris, E. E. 2023. "Durable Displacement and the Protracted Search for Solutions: Promising Programs and Strategies." *Journal on Migration and Human Security* 11 (1): 3–22.

Fotopoulos, S., and M. Kaimaklioti. 2016. "Media Discourse on the Refugee Crisis: On What Have the Greek, German and British Press Focused?" *European View* 15 (2): 265–79. https://doi.org/10.1007/s12290-016-0407-5.

Freedman, J., and G. S. de Andrade, eds. 2024. *Research Handbook on Asylum and Refugee Policy*. Cheltenham: Edward Elgar.

Freier, L. F., E. Karageorgiou, and K. Ogg. 2021. "Challenging the Legality of Externalisation in Oceania, Europe and South America: An Impossible Task?" *Forced Migration Review* 68: 23–26.

Gaynor, T. 2020. "Climate Change is the Defining Crisis of Our Time and It Particularly Impacts the Displaced," November 30. https://www.unhcr.org/news/stories/climate-change-defining-crisis-our-time-and-it-particularly-impacts-displaced.

Geiger, M., and A. Pécoud, eds. 2020. *The International Organization for Migration: The New 'UN Migration Agency' in Critical Perspective*. Cham: Palgrave Macmillan.

Georgiou, M., and R. Zaborowski. 2017. "Council of Europe Report: Media Coverage of the 'Refugee Crisis': A Cross-European Perspective." Accessed December 15, 2020. https://rm.coe.int/1680706b00.

Glazer, N., and D. P. Moynihan. 1963. *Behind the Melting Pot: The Negroes, Puerto Ricans, Jews, Italians, and Irish of New York City*. New York: Massachusetts Institute of Technology.
Hamad, A. A. 2023. "Why Does Arab Media Fail So Badly at Covering Refugee Issues?" *Al Jazeera Journalism Review*, August 28. https://institute.aljazeera.net/en/ajr/article/2309.
Handmaker, J., L. A. De La Hunt, and J. Klaasen, eds. 2008. *Advancing Refugee Protection in South Africa*. New York, Oxford: Berghahn.
Hathaway, J. C. 2021. *The Right of Refugees Under International Law*, 2nd ed. Cambridge: Cambridge University Press.
Hieronymi, O. 2005. "Identity, Integration and Assimiliation: Factors of Success and Failure of Migration." *Refugee Survey Quarterly* 24 (4): 132–50.
Hoffmann-Nowotny, H. J. 1970. *Migration: Ein Beitrag zu einer soziologischen Erklärung*. Stuttgart: F. Enke.
Horsti, K. 2008. "Eurpeanisation of Public Debate." *Javnost: The Public* 15 (4): 41–53. https://doi.org/10.1080-13183222.2008.11008981.
ILO. 2022. *Protecting Migrants in Irregular Situations and Addressing Irregular Labour Migration: A Compendium*. Geneva. https://www.ilo.org/global/topics/labour-migration/publications/WCMS_832915/lang--en/index.htm.
International Journalists' Network. 2021. "Reporting on Refugee Communities: Narrative and Research." June 16. https://ijnet.org/en/resource/reporting-refugee-communities-narrative-and-research.
IOM. 2021. *World Migration Report 2022*. Geneva. https://publications.iom.int/books/world-migration-report-2022.
Josephi, B., F. Hanusch, M. O. Alonso, I. Shapiro, K. Andresen, A. S. de Beer, and E. Tandoc. 2019. "Profiles of Journalists: Demographic and Employment Patterns." In *Worlds of Journalism: Journalistic Cultures Around the Globe*, edited by T. Hanitzsch, F. Hanusch, J. Ramaprasad, and A. S. de Beer, 67–102. New York: Columbia University Press.
Journal of Genocide Research. 2024. "Forum: Israel-Palestine: Atrocity Ccimes and the Crisis of Holocaust and Genocide Studies." https://www.tandfonline.com/doi/full/10.1080/14623528.2023.2300555.
Kraly, E. P., and B. Hovy. 2020. "Data and Research to Inform Global Policy: The Global Compact for Safe, Orderly and Regular Migration." *Comparative Migration Studies* 8. https://doi.org/10.1186/s40878-019-0166-y.
Lecheler, S., J. Matthes, and H. Boomgaarden, eds. 2019. "Media and Migration: Theoretical and Empirical Perspectives [Special Issue]." *Mass Communication and Society* 22 (6). https://www.tandfonline.com/toc/hmcs20/22/6?nav=tocList.
Lee, E. S. 1966. "A Theory of Migration." *Demography* 3 (1): 47–57.
Lengauer, M. 2021a. "Perspectives From the Middle East and the Arab Gulf Region." In *Reporting on Media, Migration and Forced Displacement: Global Perspectives*, edited by S. Fengler and M. Lengauer, 3–6. Dortmund: Erich Brost Institute for International Journalism, TU Dortmund University. http://dx.doi.org/10.17877/DE290R-22404.
Lengauer, M. 2021b. "Media Accountability in MENA Through the Perspective of the Theory of the Professions." *Journal of Middle East Media* 16: 39–89.
Lengauer, M. 2021c. "African Movements: From the Continent, Within the Continent, Within Countries." In *UNESCO Series on Journalism Education: Reporting on Migrants and Refugees: Handbook for Journalism Educators*, edited by S. Fengler, M. Lengauer, and A.-C. Zappe, 197–222. Paris: UNESCO.
Lengauer, M. 2024. "Covering Migration and Forced Displacement: Ethical Callenges for Journalism Education in the Arab World." *Ethical Space* 24 (2): 65–82.
Levitt, P., and B. N. Jaworsky. 2007. "Transnational Migration Studies: Past Developments and Future Trends." *Annual Review of Sociology* 33: 129–56.

Los Angeles Times. 2023. "Letters to the Editor: Jews Just Faced Our Worst Massacre Since the Holocaust. Here's What We Need Now." October 21, 2023. https://www.latimes.com/opinion/letters-to-the-editor/story/2023-10-21/jews-just-faced-the-worst-massacre-since-the-holocaust.

Maharat Foundation. 2016. *Media Coverage of Refugees' Issues: Lebanon, Jordan, Egypt, Morocco*. Beirut. Maharat Foundation, Arabic Network for Human Rights Information, Department o Research and Documentation (Egypt and Morocco) Website: Maharat Foundation LEB.

McAdam, J. 2018. "The Global Compact on Refugees and Migration: A New Era for International Protection?" *International Journal of Refugee Law* 30 (4): 571–74.

Migration Data Portal. 2024. "Data: Total Number of International Migrants at Mid-Year 2020." https://www.migrationdataportal.org/international-data?i=stock_abs_&t=2020&m=2&sm49=145.

OHCHR. 2023. "Journalism May Be Our Only Hope to Secure Human Rights." [Press Release], May 3. https://www.ohchr.org/en/stories/2023/05/journalism-may-be-our-only-hope-secure-human-rights.

Okunna, C. S. 2021. "Public Opinion About Migration is Mainly Positive in Nigeria." In *UNESCO Series on Journalism Education: Reporting on Migrants and Refugees: Handbook for Journalism Educators*, edited by S. Fengler, M. Lengauer, and A.-C. Zappe, 20. Paris: UNESCO.

Park, R. E. 1928. "Migration and the Maginal Man." *American Journal of Sociology* 33: 881–93.

Ravenstein, E. G. 1885. "The Laws of Migration." *Journal of the Statistical Society of London* 48 (2): 167–235. https://www.jstor.org/stable/pdf/2979181.pdf.

Rodrigo, J., and G. Priorelli. 2023. "Refugee Studies: Interdisciplinarity and Agency in Contemporary Humanitarian Crises, 1930–2020s." *Historiografías* 25: 86–131.

Sassen, S. 2007. *A Sociology of Globalization: Contemporary Societies*. London: Norton.

Scholars at Risk. 2023. "Academic Freedom and Its Protection Under International Law." https://www.scholarsatrisk.org/resources/academic-freedom-and-its-protection-under-international-law/.

Siddikoglu, H., and A. Z. Sagiroglu. 2023. "The Responses of Pakistan and Turkey to Refugee Influxes: A Comparative Analysis of Durable Solutions to Protracted Displacements." *Journal on Migration and Human Security* 11 (1): 41–56.

Smets, K., K. Lerus, M. Georgiou, S. Witteborn, and R. Gajjala, eds. 2020. *The SAGE Handbook of Media and Migration*. Los Angeles: Sage.

Speelman, L. H., R. J. Nicholls, and R. Safra de Campos. 2021. "The Role of Migration and Demographic Change in Small Island Futures." *Asian and Pacific Migration Journal* 30 (3): 282–311.

Stein, B. N., and S. M. Tomasi, eds. 1981. "Refugees Today [Special Issue]." *The International Migration Review* 15 (1–2). https://doi.org/10.1177/0197918381015001-20.

Trimikliniotis, N. 2020. *Migration and the Refugee Dissensus in Europe: Borders, Security and Austerity*. MIL: Routledge.

UNDP. 2019. *Scaling Fences: Voices of Irregular African Migrants to Europe*. New York. https://www.africa.undp.org/content/rba/en/home/library/reports/ScalingFences.html.

UNHCR. 2023. *Global Trends: Forced Displacement in 2022*. Copenhagen. https://www.unhcr.org/global-trends-report-2022.

United Nations. 2018a. "Refugees and Migrants." *Global Compact for Migration*. https://refugeesmigrants.un.org/migration-compact.

United Nations. 2018b. "Refugees and Migrants. Global Compact on Refugees." In *Global Compact for Migration: Global Compact on Refugees*. New York. https://refugeesmigrants.un.org/refugees-compact.

United Nations. 2024. "Gaza is a Massive Human Rights Crisis and a Humanitarian Disaster [Press Release]." January 30. https://www.ohchr.org/en/stories/2024/01/gaza-massive-human-rights-crisis-and-humanitarian-disaster#:~:text=Following%20an%20attack%20by%20Palestinian,human%20rights%20and%20humanitarian%20crisis.

UNRWA. 2024. "UNRWA Situation Report #108 on the Gaza Strip and the West Bank Including East Jerusalem." May 21. https://www.unrwa.org/resources/reports/unrwa-situation-report-108-situation-gaza-strip-and-west-bank-including-east-Jerusalem.

The World Bank. 2023. *World Development Report 2023: Migrants, Refugees, Societies.* Washington, DC. https://www.worldbank.org/en/publication/wdr2023.

14
CONCLUSION

Sanem Şahin

The book discussed and evidenced the intricate relationship between journalism and human rights. It explored their multifaceted connection, focusing on journalists' safety, threats to media freedom, responsibilities, and challenges of documenting human rights in conflicts, migration and climate changes, the shifts in the interaction with human rights groups and the impact of technology on human rights reporting. Each chapter demonstrated that the relationship between journalism and human rights is reciprocal as they need each other to function properly: the free press is important in safeguarding human rights, just as human rights are crucial for media freedom. Journalism's role in exposing human rights violations, holding those who abuse their power to account, and informing the public are essential for democratic societies. However, media and journalism are facing many problems, risks, and dangers globally. Deteriorating media freedom even in democratic countries, violence against journalists, economic pressures, poor working conditions, and low public trust are causing concerns among scholars, professionals, and human rights supporters.

The meaning and importance of human rights have expanded. Public perception of human rights abuses is no longer limited to political rights or problems of developing countries. Diverse issues, such as identity, health, and poverty, are covered under human rights matters, increasing their relevance and visibility. New challenges, including competition among emerging global powers, the rise of xenophobic and populist movements, and the proliferation of surveillance technologies, along with the ongoing humanitarian crises and climate change and poverty, require more scrutiny and better understanding. The public needs access to unbiased information about these developments to make informed decisions about their future, which journalism can provide.

DOI: 10.4324/9781032662589-17

Journalists, while entitled to human rights like any individual, also play a role in protecting the public's interest and human rights. Because of the significance and the risks of this function of journalism, some argue that press freedom should be recognised as a human right (Cruft 2022; Lamer 2016). As Torsner's and Sampaio-Dias, Silveirinha, and Miranda chapters explain, acknowledging journalists' unique part in safeguarding human rights is an important step in developing actions to tackle violence against them. Threats against their safety are a big concern. Journalists face many risks and dangers, such as violence, harassment, detention, legal threats, and impunity when reporting on human rights violations and therefore need greater protection and support. Women journalists are especially victims of online abuse. As women and journalists, they receive gendered-based violence. The 'chilling effect' of these attacks on women journalists has an impact on the information communicated to the public because as Pulfer (2020, 2) puts it 'half the story is never enough'.

Journalists follow legal, ethical, and practical guidelines when reporting human rights violations. Adhering to them is essential for maintaining journalism's credibility and upholding the public's trust in it. These standards become more important when working in hostile environments, such as conflicts, as White explains in his chapter. Journalists must navigate not only their own safety when facing risks like being killed, wounded, kidnapped, disinformation, and censorship, but also ethical dilemmas such as reporting facts objectively, deciding how much graphic detail to give without causing harm, protecting sources, bias towards a party, and verifying information. How journalists perceive and perform their roles in these circumstances is a widely debated topic. Both Fiorito and Selvarajah's chapters on journalists' responsibility to report, as well as Shaw's model of human rights journalism, contribute to these debates, presenting alternative approaches to journalists' roles and responsibilities when covering human rights atrocities in conflicts.

Journalism's role in the protection of human rights makes it necessary to scrutinise its practices to better understand its impact on the public's perception of human rights. Story selection and framing of human rights issues can influence how the public views and reacts to them. As the chapters in this book demonstrated, the news media can support and safeguard human rights but can also undermine them by spreading misleading information, sensationalism, and acting as a propaganda tool. Balabanova reminds us how the media's coverage of some issues such as migration erodes basic human rights. For example, when the media reiterate the political debates that deliberately ignore human rights commitments, they fail to provide the public with the necessary information. Turner presents a similar argument using the media's inadequate presentation of terrorism as an example. He explains that when the news media become a part of government efforts to manipulate public opinion, the public's right to know is weakened, leading to terrorism being poorly understood. These examples show the weaknesses, gaps, and problems in human rights news. That is why Fengler and Lengauer stress the importance of journalism training supported by research to ensure accurate and empathetic reporting on human rights issues.

Transformations in the media landscape, journalism, advocacy, and technology have created complexities for human rights reporting, which Powers describes as a 'double-edged sword'. The use of digital technology has enhanced the accessibility and reach of human rights stories and improved the verification of information on abuses. Not only journalists and human rights organisations but also individuals can document and disseminate human rights atrocities. There are more opportunities for journalists, human rights activists, and victims to collaborate and publicise human rights violations. However, digital technology has also made surveillance, online harassment and the production and spread of false information much easier and faster. The internet and social media platforms have especially become the main sources of misinformation and disinformation. They impact human rights reporting by undermining the credibility of journalistic reports, creating public confusion and polarisation, diverting journalists' resources to fact-checking rather than investigating, and increasing risks and violence against journalists.

The chapters in this book provided an overview of the immense challenges journalists experience. But they also demonstrated journalists' resilience and commitment to continue practising their profession. Driven by their dedication to truth and justice and their sense of duty and responsibility, journalists confront threats and dangers with perseverance. Sometimes, as we read in Şahin's chapter on displaced journalists, they pay a high price by having to leave their home countries. Despite these risks, journalists demonstrate remarkable strength and dedication to their work. In some cases, they acknowledge they are not just journalists and eyewitnesses but are also potential victims. For example, as Enano's chapter showed, journalists know the impact of environmental degradation will also affect them. The link between climate change and human rights has become more visible, demanding more attention and action from the international community. Journalists also adapt their practices in response to injustice and danger to ensure safety and continue working effectively. Gastelum and Franco's chapter on disappearances in Mexico demonstrated how journalists adjusted their journalism and collaborated with families of missing persons in Mexico to help them in their campaign. This adaption is a good example of journalists' renegotiation of their roles and practices according to the needs of their communities.

Looking forward

The book makes it clear that the challenges faced by journalists and the media in the context of human rights are complex and evolving. Addressing these challenges requires joint efforts from the international community, governments, media organizations, and civil society. While international mechanisms for the support and protection of journalists can be improved, governments should enact and enforce laws that uphold media freedom and protect journalists. Similarly, media organisations should prioritise the safety of their staff and provide them with training and resources. Public awareness and understanding of human rights issues are crucial in the protection of human rights and in addressing today's challenges. They will encourage individuals to advocate and defend their rights, demanding authorities to uphold them.

As it is mainly journalists who bring violations to the public's attention, it is essential for them to have the necessary knowledge and skills to recognise and report them accurately and ethically. This can be achieved with journalism training in human rights that will help them learn the legal and moral frameworks concerning human rights and communicate them with sensitivity and respect for human dignity. As journalism and human rights scholars and journalists, we hope this book will contribute to the resources supporting and enhancing journalism's role in the protection of human rights, providing the theoretical and practical knowledge needed to report on these issues effectively.

References

Cruft, Rowan. 2022. "Journalism and Press Freedom as Human Rights." *Journal of Applied Philosophy* 39 (3): 359–76.

Lamer, Wiebke. 2016. "Promoting the People's Surrogate: The Case for Press Freedom as a Distinct Human Right." *Journal of Human Rights* 15 (3): 361–82.

Pulfer, Rachel. 2020. "Half the Story is Never Enough: Threats Facing Women Journalists Worldwide and What to Do About Them." In *Half the Story Is Never Enough: Threats Facing Women Journalists*. The Canadian Commission for UNESCO and Journalists for Human Rights.

INDEX

abortion 78
abuse 1, 2, 4, 5, 7, 34, 47, 53, 54, 57, 75–78, 81–85, 89, 107, 122, 123, 198, 199; of power 1, 4, 21, 91, 95, 115
accountability 7, 28, 32, 39, 76, 80, 115, 116, 173, 179
accountable 5, 61, 83, 94, 107, 117, 163, 169
activism 21, 93
activists 4, 20, 59, 61, 63, 64, 66, 68, 155, 200; citizen 20, 61, 63, 66, 117
advocacy 6, 28, 58–66, 68, 83, 93, 110, 115, 200; groups 2, 3, 9, 15, 18, 19, 29, 35, 39, 51, 53, 59–68, 84, 86, 91–93, 101, 113, 121, 140, 145, 148, 151–54, 161, 169, 176, 184, 185, 189, 190, 198
African Charter on Human and Peoples' Rights 43
AI *see* artificial intelligence
Al Qaeda 144
Aljazeera 49–51
American Convention on Human Rights 40, 43
Amnesty International 19, 52, 55, 62, 63, 65, 69
antisemitism 123
armed conflicts 1
Article 19, 13, 30, 36, 39, 40, 43, 45, 55, 75, 79, 85, 87, 110, 112, 113, 153

artificial intelligence 20, 53
asylum seekers 19, 96, 100, 141, 184, 186
atrocities 1, 7, 46, 54, 107, 108, 111, 112, 115, 116, 144, 199, 200
authoritarian 2, 17, 41, 75
authorities 3, 9, 17, 44, 50, 52, 80, 91, 98, 109, 125, 154, 155, 157, 158, 161–64, 201; public 3, 4, 6, 9, 13–16, 19–22, 24, 35, 37, 42–45, 48, 51, 53, 54, 58, 60, 64, 65, 67, 68, 83, 86, 92, 97, 98, 108, 112, 115–18, 121–24, 129–31, 139–41, 143–45, 147, 148, 153, 155, 156, 173, 184, 189, 190, 198, 199; state 16, 17, 29, 44, 45, 51, 52, 85, 93, 101, 108, 109, 114, 115, 118, 120, 125, 126, 130, 140, 142, 147, 151, 153–57, 162, 163
Awoko 125–35

Berger 32, 33, 39, 48, 53–55, 113, 118

cancel culture 20
censorship 1–4, 17, 37, 44, 46, 79–82, 92, 199
chilling effect 2, 4, 34, 38, 81, 98, 148, 199
churnalism 64
climate 1, 2, 5, 6, 8, 16, 22, 32, 42, 54, 168–82, 194, 198, 200; change 1, 2, 4–6, 8, 16, 21, 22, 32, 42, 53, 61,

Index **203**

81, 92, 93, 116, 117, 120, 168–76, 178–82, 191, 194, 198, 200; crisis 7, 8, 16, 19–21, 23, 42, 84, 89, 99, 115, 116, 124, 151–53, 163, 164, 169–73, 175, 177–81, 187, 193, 194, 197
Committee to Protect Journalists 6, 8, 28, 49, 55, 102, 113, 118
conflict 1, 7, 18, 22, 33, 46–49, 79, 92, 107, 109, 110, 113, 115–17, 121, 122, 124, 125, 133, 142, 145, 169, 172, 185
Convention on the Prevention and Punishment of the Crime of Genocide 110, 119
convention 40, 43, 54, 80, 84, 87, 88, 110, 119, 152, 184, 191
Council of Europe 19, 24, 40, 55, 80, 87, 194
COVID-19 5, 16, 26
CPJ *see* Committee to Protect Journalists
crime 1, 3, 6, 7, 9, 35, 36, 39, 43, 47, 48, 50, 52, 55, 91, 106–12, 114–17, 119, 147, 148, 151–57, 159, 161, 163; against humanity 1, 106, 108–10, 112, 114, 152

data 4, 16, 24, 26, 104, 184, 195, 196
defamation 3, 44, 46, 57, 75
democracy 3, 29, 40, 42, 44, 50, 52, 55, 81, 82, 85, 86, 106, 107, 111, 114, 116, 117, 120, 139
democratic 2–4, 16, 17, 22, 43, 53, 75, 82, 95, 107, 139, 191, 198
diaspora 92, 101, 187
digital 3, 6, 17, 20–22, 39, 58, 60–63, 66, 76, 77, 82–84, 95, 98, 191, 200; media 1–7, 9, 13–24, 30–33, 42–56, 58–66, 68, 76, 80–86, 88, 90–94, 97–99, 101–3, 106–12, 114–18, 120, 121, 123, 125, 126, 132, 133, 139–49, 151, 152, 154, 155, 157–59, 162, 163, 170, 175, 177, 186–90, 192, 198–201
Dirty 155, 156
disappearance 7, 32, 151–53, 155, 157–59, 162–64
disasters 1, 7, 92, 142, 167, 168, 171, 175, 189; climate-related 1, 170
discrimination 7, 75–77, 79, 80, 84, 96, 100, 112, 133, 169
disinformation 4, 20, 44, 53, 76, 77, 85, 199, 200

displace 63, 92, 169
displaced 4, 7, 19, 91, 92, 94–97, 101, 102, 183, 184, 188, 190, 194, 200; internally 19, 94, 190
displacement 7, 8, 91–93, 95, 99–102, 169, 172, 183–92, 197; forced 4, 7, 8, 91–93, 98, 102, 122, 155, 172, 175, 183–92, 197
Dmitry Muratov 76
double-edged sword 6, 58, 59, 64, 68, 71, 200

ECHR *see* European Convention on Human Rights
economic 1, 2, 14–16, 19, 22, 32, 43, 44, 59, 60, 80, 83, 95, 96, 99, 101, 122, 130, 153, 154, 172, 184, 198
education 8, 32, 79, 92, 95, 97, 123, 183–87, 190–92
Edward Snowden 45, 56
elections 20, 61, 62, 139
emotional 3, 7, 77, 80, 82, 96, 99, 100, 155, 157, 159, 163
environment 3–5, 15, 21, 31, 37, 41, 53, 62, 76, 85, 102, 126, 168, 171, 173, 174; environmental 8, 32, 36, 37, 41, 146, 168, 171, 173, 174, 178, 200; sustainable 32, 43, 115, 125, 131, 168
erga omnes 110–12, 114, 116
ethnic 77, 108, 110, 114, 116, 117, 185, 186
ethnic cleansing 108, 110, 114
European Convention on Human Rights 43
European Court of Human Rights 47, 56
European Union 2, 9, 46, 56, 87, 88, 104
exile 9, 92, 93, 102–105, 119
exiled 54, 92, 94, 95, 98, 99, 102, 103
eyewitness 65

foreign journalists 1
free expression 20, 31, 43, 45, 47, 139, 141, 144, 148
freedom 1–4, 8, 9, 17, 20, 28–31, 33–35, 37, 39, 44–48, 52, 55, 57, 75, 76, 79–82, 84–88, 90–92, 94, 95, 101, 102, 106, 107, 110, 112, 114, 116, 139, 140, 143, 147, 186, 189, 192, 196, 198, 199, 201; media 2, 8–10, 14, 16, 18, 19, 22–26,

38–41, 53, 55, 56, 69, 70, 84, 87–90, 101, 103–7, 114, 117–19, 123, 134, 142, 149, 165, 188, 193–96
Freedom House 3, 9, 26, 95, 98, 103, 105
freedom of expression 1, 2, 20, 28, 30, 31, 33, 48, 52, 75, 76, 79, 81, 85, 91, 94, 95, 101, 106, 110, 112, 116
freelancers 60, 66, 151, 170, 173
French Revolution 13, 140

gatekeepers 4, 14
Gaza 1, 8, 16, 18, 24, 25, 48–50, 54, 55, 110, 118, 146, 149, 197
gender 3, 7, 33, 36, 67, 76–81, 84–86, 89, 122, 152, 154, 175, 182; gender-based 76–80, 84, 175
gendered 4, 76–78, 81, 83, 85, 199
genocide 56, 106–10, 112–14, 116–18, 122, 183
Global Charter of Ethics for Journalists 5
Global North 59, 63, 67, 187–90
Global South 17, 63, 67, 168, 170, 188, 190
global warming 168
government 3, 15, 35, 44, 45, 49, 51, 52, 54, 58–61, 63–65, 68, 93–95, 117, 120, 129–31, 139, 140, 145–47, 151, 152, 154, 157, 163, 170, 189, 199
The Guardian 45, 56, 57, 150

Hamas 1, 18, 23, 50, 57, 146, 183
Handbook for Journalism Educators 8, 190, 191, 194–96
harassment 3, 75–78, 80–86, 89, 91, 95, 98, 154, 199, 200
Hasta Encontrarles 8, 158, 159, 161–63
hate speech 44, 47, 77, 85, 122
Holocaust 47, 183, 195
hostility 3, 44, 80, 81, 96
HRJ *see* Human Rights Journalism
human rights 1–8, 13–22, 27–38, 42–48, 50, 51, 53–55, 58–69, 71, 75–77, 79, 80, 84–86, 91–95, 97, 101, 106–17, 120–33, 135, 151–53, 155, 157, 158, 162, 168–81, 183–87, 190, 191, 198–201; abuses 20; -based 8, 79, 116, 191, 199; coverage 3, 5–7, 14–16, 18, 19, 21, 23, 35, 54, 55, 58–66, 69, 86, 126–29, 131, 132, 139, 143, 146, 155–58, 172, 176, 184–90, 193, 199; international 15; international system of 13, 16; movement 5, 120, 121, 132, 155, 156, 176; news 4–8, 14–16, 20, 24, 35, 36, 41–45, 51–69, 71, 76–78, 81–85, 88, 91, 97, 102, 103, 106, 115, 116, 118, 121, 125, 127, 130–32, 142, 144, 147–50, 157, 158, 163, 173, 179, 181, 188–90, 194, 199, 200; violation 1, 2, 4–8, 14–16, 27, 28, 31–36, 38, 45, 48, 52, 61, 63–66, 77, 79, 84, 92, 107, 109–12, 114–17, 122–27, 131, 133, 151, 152, 162, 163, 168, 171, 175, 198–201
Human Rights Council 9, 25, 51, 52, 57, 76, 80, 90
Human Rights Journalism 7, 109, 119, 122, 124, 128, 134, 135
Human Rights Watch 61–64, 118
human trafficking 19, 122, 171
Human Wrongs Journalism 7, 124, 127
humanitarian 20, 25, 47, 54, 55, 105, 107–12, 152, 184, 186, 197, 198
HWJ *see* Human Wrongs Journalism

ICCPR *see* International Covenant on Civil and Political Rights
ICTR *see* International Criminal Tribunal for Rwanda
IFJ 5, 9, 56, 75, 76, 84, 88
impunity 4, 6, 31, 35, 38–40, 43, 44, 48, 50, 51, 53, 55, 56, 76, 78, 82, 84, 87, 103, 113, 164, 199
inequality 6, 23, 32, 123
International Covenant on Civil and Political Rights 30, 41, 43, 110, 112, 118, 152
International Criminal Court 49–51, 110
International Criminal Tribunal on the Former Yugoslavia 110
International Criminal Tribunal for Rwanda 106, 118
International Federation of Journalists 9, 44, 49, 50, 56, 76
international law 18, 28, 48, 51–55, 84, 107–14, 116, 152, 186
Islamic State 144, 146
islamophobia 123
Israel 1, 8, 16, 18, 23, 48, 50, 51, 54–57, 110, 195

Israeli 1, 9, 48–51, 55, 146, 183; forces 16, 48–51, 55, 63, 92, 113, 120, 121, 125, 145, 162, 183

Jamal Khashoggi 51, 54, 56, 98, 104
journalism 1–3, 5–10, 20, 27, 29–31, 35–38, 41–44, 46, 47, 50, 51, 53–60, 65–68, 75, 77–83, 85, 90, 92–95, 97–101, 109, 114, 115, 117, 120–26, 128–33, 148, 150, 152, 154–58, 163, 164, 175–79, 183, 184, 187, 190–92, 196, 198–201; advocacy 66, 69, 70, 93, 103; of attachment 109; ethical 5, 6, 31, 43–47, 83, 107, 108, 114–17, 155, 178, 180, 199
journalist 1–9, 15–17, 20, 27–29, 31–39, 41–51, 53–68, 75–86, 89–102, 105, 107–17, 119, 122, 125, 126, 133, 148, 151–56, 158–64, 167, 168, 170–81, 183–85, 187, 188, 190–92, 198–201; activist 93, 103; exiled 7, 92, 93, 102, 103, 105; female 78, 79, 84, 86, 98, 170; Journalists Killed 6, 28, 35, 39; Palestinian 9, 18, 25, 49–51, 56, 57, 183, 192; parachute 60; refugee 22–26, 70, 95, 97, 101–105, 184–186, 191–196; safety 2, 3, 5, 6, 9, 17, 27–29, 31–34, 36–38, 41, 43, 44, 47, 48, 55, 57, 75, 76, 78, 83, 84, 86, 92, 94, 95, 97, 98, 100, 101, 113, 141, 157, 168, 198–201
Julian Assange 45

LGBTQ+ 1

manufacturing consent 15
marginalised groups 20, 81
Maria Ressa 76
media: free 3, 13, 17, 20, 31, 42, 43, 45, 47, 53, 54, 112, 113, 122, 129, 139, 141, 144, 148, 163, 185, 198; independent 1, 6, 13, 17, 31, 37, 42, 44, 50, 52, 53, 91, 94, 97, 125, 155, 159, 170, 186; legacy 20, 47, 58, 61, 63, 119; social 2, 6, 14, 15, 16, 20–22, 24, 30, 42, 43, 52, 53, 61, 62, 65, 67, 68, 77, 78, 80–83, 85, 95–99, 115–17, 122, 140, 141, 151, 155, 165, 178, 180, 184, 186–88, 190, 200; Western 14

media freedom 2, 17, 92, 94, 101, 198
Mexico 7, 104, 151–59, 161, 163–66, 200
migrant 19, 23, 92, 177, 184–91, 193; illegal 19, 45, 50, 132, 141; irregular 184, 188; labour 184
migration 2, 5, 8, 19, 22, 23, 122, 169, 172, 183–93, 195, 196, 198, 199
misinformation 4, 7, 141, 143, 200
misogyny 76, 77, 82, 85
missing persons 151, 153–55, 159, 200

news: values 2, 3, 15, 39, 41, 42, 43, 85, 107, 108, 116, 123
NGOs 4, 6, 17, 58–62, 64, 66–71
Noroeste 161, 162

The Observer 46
ownership 3, 44

peace 33, 41, 50, 90, 106–9, 111, 114–17, 122, 123, 130, 143
perception 5, 16, 95, 97, 107, 176, 198, 199; public 3, 10, 17, 22–26, 41, 46, 56, 69, 70, 90, 105, 119, 195, 196, 198, 201
persecution 7, 17, 75, 91, 92, 100, 106, 163
pillars 108, 109, 111, 116
pluralism 2, 3, 31, 81, 83, 185, 186
political 42, 48
Politico 125–34
populism 6, 42, 54, 55
populist 2, 16, 44, 146, 198
poverty 5, 122, 169, 171, 172, 198
press 3, 9, 15, 20, 23, 28, 30, 31, 34, 35, 37, 39, 46, 47, 55–57, 60, 64, 65, 75, 76, 79, 82, 84, 88, 94, 117, 122, 139, 142, 143, 145, 146, 186, 189, 192, 193, 198, 199
privacy 3, 4, 33, 44, 46, 47
professional 2, 4, 5, 29, 59, 60, 64, 81, 83, 93–97, 99–102, 130, 190
propaganda 15, 44, 53, 110, 112, 144, 199
propaganda model 15
protest 25, 26, 120, 149
public interest 2, 29, 36, 44, 46, 53, 82, 95, 130
public opinion 5, 17, 54, 55, 106, 107, 116, 199
public sphere 21, 91
public trust 3, 198

R2P 108–12, 114–17; *see also* Responsibility to Protect
R2R 7, 106–8, 110–12, 114–17; *see also* responsibility to report
racism 19, 47, 122
refugee 19–23, 50, 92–97, 99–102, 105, 183–93, 195, 196
report 1–4, 7, 8, 14, 17, 24, 31, 39, 41, 52, 60, 81, 82, 89, 95, 98, 101, 105, 107–14, 116, 118, 119, 131, 133, 140, 148, 154, 156, 159, 163, 168, 169, 171, 173, 175, 178–81, 195, 196, 197, 201
reporter 50, 132, 145, 147, 148, 167, 173, 174, 176, 177, 180
Reporters Without Borders 9, 39, 50, 90, 91, 105
reprisal 2, 35
resilience 102, 159, 163, 173, 200
Responsibility to Protect 7, 108, 118, 119, 134
Responsibility to Report 7, 47, 107–9, 111, 114–16, 199
right 4–7, 17–19, 24, 27, 29–31, 33–35, 37, 41–43, 45, 46, 51, 52, 55, 75, 79, 80, 82, 84, 91, 92, 94, 96, 97, 111, 112, 114, 130, 139, 146, 148, 168, 178, 186, 199; to information 4, 6, 28, 30, 31, 33, 39, 45, 91, 92, 111, 148, 163; to know 5, 7, 30, 35, 45–47, 139, 199; to life and dignity 91
role perceptions 6
Russia 16, 18, 24, 44, 110, 119, 150

SDGs 18, 19, 39; *see also* Sustainable Development Goals
searching mothers 151
self-censorship 44
sensational 15
sexual 76–78, 85, 183
Shireen Abu Akleh 50, 54, 56
Sicarii 139, 140, 144
Sierra Leone 7, 120–22, 125, 126, 129–35
SLAPPs 46, 57, 88
source 6, 18, 34, 35, 44–46, 49, 59–61, 63–66, 81, 84, 93, 97, 98, 108, 148, 180, 184, 199, 200; official 6, 15, 44, 45, 49, 52, 59, 65, 117, 123, 148, 152, 153, 157, 158, 163
stereotypes 85, 188

strategic lawsuits against public participation 3
surveillance 1–4, 17, 45, 56, 76, 198, 200
survival jobs 96, 99
Sustainable Development Goals 18, 28, 32, 41

technology 3, 6, 21, 53, 58, 60, 62, 80, 175, 198, 200
terrorism 7, 44, 45, 130, 133, 139–44, 146–50, 199
Terrorism Act 140, 141, 148, 149
threats 2–4, 7, 13, 28, 31, 32, 34, 36–39, 45–48, 75–78, 86, 91–94, 98, 140, 141, 155, 168, 169, 198–200
trauma 16, 80, 93, 96, 99, 100, 159
trolls 77
trope 143, 144, 146

UDHR 2; *see also* Universal Declaration of Human Rights
Ukraine 16, 18, 22–24, 26, 50, 54, 61, 97, 100, 105, 110, 119, 183, 190
UN *see* United Nations
undemocratic 2, 4
UNESCO 2, 3, 8–10, 30, 31, 33–35, 38, 39, 41, 46, 48, 55, 57, 78, 86, 89, 92, 104, 105, 149, 190, 191, 194–96, 201
United Nations 17, 18, 23, 25, 38, 41, 48, 51–53, 57, 80, 90, 105, 108, 113, 149, 152, 168, 182–84, 186, 188, 196, 197
Universal Declaration of Human Rights 2, 8, 13, 29, 41, 43, 75, 119, 122, 152
user-generated content 20, 21

victim 34, 156
violence 2–5, 7, 8, 14, 20, 35, 36, 37, 39, 44, 47, 63, 75–85, 89, 91, 92, 94, 98, 100, 108–10, 115, 120–25, 129–31, 133, 140–42, 144, 146, 147, 151, 152, 154–57, 159, 163, 174, 175, 183, 198–200; against journalists 3, 4, 6, 28, 31, 33, 34, 36, 37, 48, 50, 75, 83, 91, 92, 154, 162, 198, 200; cultural 4, 7, 14, 22, 67, 77, 93, 96, 109, 115, 116, 120–27, 129, 130, 153, 184, 186, 187, 192;

online 3, 4, 7, 9, 10, 25, 40, 44, 53, 58, 61–64, 75–91, 98, 104, 105, 126, 145, 190, 191, 194, 199, 200; physical 14, 39, 43, 46, 54, 75–78, 91, 98–100, 109, 120–25, 131, 133, 155, 168, 173; sexual 75; structural 7, 16, 83, 95, 109, 116, 120–27, 129, 130, 151, 155
Violence Against Journalists 9

war 1, 7–9, 19, 23, 24, 36, 41–43, 47, 48–50, 55, 91, 97, 100, 107, 108, 110, 112, 113, 117, 121, 123, 125, 130, 146, 151, 152, 155, 156, 158, 183, 190
war on drugs 7, 156
watchdog 28, 34, 43, 46, 123, 179
whistleblowers 45
witness 8, 39, 93, 132, 145, 168, 177, 179
women 1, 2, 4, 7, 75–86, 89, 131, 132, 140, 152, 154, 161, 164, 170, 172, 199; attacks on 1

xenophobia 100, 122
xenophobic 2, 198